POUND'S EPIC AMBITION

SUNY Series,
The Margins of Literature

Mihai I. Spariosu

POUND'S EPIC AMBITION

Dante and the Modern World

Stephen Sicari

STATE UNIVERSITY OF NEW YORK PRESS

Cover photo courtesy of Mary de Rachewiltz

Production by Ruth East
Marketing by Fran Keneston

Published by
State University of New York Press, Albany

For information, address State University of New York
Press, State University Plaza, Albany, N.Y. 12246

Library of Congress Cataloging-in-Publication Data

Sicari, Stephen.
    Pound's epic ambition : Dante and the modern world / Stephen
Sicari.
        p.   cm. — (SUNY series, the margins of literature)
    Includes bibliographical references and index.
    ISBN 0–7914-0700-4 (alk. paper) . — ISBN 0–7914-0699-7 (alk.
paper)
    1. Pound, Ezra, 1885–1972. Cantos. 2. Dante Alighieri,
1265–1321—Influence—Pound. 3. Pound, Ezra, 1885–1972—Knowledge
—Literature. 4. Epic Poetry, American—History and criticism.
5. American poetry—Italian influences. 6. Medievalism in
literature.   I. Title. II. Series: SUNY series, margins of
literature.
PS3531.082C2878   1991
811' .52—dc20
                                                      90–44139
                                                         CIP

10 9 8 7 6 5 4 3 2 1

For

Mae, Mark, and Anna

CONTENTS

PREFACE

Ezra Pound exhibits what I am calling "the epic ambition" by taking as his poetic project the writing of a poem capable of incorporating and controlling the enormous amount of material to be drawn from history and politics. Not content as a successful poet of short lyrics, he turns his talents to the genre requiring the capacity to incorporate the totality of one's "lyric" observations into a sustained and satisfying unity. In this poet's hands, the epic becomes an accumulation of fragments held together and mastered by a unifying vision. Compelled by his desire to become the dominant poet of his age, he embarks upon a poem seeking mastery over the particulars of his culture, interpreting the past and prescribing the future. In doing so, he assigns to poetry a most ambitious role, to lead its readers away from a present state of cultural corruption and toward a new order based upon the poet's own visionary experience. The "epic ambition" in Pound is best seen in his relentless efforts to earn for himself as poet a position of dominance over his culture.

The Cantos is about Pound's efforts to master Western history. While his definition of an epic as "a poem including history" (*LE* 86) or "a poem containing history" (Hall 57) is deliberately reductive, it nonetheless testifies to a fundamental conviction, that the epic poet works to fashion a poetic form that can contain what we normally think of as the concerns of history. In fact, as my study demonstrates, the chief problem of the epic in the modern world is the problem of form: how can poetry confront, include, provide meaning to, and thus master the violent and complex world of history?

The underlying thesis of this study is that Ezra Pound came to define his own poetic project through an astute and continuous reading of Dante's *Commedia*. Pound's reading of Dante, eccentric though it may be, identifies certain aims and strategies in the medieval epic that he hopes to adapt to his "modern" concerns. Most importantly, he finds in the *Commedia* a formal principle

capable of organizing the diverse cultural material that the genre
compels to be "included."

In one fundamental way my argument goes against the grain
of much recent Pound criticism: whereas much of the effort lately
has been to understand and appreciate the fragmented nature of
The Cantos, my work renews the dominant focus of Pound's early
commentators in looking for a structural or formal principle that
organizes the poem's heteroclite material. I began, however, with
little sense of the possibility for such a discovery; I had undertak-
en to trace Pound's reading and use of Dante in *The Cantos,* hoping to show that Pound was consistent and penetrating in his
understanding and application of the *Commedia* to the conditions
of the modern world. But, as I gradually came to see, Pound found
something quite useful in his lifelong reading of Dante, a structural principle both traditional enough to provide coherence and
stability and flexible enough to allow for the integration of diverse
material into a single unified journey of redemption. This principle
of formal order lies in the composition of the epic figure of the
wandering hero.

It has been over twenty years since the last major attempt to
find such order: Daniel Pearlman's *The Barb of Time: On the Unity
of Ezra Pound's* Cantos, published in 1969. Pearlman was able to
offer some new and important readings of individual cantos, but
his sense of order now seems too mechanical to be of any lasting
value. He too believed that the clue to Pound's epic lies in Dante,
for he divides his book into an *Inferno,* a *Purgatorio,* and a *Paradiso.* But it is precisely this kind of superficial order that Pound
did not look for when reading Dante. If the early efforts to find
unity in *The Cantos* led to artificial and reductive boundaries to be
imposed on the dazzling surface of the poem, any attempt coming
after two decades of rigorous analysis of the poem's multifarious,
highly charged, sharply fragmented material must look for a structural principle that provides order without losing the poem's vivid
sense of multiplicity and diversity. One must take into account the
many different directions and tensions generated by the poem's
material as one looks for the possibility of order.

My study has the potential to return Pound scholarship to its
earlier focus—the search for unity—without sacrificing the wonder
and brilliance of what the poem manages to include. If there is
order in *The Cantos,* it is achieved only through the tremendous
effort of a poet whose "will to order" was set against his commitment to depict what he saw as the chaos of the modern world. By
reading Dante, Pound develops and deploys his own version of the

epic wanderer whose journey strains toward order amidst the seeming anarchy of Western history.

I am hardly the first reader of *The Cantos* who has suspected that Dante's work plays a significant part in shaping Pound's ambitions to write an epic. A number of the best books about Pound— including Pearlman's, Peter Makin's *Pound's Cantos,* Wendy Stallard Flory's *Ezra Pound and* The Cantos: *A Record of Struggle,* and Kenner's *The Poetry of Ezra Pound* and *The Pound Era*—mention his use of Dante. And James Wilhelm has written a full-length study *Dante and Pound: The Epic of Judgment,* which testifies to Dante's general lifelong importance to Pound.

But my study is the first to show, canto by canto and section by section, how Pound uses the epic tradition as understood by Dante to organize his own "long poem including history." An informed reader will be able to see, perhaps for the first time, the unity, cohesion, and systematic growth of the poem toward climaxes of light in the final cantos. My argument is that, while Pound intends to include whatever significant details he finds in his study of the Western past, he also hopes to organize the multifarious material he happens to accumulate into a coherent unity through the use of a multifaceted wanderer he creates out of an inherited epic tradition. As the material of the poem grows ever more diverse, he continues to describe and develop the movement of this epic wanderer whose journey is intended to integrate the material into a satisfying whole.

In the following chapters I shall demonstrate that the unifying principle of *The Cantos* is the theme of the wandering hero who is, from the very first canto, a conflation of various figures from the epic tradition the poet inherits and interprets. As the poem expands its focus and develops new aims, Pound adds and emphasizes new dimensions to his wanderer and these serve to organize the various sections and to establish connections to the earlier cantos. In my introduction I show that Pound arrives at this strategy through a careful and insightful reading of how Dante established his own journey of redemption as the unifying principle of the *Commedia.* Pound then writes his own journey in the wake of those journeys recorded in the epic tradition of which Dante has given the last great and, thus far, fullest expression.

Each of the next four chapters follows Pound's writing of *The Cantos* from beginning to end, tracing for various sections of the poem the way Pound articulates his present purposes through the use of his own composite wanderer. In the first chapter, the wanderer is chiefly an exile seeking the purity of the original human consciousness that the poet regards as one's private "home." This wanderer is composed of the cunning and nostalgic Odysseus of Homer's epic, the strong-willed but reckless Ulysses of *Inferno* XXVI, and the Dante who manages to achieve the divine consciousness that glimpses a vision of ideal and perfect justice. In those cantos of the first fifty-one that present this wanderer, Pound brings to the forefront the courage, guile, and strength needed to escape the confines of a corrupt culture and return to a natural and original health.

The second chapter describes how this centrifugal wanderer becomes the center of a new order as the exile becomes a Fascist, as the alienated and lonely wanderer becomes the poet of an ideal state. Here, Pound watches how his own version of the epic hero provides a model for political action that might explain the actions of past historical figures and of Mussolini in the present. He adds Confucius and John Adams to the composition of his hero in the next set of cantos to indicate the poet's ambition to become the sage who counsels political leadership, the poet whose wisdom can direct the political regeneration of his homeland.

In the third chapter we follow as Pound seeks a way to continue his epic of hope for political regeneration after the fall of Mussolini and his own internment as an accused traitor. The famed *Pisan Cantos* are the poet's effort to find consolation for the fall and hope for the future in his own status as prophet of the ideal city recently crushed but still and always possible. To announce and organize this tremendous ambition, he emphasizes Dante's purgatorial journey and adds Aeneas and a certain aspect of the Hebrew prophets to the already complex wanderer. In these most personal cantos Pound asks not to be forgiven but to be considered a prophet whose vision records a goal for future generations to receive and implement. The relation of the poet to the process of history is given its most ambitious expression.

The fourth chapter examines how, in *Section: Rock-Drill* and *Thrones de los Cantares,* which were conceived and executed while he was confined to a psychiatric institution, Pound devises his most original use of the motif of the journey and adds to the epic tradition a new version of the wandering hero. The wanderer is now voyaging through a sea of historical texts that he himself has accumulated; if he can arrange and organize these texts into a perfect pattern of ideal justice, he will transcend the limitations of history and achieve a consciousness of ideal justice. Even here, however, the poet is careful to align his hero with the tradition he has been following; the Dante of *Paradiso* is once again called upon—but in a more innovative way than in the early cantos—to provide the new focus.

In the conclusion we turn to the *Drafts and Fragments* that end the poem's long journey and question whether Pound brings the epic to a satisfying conclusion. I will argue that Pound sings a palinode to the earlier political goals of his wanderer and reasserts the value of the spiritual journey described in *Rock-Drill* and *Thrones*. Since the process of achieving the blessed state is, in this human life, now understood as endless and always to be repeated, the silence that ends *The Cantos* is a fitting if not totalizing conclusion. Through the detailed analyses of the various sections of this poem, I hope to demonstrate the bold claim that we can best read *The Cantos* as a dazzling array of finely wrought fragments straining to achieve order and unity through the deployment and development of Pound's wandering hero. Perhaps readers of this important poem will begin once again to appreciate the poet's strenuous effort to make an order out of chaos and understand why Pound hoped to be classified among "the lovers of ORDER" (*J/M* 128).

A first book is also an only book, and I would like to take this opportunity to acknowledge several people who have influenced my thinking and writing. My first thanks are to Alfred DiLascia of Manhattan College whose rigorous and comprehensive approach to "the text" I hope one day to make my own. I also wish to express my gratitude to Daniel R. Schwarz of Cornell University, who directed the dissertation that led to the conception and execution of this book; and to Paul Sawyer (of Cornell) and Jon Stallworthy (formerly of Cornell and now at Oxford), who offered such sensitive criticism of that dissertation that I saw early on and clearly what further work I had to do to write this book.

I have a special debt to Giuseppe Mazzotta of Yale University, whose understanding of Dante I have tried to acquire, who suggested what I hope are fruitful ways to apply the study of Dante to modernist poetry, and who has been encouraging me to write this book for the past six years or so. Thomas Heffernan of Adelphi University read the manuscript chapter by chapter and influenced its final form with his perceptive comments.

In addition, grateful acknowledgment is given to New Directions Publishing Corporation and Faber & Faber Ltd. for permission to quote from the following works of Ezra Pound:

The Cantos (Copyright © 1934, 1937, 1940, 1948, 1956, 1959, 1962, 1963, 1966, and 1968 by Ezra Pound)

Finally, I wish to acknowledge the loving support of my wife and the joyful example of my children.

ABBREVIATIONS

CEP *Collected Early Poems*
Con *Confucius*
GB *Gaudier-Brzeska: A Memoir*
GK *Guide to Kulchur*
I *Impact*
J/M *Jefferson and/or Mussolini*
LE *Literary Essays*
P *Personae: Collected Shorter Poems*
SL *Selected Letters of Ezra Pound,* ed. D. D. Paige
SP *Selected Prose,* ed. W. Cookson
SR *Spirit of Romance*
T *Translations*

INTRODUCTION
THE EPIC AMBITION: READING DANTE

Ezra Pound's ambition was to write the great epic poem giving voice to the culture he inhabited and directing it to its best imaginable ends. This poem, he hoped, would connect the present cultural moment to certain monuments of the past in such a way that the present is seen as both a result of that past and the beginning of a movement to another end still in the future. A certain few poets have accomplished this for their times: for Pound's purposes, these will be Homer in the *Iliad* and the *Odyssey*, Virgil in the *Aeneid*, and Dante in the *Divina Commedia*. Pound's ambitious hope was to write the next great epic in a sequence of epic poems that have defined the West and directed it to its greatest achievements.

A poet who develops this "epic ambition" becomes acutely self-conscious of his own position in the linear movement of literary history. While it is probably true to say that many great writers have examined the past monuments of their literary tradition with an eye to their own place at the "end" of this progression, as its culminating figure, Pound's case may be somewhat different in the urgency he exhibits in actively creating the tradition he plans to fulfill. The modern poet differs from his predecessors in his radical conviction that the wholeness of one's cultural past has broken down and that the poet's mission is first to make a tradition in which one's own work fits. No longer can one rest content with the sense of a linear progression of a continuous past unfolding into the present moment; no longer can tradition be unconscious. What is "modern" about Pound's "high modernism"[1] is its criticial self-awareness that the present cultural moment is no longer connected to a stable tradition of past greatness but instead seems rootless and undirected. The self-consciously "modern" epic poet first must reassemble a cultural past and establish the connection of that past to the present moment before the poem can focus on current concerns and present needs.

Pound turns to Dante as his primary precursor because the *Commedia* is the last great epic to achieve this place of prominence in western culture. He would be quick to notice as he reads the *Commedia* that Dante labors strenuously to place his work in relation to Virgil's and Homer's epics; that in expressing a comprehensive evaluation of his culture, Dante shows an awareness that his is a continuation of the efforts of earlier great poets in the epic. Pound's practice in *The Cantos* indicates that he saw as an essential aspect of the epic the inclusion of a past tradition of journeys which the present one continues and makes new for the contemporary scene. The "modern epic" first renews a tradition by which the reader can measure a strikingly "new" journey undertaken for the modern world. As Virgil includes and continues Homer's story, and as Dante makes Virgil a guide he will surpass and conclude, so Pound writes of an epic journey undertaken within and continuing this tradition of which the *Commedia* is the last great culmination.

The Cantos is written primarily in Dante's wake. It is not simply that he aspires to write "an epic of judgment"[2] generally similar to and rivalling Dante's; that much is true, but the actual terms of the judgment and the very form of the epic are informed by what Pound discerned as the organizing principle and controlling metaphor of Dante's epic. *The Cantos* is given direction and meaning by Pound's response to Dante's creation and deployment of the figure of the wandering hero. In his reading of Dante's medieval epic, Pound finds a principle of organization he can adapt for his own "modern" needs. It is from Dante and the epic tradition that Pound learns the formal principle enabling him to express his epic ambition.

It is easy for a casual reader of the *Commedia* to underestimate the composite nature of the chief figure, a man named Dante in the poem who undertakes a journey from a lost wood, through hell, up the mountain of Purgatory, and through the various heavens until he achieves union with God. Dante the poet is constantly measuring his pilgrim-hero against other famous wanderers from the literary tradition he inherits, most particularly Ulysses and Aeneas. In a way that Pound renders even more complex, Dante fashions his pilgrim out of the material of an epic tradition he adapts to his own needs and purposes. It is Dante's innovative use of the materials of a rich epic tradition for his own ends that Pound adopts as the organizing principle of *The Cantos*.

Dante's decision to define an epic tradition in which his own journey takes place is most evident in his creation of a radically new version of the Ulysses story. Instead of an Odysseus who yearns for home and manages a return in which he reclaims his former identity as prince, husband, father, and son, Dante invents a Ulysses who forsakes even a brief stop in Ithaca and who instead journeys beyond the assigned limits of the world toward new experience. What Dante accomplishes with his version is to complicate what "home" means to the exiled and alienated wanderer. Odysseus seeks and manages a return to the very condition he left, to the familiar and comfortable world of relations and duties left behind entirely against his will. His exile is purely involuntary, whereas Dante's Ulysses chooses to wander. He chooses the condition of exile because for him home is not the world of relations and duties that he has come to know and which gave him his former identity; rather, "home" is a return to the lost original consciousness that has access to the "new," the consciousness that marvels at all aspects of experience as if each moment were fresh and unique. It is in search of original experience that he travels beyond Gibraltar in the wake of the sun.[3] Dante compares the journey of his pilgrim to that of his newly invented Ulysses (and not Odysseus) because he too does not seek a return to the familiar world but to the original experience of humanity figured by the earthly paradise of Eden. He measures the pilgrim's deliberate journey to origins against Ulysses' reckless one.

Dante's creation of Ulysses also allows him to endow that wanderer with the poet's talent and so identify his own poetic project with Ulysses' craft. In this way Dante can articulate the poem itself as a version of a dangerous quest for new and wonderful experience. Ulysses is consigned to hell as a false counsellor, for he misuses the powers of language by persuading his companions to break God's decrees and travel after forbidden knowledge. The relation of language to truth is put in doubt by Ulysses' powerful rhetoric. As Giuseppe Mazzotta remarks, Ulysses "is a constant reminder to the poet of the possible treachery of his own language and the madness of his own journey" (105). We will see in the first chapter how Dante recalls Ulysses "mad flight" regularly to define his own quest, that of leading fit readers on the dangerous journey from the dark wood, back to Eden, and then to paradise; a journey enacted by means of the poet's use of language which has been made dubious by Ulysses' example. Dante reminds himself that he too might be leading his companions to their doom. He employs the classical metaphor of navigational voyage for the act of writing (Mazzotta 144-45) and so makes his quest an alternative to Ulysses'.

While the Ulysses of *Inferno* XXVI is largely his own creation, Dante also relies on the classical wanderer who dominates the epic tradition inherited by the medieval world. By making Virgil his guide through hell and purgatory, Dante invokes comparison of his quest with that of the Roman hero Aeneas. Mazzotta demonstrates that Dante often indicates his own sense of purpose and direction by distinguishing between the fates of Ulysses and Aeneas. For instance, Dante notes that while Ulysses travels westward in the sun's tracks searching for a perfect return to literal origins, Aeneas travels westward and stops. The Roman learns to overcome what Mazzotta calls the "illusory nostalgia" for a "perfect return to the point of origin" and work for the eventual renewal (and not duplication) of the greatness and splendour of those origins. Aeneas learns that he cannot escape history by recreating Troy but must wait for the development, over a long period of time, of the sequence of events that lead to the renewal of Troy in the greatness of Rome. Through this figure and his difference from Ulysses, Dante "asserts the discovery of the linear, open-ended translation of history" (Mazzotta 102). Dante establishes his own historical attitudes and convictions by aligning his wanderer with certain aspects of Virgil's hero. What I wish to emphasize is the process by which Dante articulates his own direction and purposes by writing his pilgrim's journey over the palimpsest of an epic tradition he is interpreting. It is Pound's discovery of this aspect of the *Commedia* that allows him to begin work on *The Cantos*.

One must recall that Pound begins his "poem including history" amidst the devastation of the First World War. As technological advances once deemed blessings and certain signs of progress turn monstrously on their creators, it was only logical for Pound to conclude that civilization as the West had seen it had developed only to destroy itself, and that a new way of organizing a culture must be found by the artists. He searched the past for a tradition embodying some principle of order around which a new civilization might be organized; he looked especially to Dante's example for such a principle because Dante had also sought a relation to a past tradition that his own work would fit into and culminate. Pound grappled with this problem of finding a formal principle for his epic poem until he came up with the composite wanderer he sends on his journey in what came to be the opening canto. The wanderer in Canto I is Pound's unique synthesis of Homer's Odysseus, Dante's Ulysses, and Dante's pilgrim, as well as certain elements of the Anglo-Saxon wanderer theme. When he was beginning his poem in the early war years Pound may have been tentative about discussing his plan and his principle of construction; but in 1944, in a period of both personal and public crisis, and when the poem is over seventy cantos long, Pound has no trouble in identifying his "precursor text":

> For forty years I have schooled myself, not to write an economic history of the U.S. or any other country, but to write an epic poem which begins "In the Dark Forest" crosses the Purgatory of human error, and ends up in the light, and "fra i maestri di color che sanno." (*SP* 167)

Pound attempts to establish his authority to speak on "The Economic Nature of the United States" by appealing to his study of Dante's spiritual journey from darkness to the light of the heavenly intellect. He justifies, to an Italian audience (for the essay in question was written in Italian), his pretensions to speak on the economic ills that were destroying civilization by claiming to have earned the status of an epic poet who has journeyed from the darkness of economic ignorance to the enlightened state of quick and total apprehension. Apparently, to Pound's way of thinking, the person who earns the right to be called an epic poet discovers a principle of order enabling him to speak on any aspect of "history." And it is "fra i maestri di color che sanno," among the masters of those who know, that he has planned and executed his epic. He had already offered a detailed explanation of this phrase from *Inferno* IV describing Aristotle:

> When first read, the phrase, "*maestro di color che sanno*" seems a general and generous compliment. The beauty of the twilight scene takes full possession of the reader. Limbo is divested of its defects. Only today do I stop to take count of the *sanno* as the mot juste, a graded and measured word, not merely two handy syllables fitting the metre.... (*GK* 317)

What the phrase has come to mean to him is "Master of those that cut apart, dissect and divide. Competent precursor of the card-index" (*GK* 343). He situates the writing of his epic "among the masters of those who" cut and dissect experience into small and isolated segments arranged according to an arbitrary principle (the alphabet, for instance); he writes from within limbo, whose only defect (once hardly noticed but now prominent) is that it never receives the light which emanates from God. Without this light, knowledge achieves no orderly whole but remains discrete fragments in arbitrary and partial relations. He places himself in the company of those whose keen analytical intelligence is not guided by God's splendour; the poem he is following, however, goes well beyond limbo: Pound's reading of the *Commedia* in *The Spirit of Romance* emphasizes the gradual strengthening of the visionary faculty until it sees God's light pouring through the universe. Anyone who claims that Pound secularizes the *Commedia*[4] ignores the poet's praise of *Paradiso*: "Nowhere is the nature of mystic ecstasy so well described as here" (141); "no man who has not passed through, or nearly approached, that spiritual experience known as illumination—I use the word in a technical sense—can appreciate the Paradiso to the full" (144). In his epic Dante certainly dissects experience into finely discriminated aspects but the medieval poet puts all that he has cut apart into an finely graduated hierarchy whose ordering principle is God's light.[5] Pound emphasizes this synthesis of knowledge when he notes that "Dante put Aristotle in Limbo, having, can one say, worked his way to the other side of the cosmos to get his limbo in proportion" (*GK* 343). Pound claims to follow the example of an epic that organizes all aspects of human experience according to a principle discovered at the end of a journey "to the other side of the cosmos." The epic poet takes the fragments of his culture and puts them back into perfect order.

Pound seeks not simply to gain knowledge of the unknown; such a desire would identify him with Dante's Ulysses. He emulates Dante himself, who is able to organize and give order to all knowledge. So he too undertakes a journey, but still he cannot simply follow Dante. For one thing, such imitation would be servile, and Pound's ambition is not to copy Dante's achievement but to accomplish the same comprehensive scope and authority for his age and nation as Dante did for his.[6] But, more pointedly, Pound insists on a distinction between the orderly medieval world with its established and coherent tradition and the relatively rootless and anarchic conditions of the modern age. To this end he notes the inadequacy of Dante's model for a modern voyage: "I haven't an Aquinas-map; Aquinas not valid now" (*SL* 323); "Stage set à la Dante is *not* modern truth. It may be O.K. but *not* as modern man's" (*SL* 293). While the medieval poet could rely on a ready-made map and acted upon a stage firmly established, the modern poet must depend chiefly on his own wit and courage in navigating the journey back home. But it is the reckless Ulysses of *Inferno* XXVI more than Homer's Odysseus who inspires Pound. In a late interview conducted by Donald Hall after *The Cantos* were more or less finished,[7] Pound explains in terms that recall Dante's Ulysses the difficulty of a modern poet to assume the epic project:

An epic is a poem containing history. The modern mind contains heteroclite elements. The past epos have succeeded when all or a great many of the answers were assumed, at least between author and audience, or a great mass of audience. The attempt in an experimental age is therefore rash. (Hall 57)

It is Dante's epic project that is undertaken but with the rash spirit of Dante's Ulysses. And the project when undertaken in the "modern world" is rash, but not necessarily doomed to failure. The epic poem in the modern age with its extraordinary proliferation of detail and data which must be "contained" is the attempt of the rash man who has no map to follow. Like Ulysses, the modern epic poet must search, on his own and without any guidance or external discipline, for the principle that can form an order out of the chaos of "heteroclite elements." Hugh Kenner noticed this aspect of Pound's epic when he argues that the adoption of Odysseus as the figure for the opening canto is the poet's "most radical decision: to experience the poem as he wrote it, himself committed to all he wrote, himself actually Odysseus en route" (*Era* 379). It is an act of daring rivalling Dante's Ulysses: "Pound hoped to become, while writing the poem in public, the poet capable of ending the Cantos" (*Era* 377). Though Kenner is referring to Homer's Odysseus, it is Ulysses' daring voyage to the unknown (and not Odysseus's journey to the familiar) that is described. The writing of *The Cantos* is itself figured as a daring journey out into the unknown whose destination is, at the outset, unimaginable. As it was for Dante, the actual writing of the epic poem is assuming characteristics of the epic journey. If Pound exhibits more sympathy with Ulysses than Dante allowed himself, it is because the modern journey, whose aims and destination are defined by Dante, is made in Ulysses' spirit of reckless abandon and bold independence.

One might object at this point that sufficient attention has been paid to the figure of Odysseus in *The Cantos*. In fact, in his effort to understand this poem "from the vantage-point of its ambition as a modern epic," Michael Bernstein denies the usefulness of exploring any further the role of the epic wanderer:

Although the Homeric epics and the *Divina Commedia* exerted an immense influence upon Pound's conception of his work, to read *The Cantos* largely as an attempt to adapt their techniques to the contemporary world would leave unanalyzed the specific structural difficulties and thematic intentions of that poem. (11)

We must be alert to the way Pound decides to develop and deploy his own version of the wandering hero, a version he makes by conflating various aspects of several famous wanderers. Bernstein suggests that Homer and Dante might have helped Pound begin his epic but that he does not keep their models in constant view as he executes his own project. Bernstein asserts that we cannot, for instance, use any paradigm based on Homer or Dante to read the Chinese History Cantos because "[l]arge sections of the poem simply do not fit such a paradigm or belong within so fixed a scaffolding" (170). But Pound's use of the epic paradigm of the wanderer is not fixed or static; nor does he follow Dante by imitating the *Commedia*'s "scaffolding," its neat division into three distinct and separate aspects of experience. On the contrary, Pound finds in Dante's epic the elastic form he needs. He follows Dante's example not in a superficial borrowing of general outline but in continually indicating his poem's changing relation to previous epic journeys, by creating his own distinct purpose and destination by emphasizing the particular aspects of established epic heroes that fit his present needs. There is at the heart of *The Cantos* an ambivalence between a reliance on tradition and an acute sense of his own original position as an epic poet in the modern world: he works to fit his unique needs and purposes into an already established tradition that he is interpreting and hoping to culminate. He takes whatever he needs from the tradition not only to provide continuity between his journey and those of other epic heroes but also to provide internal coherence as the poem's interests and goals change. Indeed, Pound's wandering hero undergoes a significant and deliberate development as *The Cantos* grows in scope and purpose.

Pound indicates that it was his decision to deploy this composite and ever-shifting wanderer that enabled him to begin the epic task. In the same late interview, conducted by Hall, he recalls his early search for "form":

> The problem was to get a form—something elastic enough to take the necessary material. It had to be a form that wouldn't exclude something merely because it did not fit. In the first sketches, a draft of the present first *Canto* was the third. (38)

When discussing his search for form, the poet refers to his decision to make Odysseus's descent to the underworld the opening canto, as if this shift solved his formal problem. Pound's genius is in devising a figure flexible and adaptable enough to open the poem to new material and new scope, yet traditional enough to provide recognizable shape to the poem's meaning and intentions. As his needs change, the poet adds new layers and meanings to the journey his Odysseus has undertaken. Pound's wanderer is not a fixed form whose journey always has the same destination and the same method, but "elastic enough" to include any new material that the poet has discovered and chosen to include. Despite Bernstein's claims, we can follow the poem's thematic intentions and structural developments by watching carefully the various additions Pound makes to his wandering hero, for these additions announce and shape the changing emphases and intentions that *The Cantos* comes to embrace.

Pound's formal difficulties in beginning his epic have some important implications for the study of modernism in general. To write a modern epic Pound had to worry more than his predecessors in the genre about the nature of the container designed to hold all relevant aspects of "history." He knew that, while he could not borrow traditional modes of versification nor the major forms of the epic tradition, he could not allow the fragmented anarchy of the modern world to dictate an aesthetic decision to ignore order and form altogether. This tension—between the pull toward chaos urged by the state of the modern world and the need for form dictated by the nature of poetry and all art—may be the tension that best accounts for the texture of *The Cantos* and the works of high modernism in general.

If Pound follows Dante in constructing a wandering hero comprised of aspects of previous heroes in the epic tradition, he must make Dante fit his own needs by making the figure more flexible and adaptable and so open to the vaster array of "heteroclite elements" contained by "the modern mind." As Pound "modernizes" Dante in the question of form or organizing principle, so he must bring Dante up to date regarding material. Two recorded comments of his describe his poem as such an updating: "Dante has said everything there is to be said, so I start with Malatesta" (*Disc.* 159); "the first thing was this: you had six centuries that hadn't been packaged. It was a question of dealing with material that wasn't in the *Divina Commedia*" (Hall 38). The first remark comes in the course of introducing his daughter Mary to *The Cantos*, and he explains that he turns to Sigismundo Malatesta as the first "historical" (as opposed to mythic or literary) figure to be included because he is the first attractive personality to live after Dante; that is, his first strategy for "including history" is to supplement Dante's epic by making it factually current. The second comment is once again from the Hall interview, and it continues

Pound's "search for form" discussed above. The form must be able to "package" the six centuries since Dante; the form sought by modernizing Dante's journey must be a fit container for the material that updates the *Commedia*.

What principle governs the selection of material? How does the poet decide if some detail discovered on the course of his journey is relevant to his epic ambition of modernizing Dante? It seems pointless to say that Pound has found a form that can include everything; even if that were possible, only certain things get into the poem, and it seems reasonable to suppose that some principle governs the selection. As Pound reviews his poem in 1962, it is to the *Commedia* he turns to explain his principle of inclusion: "I have made the division between people dominated by emotion, people struggling upwards, and those who have some part of the divine vision. The thrones in Dante's *Paradiso* are for the spirits of the people who have been responsible for good government" (Hall 58). He explains that he has organized various aspects of human behavior according to the divisions established by Dante: into a hell where people have subjected reason to desire and so are "dominated by emotion"; into a purgatory where people work to purge themselves of sinful emotion and so are "struggling upwards" to Edenic purity; and into a heaven where people act according to "the divine vision." He has been looking to discover and amass enough examples of human behavior that will provide a reliable and sufficient guide for responsible public action. Even before he had undertaken *The Cantos* he had understood Dante's epic as "an expression of the laws of eternal justice" (*SR* 127). His emphasis, both in 1912 and fifty years later, is on accumulating examples of people with the capacity to see and act upon a divine vision of perfect justice, enough examples from which it is possible to formulate "the laws of eternal justice." Pound's early search for form was for a package that does not exclude any material; but as the epic develops in his thinking and in practice, the poet increasingly recognizes that his form was fitted to incorporate the material needed to "modernize" Dante's epic subject of ideal justice.

Pound's modernist obsession with finding and describing a useable past does not necessarily indicate a nostalgia which despairs about one's present prospects. Donald Davie looks at Pound's explicit use of Homer's Odysseus as just such a sign of the poet's backward-looking nostalgia, an attitude that "comports better with elegy than with epic" (*Sculptor* 32). But once we realize that Pound's wanderer is not Odysseus but a more complex and multi-faceted figure, we are free to see that Pound's nostalgia functions in a way that leads to and supports the epic scope. For by following Dante's form and matter, Pound understands that nostalgia can be more than intense longing for a previous condition; it can be the desire that directs one's behavior in the present toward a goal in the future that takes its shape from a vision of original perfection. By reading Dante, Pound knows that nostalgia can be future-oriented, that "home" can be a goal to aim for. In 1912, before *The Cantos* is begun and while he is studying Dante, Pound recognizes that a desire for "a return to origins" does not have to be sentimental longing for an impossible past:

> A return to origins invigorates because it is a return to nature and to reason. The man who returns to origins does so because he wishes to behave in the eternally sensible manner. That is to say, naturally, reasonably, intuitively. He does not wish to do the right thing in the wrong place, to 'hang an ox with trappings', as Dante puts it. He wishes not pedagogy but harmony, the fitting thing. (*LE* 92)

Pound invests quite early in his poetic career in a myth of healthy and pure origins. Nostalgia is not, as it was for Homer's hero, the desire to return to the place he left behind but the longing for a return to an original health where one learns to "behave in the eternally sensible manner." "Home" is not the final goal but the first step in "invigorating" humanity so that it can do the "fitting thing" and find "harmony." Like Dante's pilgrim (and the apparently casual reference to Dante in the passage indicates that the *Commedia* was on his mind when formulating this idea), Pound hopes to return to an original state from which he can work toward the harmony of an integrated vision of humanity and its history. The classic example of nostalgia in the Western literary tradition, Homer's *Odyssey*, is used by this poet to indicate his longing for a world in which one feels "at home"; but Pound conflates Homer's wanderer with Dante's to indicate that his nostalgia is not wistful longing for an irrecoverable happiness but a practical historical goal. With Dante as his chief model, he understands origins as the basis for healthy human action that can transform the world into a true and satisfying home for all humanity. In Pound as in Dante, nostalgia is made the motive for a political program that has as its goal the recovery of "home."

Pound's understanding of the epic project helps us see modernism's purported nostalgia in a new light. For the modernists who look to the past for order and tradition—especially Yeats,

Joyce, Hulme, and Eliot, all friends and associates of Pound's—are not locked into a backward-looking posture in which one indulges in wistful longing for lost comfort. The modernists in general and Pound in particular turn to the past to see what can be renewed (and not merely repeated), what can be taken and used as the basis for a new moment of cultural health and integrity. Nostalgia is made progressive as the past is understood as the storehouse of images and concepts that can be made the goals of a new order in the modern world.

It is also important to note that we are not necessarily trying to understand Dante's formulation of various issues but are primarily following Pound's private, perhaps eccentric reading of Dante. It is a reading that can be characterized as post-Romantic, by which I mean that Pound emphasizes the aspects of Dante's epic that match the needs and purposes of a poet who comes after the Romantic period. "A return to origins" is a motif that certainly exists in Dante, but it receives its special prominence in *The Cantos* because Pound was nurtured on the aims and methods of poets who believed that humanity's natural state was pure and innocent and that the poet's task is to bring humanity back to such a condition.[8] Pound's reading and application of Dante can be placed within the tradition described by M. H. Abrams in *Natural Supernaturalism:*

> The basic categories of characteristic post-Kantian philosophy and the thinking of many philosophical-minded poets, can be viewed as highly elaborated and sophisticated variations upon the Neoplatonic paradigm of a primal unity and goodness, an emanation into multiplicity which is *ipso facto* a lapse into evil and suffering, and a return to unity and goodness. (Abrams 169)

Pound is "romantic" in his belief in the possibility of a return to origins that are healthy and pure ("a primal unity and goodness") and that can ground a natural (compare Coleridge's "organic") growth toward human perfection. But he enacts what can be called a modernist variation upon the Neoplatonic paradigm Abrams has articulated. For by following the "romantic" Dante he has created, Pound comes to the conviction that the attempt to return humanity to goodness and unity can only take place within the complex and violent world of history. If "history" is the result of the fall from innocence, it must, in Pound's estimation, also be the locus for the process of redemption, whether such is conceived as personal and spiritual or public and secular. One aim of the present study is to articulate how, in its relation to Dante, Pound's "modernism" consists of a keener consciousness of poetry's complex relation to something called "history" than exhibited by the Romantic poets, and that Pound bases his thinking about this in a reading and application of Dante's epic. For though Dante seeks a return to an Edenic state, he never allows himself to forget the effects of history upon the individual and the necessity of developing the proper relation to the demands of history. Simply put, Pound's romantic aims are disciplined by his reading of the historically acute Dante. When we recall that Eliot and Joyce also revere Dante, we may wonder to what extent is what we call "high modernism" the effect of Dante upon the romantic sensibility.[9]

By watching the deployment and development of Pound's complex wanderer, we can follow the poet's growing understanding of the possible relations of poetry to history, an understanding constantly measured and marked by references to Dante and the epic tradition. Pound takes very seriously his pithy definition, that "an epic is a poem including history." *The Cantos* is always about history, about the world of public affairs, about political structures and institutions that determine the quality of actual human existence. It is Dante who teaches Pound that he cannot wake from the nightmare of history but rather must always confront it and seek to exert power over it. This lesson from Dante distinguishes Pound's modernism from certain limitations of the Romantic sensibility. Abrams notes in the Romantic period "a widespread shift in the basis of hope from political revolution to the powers inherent in human consciousness" (Abrams 65). Pound is romantic in that he too turns to the powers of the human mind as the basis for regeneration but he does not relinquish the hope for a political regeneration until, very late in *The Cantos*, he reconsiders his political efforts (and, even then, politics is not abandoned as a value in the poem); the attainment of an original health for the individual human consciousness becomes, in Pound's qualified romanticism, the ground for healthy and constructive action in the realm of history. Unlike his friend T. E. Hulme, Pound does not reject romanticism out of hand, but, by interpreting and following an epic tradition in general and Dante in particular, he becomes acutely aware of the problems and dangers attendant to certain romantic aims and conceptions, most notably the movements toward the personal and away from the public; toward the internal away from the external; toward nature and away from history. Pound's modernism is a romanticism tempered by a careful reading of an epic tradition that has attempted to "include history."

We can infer, from his definition of the epic but more pointedly by his practice in *The Cantos,* how Pound reads the great tradition of epic poems, each of which in his estimation aims at "including" the "history" of its culture in an effort to prescribe a mode of behavior for that culture. When he turns to what he considers the major poems of the epic tradition, he discovers that each presents some great achievements from its cultural past in order to provide the present with its identity and purpose, a goal which in turn presumes a plan for future action and development. In Pound's reading, the epic is the poem capable of connecting the past and present by means of a masterful narrative that serves as a principle of cohesion for its culture and prescribes a direction for that culture toward the future. The poet of *The Iliad* recites a legendary story of past greatness designed to provide an ideal of valor and strength around which a people emerging from primitive conditions can unite and build a civilization. Equipped with a more sophisticated understanding of history as a line of continuity connecting points from various epochs in meaningful, usually causal relations, Virgil turns to the mythic past of Homer's world to describe a figure whose mission is to begin the process of history that will culminate in the grandeur of the present moment, the early years of Imperial Rome: in this way Virgil defines his present moment in terms of an epic past. Dante makes use of the past when he measures his unique journey against those of other wanderers in the tradition, especially Ulysses, Aeneas, and Saint Paul. He also works assiduously to include numerous details—that is, actual and mythic figures as well as references to important public events—from the past in his poem, a past understood and explained from the perspective of a timeless beatitude. No poem includes more material from his culture's past in the attempt to organize it all into a perfect unity than the *Commedia,* unless that poem is *The Cantos.* Even in its obsession to include and explain as much from the past as possible, Dante's epic is Pound's first model.

Perhaps a central characteristic of "high modernism" is a radical awareness of the past's demand upon the present to be accounted for as the basis of that present. Out of the material of the past the poet strives to form an order, a tradition, upon which he can write his own original work of his individual talent. We can ground an understanding of this school of modernism in the tension between Pound's reverent awareness of his place in a well-defined and dense tradition and his ambition to write a wholly original poem adapting this tradition to present conditions and bringing it to a new culmination. It is not only true of Pound but of

Joyce and Eliot as well to say that the modernist author seeks to include and surpass the tradition he has inherited. As Eliot mimes what he considers a breakdown of culture with the fragments of *The Waste Land,* which are assembled with some urgency to shore the poet against the ruins and so provide him with some measure of coherence and identity, so Pound includes an enormous array of details from his culture's past as he seeks to interpret that past and direct the present. And as Joyce includes as continual subtext what we have come to call Homeric parallels to provide depth and grandeur to his own story of a present-day Dubliner named Bloom, so Pound presents his quest for knowledge and beatitude in terms of a tradition of epic wanderers whose similarly motivated journeys provide direction and purpose to Pound's. These three modernists exhibit a fundamental tendency to write their ambitious projects over the palimpsest of a powerful tradition they seek to renew and culminate. They exhibit the need to place their own "modern" understanding of the world in terms of a tradition of poems that have similarly sought to interpret and thus master their cultures.

This demand for the epic to master history is the primary impetus to Pound's search for a principle of organization and unity. Pound's definition of the epic as a long poem containing history can be understood as a call for a "major form" capable of "containing" the enormous array of material in "history," which is understood by Pound primarily as records from the past capable of representing that past to the present. This major form, which Pearlman defines as "an over-all design in which the parts are significantly related to the whole" (3), lies in the figure of Pound's composite wanderer, who, standing for the poet himself, confronts all sorts of records from the past and hopes to have them cohere through the strength of his personality. We should not be surprised that *The Cantos* undergoes striking and significant changes in direction and purpose when we recall that the poem defines a journey almost fifty years in the making. As he changes his understanding of the nature of his journey, his understanding of history and of his role in the historical process undergo several large shifts and a number of smaller adjustments. Pound devises his composite wanderer as his organizing principle in order to announce these changes and provide them with a rigorous sense of meaningful development. We can read *The Cantos* as an organized and perhaps even unified whole only if we grasp how this wanderer is made to function in every aspect of the poem.

The danger of my approach is that, in looking for formal

order, I may overlook the disarray of the poem and ignore its striking appearance of chaos. As one traces the developments in the figure of Pound's wanderer, one must not forget that the poem's overall appearance and texture remain predominantly chaotic; in fact,
I note and try to account for a rather obvious fact, that *The Cantos*
becomes increasingly fragmented and ever more anarchic as the
poem continues. At the heart of this apparently open-ended and
radically fragmented poem lies a narrative line surrounding the
figure of the wanderer, a narrative line providing coherence and
cohesion to the heteroclite material. *The Cantos* is written in the
tension between anarchy and order, chaos and unity . Pearlman (4)
recognizes that Pound's wanderer may be a "unifying metaphor"
for the poem but denies it the supreme role I have assigned it, as
the "plot" of *The Cantos*. Against the pull of highly charged,
exquisitely rendered but apparently randomly assorted details,
Pound deploys this figure whose journey, though ever-changing, is
the narrative basis for the rest of the poem. In short, I shall argue
that we can read *The Cantos* as a dazzling array of finely wrought
fragments straining to achieve order and unity through the
deployment and development of "the Ulysses theme"[10] as filtered
through the epic tradition as defined by Dante.

1 ❦ THE WANDERER AS EXILE:
THE QUEST FOR HOME

From the very beginning of his work on *The Cantos* we can discern the importance of the figure of the wandering hero to Pound's conception of his epic's scope and purpose. His decision to place his translation of Book XI of the *Odyssey* as the opening canto, after its placement in the first schema as the third canto, is evidence enough that Pound's Odysseus plays a significant role in the early conception of *The Cantos*. In this chapter I shall examine how Pound develops his own version of the wandering hero and deploys him in the first fifty-one cantos to establish the initial direction and goal for his epic.

In the early cantos he follows Homer's Odysseus closely, for this heroic wanderer is characterized by an individualistic morality and cunning that the poet wants to adopt:

> The *Odyssey* high water mark for the adventure story, as for example Odysseus on the spar after shipwreck. Sam Smiles never got any further in preaching self-reliance. A world of irresponsible gods, a very high society without recognizable morals, the individual responsible to himself. (*GK* 38)

By the time he writes these words, Pound has become a spokesman for Italian Fascism, and the general lack of social responsibility in the Homeric world is a certain and serious defect that reminds the poet of the current condition of most western states (excepting Italy and possibly Germany). When cut off from any cultural tradition that can provide responsible moral leadership for one's journey, the heroic individual must emulate the "self-reliance" of Odysseus and adopt the pose of an "adventurous" wanderer working in isolation from the rest of his culture, responsible only to himself. One can rely only on his own wit and must ignore the conventional morality that serves to repress the will that alone can bring one to a different destination. And Homer's hero provides for the modern poet such a destination in his intense longing for a return to a lost home. Pound begins his epic with Book XI of the *Odyssey,* in which Homer's hero descends to the underworld to hear Tiresias' counsel about how to return home, in order to align his quest with Odysseus's. The poet considers that the modern world is cut off from any leadership or cultural authority that can provide the structures and categories of experience that fulfill desire and establish the comfort and ease associated with home. In Pound's estimation, "home" is nowhere to be found in the present state of culture and so he must wander in search of it. Pound's state of exile might be said to differ radically from Odysseus's: after all, the Greek was prevented from returning home by spiteful Neptune while Pound voluntarily adopts this pose. But, while his exile is a willed decision, it is the failure of his culture to provide a "home" that impels his wandering. Pound shares with Homer's Odysseus an intense nostalgia that propels a lonely journey guided only by one's native wit, what Homer calls "polumetis." As Pound describes Odysseus's wit in a letter to W. H. D. Rouse, "'[W]hen a man's got a mind like that even the gods respect him'" (*SL* 270).

But Pound's wanderer is not a simple replica of the Homeric model. This poet works with great care to find a way for his individual talent to draw upon and advance a larger tradition of epic wanderers than the Homeric epos provide. He turns to Dante, who also sought to place himself in a tradition of wandering heroes that he hoped his own work would culminate, for a more refined and spiritual understanding of nostalgia. For Dante too is a wanderer seeking a lost home, but that home becomes more than the place he left behind; Pound calls upon Dante to suggest that the "home" to be sought in *The Cantos* is similar to the earthly paradise of Eden, now lost beyond memory and regained only by the terrifying descent to hell and the painful ascent up Mount Purgatory. One ought to be struck by the absence of any mention of *The Cantos* in W. B. Stanford's classic account of *The Ulysses Theme.* In his final chapter, "The Re-Integrated Hero," Stanford credits James Joyce with successfully solving "a radical antinomy in the [Ulysses] tradition—the conflict between the conceptions of Ulysses as a home-deserter and as a home-seeker" (Stanford 215). Pound too seeks to reconcile these contrary motions, and he does so by reading Dante.

The Dantesque Paradigm: The Return to Origins

Ulysses is central to the *Commedia.* In *Inferno* XXVI, Dante hears the story of Ulysses, a voyager who disdains a return to Ithaca, his literal home, and who instead seeks the intensity of new and for-bidden experience. Employing Joyce's terminology, Stanford calls this Ulysses the "centrifugal" wanderer (Stanford 181), one whose thirst for new experience is so compelling that no obligation—"not fondness for a son, nor duty for an aged father, nor the love I owed Penelope"—could conquer it. He has been consigned to hell as a "false counsellor," for he in turn incites his companions to abandon in like manner the bonds of affection and duty that support civi-lized life. Ulysses and his companions break free from the Homeric version of "home" and all its "centripetal" obligations and travel beyond the Pillars of Hercules, beyond the assigned limits of our allotted experience. At last Ulysses sights a mountain, at which point a storm arises and sinks his ship. This journey, away from the familiar and toward experience as yet undifferentiated by human categories, ends in a violent storm of chaos that over-whelms the centrifugal wanderer.

While briefly noting that Dante might be "condemning a ten-dency to over-adventurous speculation and research in his own mind" (182), Stanford does not appreciate the central role Ulysses plays in Dante's epic. As Giuseppe Mazzotta remarks, "Ulysses will appear, even in *Paradiso,* as a constant reminder to the poet of the possible treachery of his own language and the madness of his own journey" (Mazzotta 105). Dante recognizes that his poetic lan-guage leads us on a quest that nearly duplicates Ulysses'—after all, what is the *Commedia* about if not what Ulysses seeks, "expe-rience of the world and of the vice and worth of men"? In addition to Homer's centripetal wanderer, Pound responds to Dante's treat-ment of Ulysses as he deploys that figure in *The Cantos.*

Inferno I opens as the pilgrim awakens "within a dark wood where the straight way was lost." He is stricken with fear, but soon he takes hope at the sight of a hilltop clothed with the sun's light. The pilgrim decides to climb this hill to reach the comforting light, but three wild beasts block his easy ascent and send him scurrying back. John Freccero demonstrates that in *Inferno* I Dante is taking issue with the Platonic conception of transcen-dence, that one can achieve a transcendent experience by means of a direct ascent to the light (Freccero 6–11). The opening canto insists that the path to God's light is no easy and direct ascent.

Freccero argues that Ulysses' voyage recounted in *Inferno* XXVI recalls the pilgrim's own aborted journey that the three beasts cut short: "In Dante's reading, as in the reading of the [medieval] neoplatonists, the voyage [of Ulysses] was an allegory for the flight of the soul to transcendent truth" (15). He then demonstrates how *Inferno* I, Inferno XXVI, and *Purgatorio* I are all connected by the image of shipwreck (23). "[I]n the first canto of the poem," he notes, "the pilgrim seems to have survived, by pure accident, a metaphorical shipwreck of his own":

> And as he who with labouring breath has escaped from the deep to the shore turns to the perilous waters and gazes, so my mind, which was still in flight, turned back to look again at the pass which never let any go alive. (*Inferno* I, 22–27)

While Ulysses' fate is to die at sea, "as One willed," the pilgrim is spared. At the end of *Purgatorio* I, having just completed the descent to hell that becomes the ascent up Mount Purgatory, he recalls both his own earlier survival and Ulysses' death by water:

> We came then on to the desert shore that never saw man sail its waters who after has experience of return. (*Purgatorio* I, 130–132)

We are meant to recall that Ulysses drowns just as he sights a mountain that no one ever saw before, a mountain that in the medieval geography Dante follows can only be Mount Purgatory. As the pilgrim embarks on his own purgatorial experience up this mountain, the poet recalls Ulysses who failed to see the need for purgation before he set sail for ultimate experience. Unlike Ulysses, Dante undergoes purification as preparation for the return to an original state.

As Dante climbs Mount Purgatory, he purges sin after sin until he is free of all contamination. At the top of this mountain he enters Eden. Wandering in the earthly paradise, he recalls the experience of *Inferno* I:

> Already my slow steps had brought me so far within the ancient wood that I could not see the place where I had entered. . . . (*Purgatorio* XXVIII, 22–24)

The "ancient wood" here recalls the "dark wood" of *Inferno* I. There, Dante was in a wood darkened by his own sin; here, he meanders in an ancient wood that is the place of humanity's pure origins. The difference between Dante and his Ulysses is not in their ambitions, for both seek transcendence of the present human condition bound by space and time; but in their methods, for Dante sees the need to purify himself of the stain and contamination that being in space and time has placed upon him before he can reach the purity and health of a lost home. Both seek to move away from the conditions of the present, but Ulysses' voyage is a reckless attempt at escape while Dante's is a more deliberate effort at purification.

Like Ulysses, Dante may forsake his present home, his present culture that is contaminated by sin; but in his movement away from that home, he manages to reach his original home, Eden, whence he can ascend to his final home, union with God. The solution of a "radical antinomy" with which Stanford credited Joyce was achieved centuries earlier by Dante: the centrifugal impulse away from home has been reconciled with the centripetal impulse to find home. In precisely this pattern Pound deploys his Ulysses.

Cantos I–VII

Within this Dantesque paradigm, however, Pound still relies on Homer's hero; in fact, throughout *The Cantos,* Pound's wanderer is called either "Odysseus" or "no man," but never Ulysses. While I shall argue that Dante is the poet's main model, he needs the Homeric wanderer to emphasize that the modern journey to origins is an unmarked, unaided, and isolated endeavor: "I haven't an Aquinas-map; Aquinas *not* valid now" (*SL* 323); "Stage set à la Dante is *not* modern truth. It may be O.K. but *not* as modern man's" (*SL* 293). All three epic wanderers—Homer's Odysseus, Dante's Ulysses, and Dante the pilgrim—are present in Canto I.

As Ronald Bush has noted (133), the very first of *The Cantos* begins precisely where Dante's Ulysses begins his personal narrative: "When I parted from Circe, who held me more than a year . . . I put forth on the open deep with but one ship and the company which had not deserted me." The fact that the poet translates Andreas Divus's medieval Latin translation of Book XI of the Odyssey is evidence enough that Pound's wanderer is based on Homer's centripetal, home-seeking Odysseus.[1] Moreover, Pound finds a "crime and punishment motif in the *Odyssey*" (*LE* 212–13), and the descent to the underworld, which he reads as a ritual of purification (Bush 132), might indicate that he does not need Dante's pilgrim as an example. As if to foreclose such a misreading, Pound follows Divus's mistranslation in which Tiresias asks Odysseus why he descends a second time. I imagine that Pound would have been aware that this is an error on Divus's part and that he leaves it uncorrected because it serves his own purposes:

to indicate that this is not simply a copy of Odysseus's descent but
a "second" version, something new and distinctly his own. After
Tiresias' prediction of Odysseus's lonely return through spiteful
Neptune, the poet abruptly halts his translation of the Latin text:
"Lie quiet Divus." The reader cannot fail to notice that a sharp
break has occurred in the narrative, a break designed to cause the
reader to take special note of the way the poet has chosen to continue Odysseus's wandering. The ritualistic solemnity of Pound's
translation is suddenly broken by an agitated voice that pedanti-
cally cites his source:

> Lie quiet Divus. I mean, that is Andreas Divus,
> In officina Wecheli, 1538, out of Homer.   (I/5)

Pound shifts for a moment to an editorial voice unnerved by
the prospect before him: an Odysseus who ignores Ithaca and Penelope's arms and who travels instead toward unknown experience,
uncharted seas. Rather than look upon and follow the centrifugal
movement that is about to take place, this editor retreats to the
shelter of scholarly pursuits. But the poet resumes his narration,
again in a solemn voice but no longer following Homer's hero:

> And he sailed, by Sirens and thence *outward and away*
> And unto Circe.
>   Venerandam,
> In the Cretan's phrase, with the golden crown, Aphrodite,
> Cypri munimenta sortita est, mirthful, orichalchi, with golden
> Girdles and breast bands, thou with dark eyelids
> Bearing the golden bough of Argicida. So that: (I/5, my italics)

This Odysseus sails "outward and away," a distinct centrifugal movement away from all known and familiar bonds. Homer's
Odysseus has given way to Dante's Ulysses; the model of the
home-seeker is abandoned at this point and replaced by the reckless home-deserter who seeks new experience. Pound's wanderer,
however, does not drown but attains instead a vision of the divine.
By breaking free of all constraints and structures that "home" may
come to stand for, he can return to humanity's first home, its original consciousness that can see "gods float in the azure air" (III/11).
Forsaking Penelope, he finds "Aphrodite," a visionary experience
of love and delight that is his true home.

Canto I establishes the initial and fundamental identity of
Pound's wanderer: the wit and nostalgia of Homer's Odysseus, the

daring recklessness and intensity of desire of Dante's Ulysses, and the successful attainment of divine experience of Dante the pilgrim. The "So that:" ending the canto indicates that, with this figure developed and deployed, we are ready to embark on the epic journey away from the present corruption and back toward an original home.

The lines that celebrate the vision of Aphrodite come from Georgius Dartona's medieval Latin translations of the First and Second Homeric Hymns to Aphrodite and the First Hymn to Hermes. Pound's decision to translate these and Divus's medieval translation of Book XI of the *Odyssey* suggests his historical approach to the examination of culture. He proceeds backward in time until he finds an artifact that indicates a place and time that last had contact with the vigor and insight of the Homeric original. The early Italian Renaissance (still writing in Latin, at least in this instance) was the last moment in Western cultural history that enjoyed vital contact with the pagan world of energy and immanent divinity (see Makin, *Pound's Cantos* 127). And Pound does not translate Divus into modern English; instead, he chooses the measure and diction of Anglo-Saxon verse because, in this poet's estimation, poems such as "The Wanderer" represent the last time in English literary history that a poet manifested an understanding and appreciation of the hardships, toils, and pains of exile and the subsequent intensity of nostalgia akin to Homer's.[2] The opening canto returns the modern world to its last moment of cultural health, the last time it had contact with the vigor and beauty of "the original world of the gods" (*SL* 210).

In 1917, when Pound was working on this canto, Rudolf Otto was advancing a similar conception of the human mind. For Otto, the holy "is a purely *a priori* category," "an original and underivable capacity of the mind implanted in the 'pure reason' independently of all perception" (112). Otto makes the bold claim to have isolated an "original" category of the mind, a mode of perception natural and given as opposed to artificial and constructed. Canto I suggests that the original and natural human consciousness is one that sees the presence of the holy in the world. The home Pound's Odysseus seeks and glimpses is not a place but a way of being, not the familiar world of civilized duties but the lost and recoverable consciousness we originally enjoyed. Pound's insistence that "the gods exist" (*GK* 125), that pagan myths of gods and goddesses "are . . . *real* " (*SP* 92), strongly resembles the thesis of another neo-Kantian philosopher of Pound's time, Ernst Cassirer, who describes what he calls the "mythic consciousness." Visions of gods and daemons occur when the mind:

is captivated and enthralled by the intuition which suddenly confronts it. It comes to rest in the immediate experience; the sensible present is so great that everything else dwindles before it. For a person whose thinking is under the spell of this mythico-religious attitude, it is as though the whole world were suddenly annihilated; the immediate content, whatever it might be, that commands his religious interest so completely fills his consciousness that nothing else can exist beside and apart from it. The ego is spending all its energy on this single object, lives in it, loses itself in it. (32–33)

We can apply Cassirer's thesis to the end of Canto I, when Odysseus attains a vision of Aphrodite, to assert that the wanderer has managed to break free of all structures and categories that constitute the familiar objects of a secular world and has returned to an original consciousness whose intense concentration on the phenomenal world has resulted in the manifestation of the goddess. One accomplishes this return by "annihilating the world," by destroying the structures that determine our modern debased consciousness. Without these corrupt categories to interfere with our experience of the phenomenal world, one is free to become immersed in the intense concentration upon any object that "enthralls" or "captivates"; then, "the spark jumps across somehow, the tension finds release, as the subjective excitement becomes objectified and confronts the mind as god or daemon" (Cassirer 33). The philosopher is trying to explain why human beings originally saw gods and daemons, while the poet implies that his wanderer has actually returned to that original and healthy state. Canto I culminates in an experience of original beauty and divine splendour to announce that the first goal of the epic hero's wandering is to return to the purity of our lost origins, to a consciousness as it was originally and naturally constituted before the ill effects of history. In this way his project is aligned with the Dante who seeks and manages a return to the earthly paradise of Eden, where, after a certain ritual of purification, the pilgrim gains access to the divine splendour operating within the natural order. For Pound as well as the Dante he has invented, "home" is a state before history in which the human mind "sees" the holy in the world.

Canto II quickly resumes the depiction of an Homeric world by means of allusion to and translation of some lines from *Iliad* III that focus on Helen. The old men of Troy complain about her presence while admiring her almost divine beauty. Because she is ship- and city-destroying, she ought to be sent back to the Greek ships.

Though "blind as a bat," "poor old Homer" was able to represent, in words, the beauty that leads to the destruction of Troy, which functions for Pound as the first manifestation of the ideal city that will play an increasingly central role in his political theorizing. The poet then moves to the *Odyssey*, Book XI again (a purely mechanical connection to the previous canto that nonetheless serves to form a pattern of Homeric values) with the story of Tyro, who was raped by Poseidon; from this violent encounter with the god, she gives birth to Pelias and Neleus, great servants of Zeus. Sexual desire and female beauty can lead either to great destruction or construction, to the ruin of a world or to its establishment and strength. Pound's innovation in telling this story is to depict Tyro and the sea god locked in the act of love that will produce the great heroes. The Homeric world of pagan reverence for sexuality leads to the visionary experience of Canto I, to the conception of heroic strength, or to the utter destruction of the ideal city.

This scene modulates into the main action of this canto, Acoetes' narrative of the danger and glory of Dionysius. Those who do not recognize the divine in this boy are transformed into brutes, while the one who does see the presence of a god is spared and becomes a devotee. Acoetes is telling his story to Pentheus as a warning to that young king to end his opposition to Dionysius and to join the worship of the god. Acoetes' line—"I have seen what I have seen"—presents the attitude of one who has been a witness to the power and greatness of the god but who cannot explain or defend his vision. Acoetes is witness to the twin possibilities of the divine already established through Homer. The canto ends back with the seascape where Tyro and Poseidon lie together, the natural beauty of the world depicted as the proper setting for the manifestation of the holy. The modern secular world is in the position of Pentheus, who relies on the powers of human reason and so ignores the warning to his destruction. While Canto II does not present Odysseus, it has created an Homeric frame for the story of another wanderer, Acoetes, who has seen and believes. Something has been added to the figure of the wanderer, the role of witness (but not yet of prophet).

The next canto follows thematically, in that Pound himself is a witness in a similar way, and we can either accept his warning or, like Pentheus, become victims of our worldly scepticism.

Canto III is an important "wanderer" canto because in it the poet establishes himself, in his own person, as an exile whose visionary gift reminds us of the Odysseus from Canto I. He includes a very specific and real situation from his own past as relevant material for his epic:

> I sat on the Dogana's steps
> For the gondolas cost too much, that year,
> And there were not "those girls", there was one face,
> And the Buccentoro twenty yards off, howling "Stretti",
> And the lit cross-beams, that year, in the Morosini,
> And peacocks in Koré's house, or there may have been.
>   (III/11)

He recalls his visit to Venice in 1908, when he left America for Europe to become a poet. Elsewhere, he will also recall this period of his life as a time of near despair, when he almost threw his manuscript of poems that becomes *A Lume Spento* in the water. Not even twenty-three, he finds himself unknown, impoverished (he cannot afford to ride in a gondola), and with doubtful prospects. Other young men would despair and chuck the poems in the canal, but this young man instead manages to achieve a visionary experience:

> Gods float in the azure air,
> Bright gods and Tuscan, back before dew was shed.
> Light: and the first light, before ever dew was fallen.
> Panisks, and from the oak, dryas,
> And from the apple, maelid,
> Through all the wood, and the leaves are full of voices,
> A-whisper, and the clouds bowe over the lake,
> And there are gods upon them,
> And in the water, the almond-white swimmers,
> The silvery water glazes the upturned nipple,
>   As Poggio has remarked.   (III/11)

Instead of despair, the young poet enjoys a vision of beauty and delight as he gazes over the Grand Canal, transforming the secular scene before him into a pagan world where divine and semidivine creatures play. The scene he conjures is remote in time, "back before dew was shed," "before ever dew was fallen"; it is an original world, where "the first light" shines. He is blest with Cassirer's "mythical consciousness," able to transform the objects of reality into holy objects. It is all "as Poggio has remarked"; as in Canto I, he turns to a medieval Latin text to aid his concentration. This again marks Renaissance Latin Italy as the last time, language, and place that had vital contact with the "first light." This canto is important because it is Pound's claim that he has a visionary capacity, that he had it as a very young man with no prospects:

this capacity is his stength and distinction. Pound himself becomes part of the wandering figure he is developing in these early cantos.

This canto divides neatly into two fragments of almost equal length, and their juxtaposition is telling. The other fragment is from the Spanish epic poem *Cantar de mio Cid;* Pound quotes from Part I, "The Exile." While this hero is meant to remind one of the composite Odysseus of Canto I, he also develops the character of the young poet already presented. As an exile, an outlaw, a man whom the authorities oppose and want to control, Ruy Diaz enables Pound to enlarge his own sense of isolation and danger. Like the young Pound, this resourceful bandit is out of funds, and economic privation is the main weapon that the powerful use to break its heroes. But as the young poet avoids despair and sees the gods, so myo Cid is able to transform his penury into capital. He fools Jewish moneylenders into thinking that a sealed trunk weighted down with sand actually contains gold. With such collateral, he is given the money he needs to raise an army and continue his outlawed existence.

The juxtaposition of these two fragments does more than present the poet himself as an outlawed hero whose cunning enables him to rise above the conditions of the present and continue his heroic enterprise. It also has aesthetic implications. Perhaps the vision of the gods that the young Pound manages is not "true" just as Diaz's sand is not gold.[3] The greatness of both cunning heroes—myo Cid and Pound—lies in their ability to transform the worthless into the fruitful. Sand is not gold anymore than the poet's words depict or represent anything really "out there." But somehow the poet's language can create an illusion that works, a fiction of origins that can make a real difference. This canto suggests that the poet is aware that he is constructing a myth of origins that may or may not be true; the "truth" factor is not the important matter, what matters is that it makes of human origins the capacity to feel joy and delight. He creates a fiction, that human origins are healthy and holy, so he can restore humanity to a health it may never have enjoyed. Origins are a place for the poet to work, a place of power in that they are constructed foundations capable of determining the version of humanity and the culture to follow. I do not wish to provide a method of deconstructing Pound; rather, I wish to suggest that he has the essential insight of the deconstructionist, that origins are a construct the powerful establish and control. The poet is an outlaw like myo Cid because the system in place at present recognizes the implications of the poet's cunning skill.[4]

The next three cantos introduce the troubadours of Provence

and Tuscany as another component of the wanderer. These singers wandered throughout southern Europe, celebrating the joys of sexual love, female beauty, and heroic warfare. After Canto III in which Pound's poetic gift is made part of the wanderer's nature, these cantos connect this poet with a tradition of wandering singers who, he believed, had a secret and outlawed religion with ties to the pagan past:

> Provence was less disturbed than the rest of Europe by invasion from the North in the darker ages; if paganism survived anywhere it would have been, unofficially, in the Langue d'Oc. That the spirit was, in Provence, Hellenic is seen readily by anyone who will compare the *Greek Anthology* with the work of the troubadours. (*SR* 90)

Ascetic and orthodox Christianity had less effect, Pound asserts, in Provence than in the rest of Europe and so an "unofficial paganism" survives there and reaches Tuscany in the thirteenth century. The orthodoxy is threatened by this pagan heritage:

> If a certain number of people in Provence developed their own unofficial mysticism, basing it for the most part on their own experience, if the servants of Amor saw visions quite as well as the servants of the Roman ecclesiastical hierarchy, if they were, moreover, troubled with no "dark night of the soul," and the kindred incommodities of ascetic yoga, this may well have caused some scandal and jealousy to the orthodox. (*SR* 91)

Peter Makin shows that the troubadours were part of a religious cult that the orthodoxy considered heretical (see *Provence* 217ff). So Pound adds another dimension to his wanderer to place him in a poetic tradition whose celebration of erotic love renders it outlawed and which "culminated in Dante Alighieri" (*SR* 88–89). "I am constantly contending that it took two centuries of Provence and one of Tuscany to develop the media of Dante's masterwork" (*LE* 9–10). It is safe to assert that even this addition to the wanderer theme has its purpose in deepening Pound's relation to Dante.

Pound has each of these three cantos begin in ways that recall the opening cantos in order to connect the troubadours to the wanderer theme there established. Canto IV opens with a sketch of a burning Troy, which reminds us of Helen from Canto II whom the old men feared would bring doom to the ideal city. A ref-

erence to Cadmus follows in his aspect as founder of the fabulous
legendary city of Thebes. Troy and Thebes are presented as realized examples of the ideal city that depend somehow on the pagan
reverence for the divine that troubadour song preserves. The canto
next presents two stories from Ovid that are retold in Provençal
legend: the story of Ityn is paralleled in the life of Guillems de
Cabestanh and the story of Actaeon in the life of Peire Vidal.
These couplings suggest a continuity from Ovid through the
Provençal singers, as do the many name places included, either
from Ovid's *Metamorphoses* or from Pound's own walking tour
through Provence in 1912. Ovid, one of the few "safe guides in religion" (*SL* 183) because he is the least dogmatic and merely witnesses the appearances of the divine (Bernstein 76–78), is implied
to be the classical source of the later singers. The canto also
includes scraps from Catullus and Arnaut Daniel, furthering the
sense of a survival of a tradition of erotic love songs from classical
Rome through the time of the troubadours.

Canto V begins with "Ecbatan, City of patterned streets,"
another historical manifestation of the ideal city that is now made
the product of the poet's "vision":

> Measureless seas and stars,
> Iamblichus' light,
>   the souls ascending,
> Sparks like a partridge covey,
>   Like the "ciocco", brand struck in the game.
> "Et omniformis": Air, fire, the pale soft light.
> Topaz I manage, and three sorts of blue;
>   but on the barb of time.
> The fire? always, and the vision always ...   (V/17)

As in Canto III, Pound presents his own visionary capacity as
material for his epic; it is relevant for this poet to inform his reader of what sorts of visionary experience he can "manage." It is
worth noting that, among other medieval Neoplatonic sources, he
alludes to *Paradiso* XVIII, Dante's image of sparks flying upwards
from a burning log that describes the souls of blessed warriors rising to form a great eagle. Pound implies that his vision of the ideal
city is in the tradition of Dante's heavenly city; a further layer has
been added to Pound's wanderer, as one whose vision reaches transcendent knowledge of heavenly justice and harmony. The canto
then connects this vision of the ideal city to the singers of erotic
love songs—Catullus, Sappho, Poicebot, and Pieire de Maesnac

(once again, a grouping of classical and Provençal poets implying an unbroken tradition)—in his effort to place his own poetic gift in a sacred (though largely secretive and scandalous) tradition. Pound more explicitly connects the story surrounding Pieire de Maesnac with the visionary city: the singer steals the wife of De Tierci (who is compared to Menelaus) and a war ensues, "Troy in Auvergnat" (18). The vision of the ideal city is somehow dependent on a poetic tradition Pound is working to establish in these cantos and into which he will fit himself.

Peter Makin calls Canto VI "a history of the Provençal civilisation," and his description of it confirms my thesis, that Pound uses this tradition to approach Dante:

> The Canto begins with the first known troubadour, William IX of Aquitane (1086–1127); moves to the marriage of his granddaughter Eleanor with Louis VII of France, to her second marraige with Henry II Plantagenet, and her relations with Bernart de Ventadorn; and shifts finally to Sordello, one of the last great troubadours, an Italian, whose lady Cunizza was known to Guido Cavalcanti. What this canto says is that there was a continuity from the circle of William IX of Aquitane right through to the circle of Dante.... (73)

Pound begins the canto in a way that connects this troubadour tradition to the figure of the wandering Odysseus:

> What have you done, Odysseus,
>   We know what you have done...
> And that Guillaume sold out his ground rents
> (Seventh of Poitiers, ninth of Aquitain).   (VI/21)

It is as if Guillaume sells his ground rents (in order to go wandering on a Crusade, Makin tells us, p. 75) as a result of what Odysseus has done. This enigmatic statement (for, after all, I hope I have shown that it is not self-evident what Odysseus has done) seems to have no other role in the canto than to place Pound's Odysseus—Pound's unique and labored version of the wandering hero—as the controlling figure of the canto's material.

While one purpose of Cantos IV through VI was to establish a tradition of wandering love poets, Canto VII presents another important addition to his model of the wanderer as he completes his initial development of this figure, an addition that renders Dante's example central to the epic's purposes.

First he establishes a literary tradition in which he seeks to operate as a poet/wanderer himself. He begins by recalling the scene out of *Iliad* III where the old men complain about Helen even as they praise her beauty. But this time she is connected to her later incarnation as Eleanor of Aquitaine, who was the subject of the previous canto and of whom Bernart de Ventadorn, Bertrans de Born, and Arnaut Daniel all sung (Makin 132). Then he turns to a passage from Ovid's *Ars amatoria* that gives advice to young men about how to seduce beautiful girls. What these two episodes establish are the powers and dangers of female beauty. Then comes a fragment from Bertrans de Born's poem that celebrates the coming of spring—not for its renewal of sexual passion and love but for the return of the glory of battle. Bertrans's poetry rails against those too cowardly to enjoy in warfare the same aesthetic delights as in love: his "propaganda is against fear" and his belief is "in the contagiousness of courage" (Makin 42, 44). The inclusion of Bertrans's ethic prepares the way for Dante's complex vision from *Paradiso* XVIII where the souls of the blessed warriors fly upward like "ciocco" to form a great eagle that is the heavenly symbol of the strength and vision required for the achievement of harmony and justice. Sexual love for women as sung by Homer and Ovid is the stuff that incites warriors and rulers to aim for heavenly justice in Dante. Pound then jumps more than five centuries, from the heaven of Dante to "the age of prose" that documents the bourgeois materialism of Flaubert's France. The contrast is drastic, from a world of great passion and courage to the precise depiction and diagnosis of a decadent world of sterile emotion and ornamental bricabrac. This great tradition ends with Henry James, whom Pound presents lifting his old voice above the others. He is compared to Sordello from *Purgatorio* VI, who watches Dante and Virgil pass *"con gli occhi onesti e tardi"*—"with eyes honest and slow." James is like this watchful couching lion who comes to recognize the poets as fellows and guides them only as far as the entrance to Purgatory proper (which is still denied him). Or James is like those great poets of antiquity from *Inferno* IV (Dante's limbo). Their solemn movement—*"grave incessu"*—announces their difference from the rest of those in this dimly lit part of hell whose only pain is the eternal loss of hope. In that canto Dante associates himself with great poetic forebears and indicates that he is both one of their number and beyond them, for he will leave hell, climb the purgatorial mountain, and achieve union with God. James then is the watchful artist who, in "weaving an endless sentence," mimes the mental paralysis of the modern bourgeois culture and who leads the poet someway toward a purgatorial experience denied himself.[5]

The prose tradition of Flaubert and James provides the context for a depiction of Pound himself, seeking buried beauty as he climbs the stairs of Purgatory:

> We also made ghostly visits, and the stair
> That knew us, found us again on the turn of it,
> Knocking at empty rooms, seeking for buried beauty;
> And the sun-tanned, gracious and well-formed fingers
> Lift no latch of bent bronze, no Empire handle
> Twists for the knocker's fall; no voice to answer.
> A strange concierge, in place of the gouty-footed.
> Sceptic against all this one seeks the living,
> Stubborn against the fact.   (VII/25)

The decadent world created by the bourgeois consciousness that sees no value other than accumulation of material has been bereft of the true beauty that the poet seeks. Pound has indicated a literary tradition of sexual passion, courage, and beauty that has been brought to the modern age only in the guise of prose fiction—Flaubert and James—which can diagnose the disease of the modern world. Pound picks up after James as the poet succeeds the master of English prose and seeks to uncover the beauty that the bourgeois mind has buried. Only the poet can find and record this beauty, which he believes still exists though the "facts" presented by the prose writers would indicate otherwise. He is "sceptic against all this," disbelieving that only the gross and ornamental bricabrac of the bourgeois world exists. The poet is a purgatorial figure who works to restore our vision to the beautiful, as Homer, Ovid, and Dante saw it. He establishes his own project as the creation of an epic poem in the age of the novel, an attempt to write in a genre appropriate to heroic ages and to be made vital once again. The first step in the restoration of the epic poem in the "modern" age is the heroic search for beauty in a culture that seems to have lost its capacity to see the beautiful.

Pound regards himself as an epic poet in the age of prose. After some lingering in the debased and sordid "contemporary" world, Pound resumes the theme of eros that earlier in the canto was seen as culminating in Dante's heavenly vision:

> The sea runs in the beach-groove, shaking the floated pebbles,
> Eleanor!
>   The scarlet curtain throws a less scarlet shadow;
> Lamplight at Buovilla, e quel remir,

                    And all that day
Nicea moved before me
And the cold grey air troubled her not
For all her naked beauty, bit not the tropic skin,
And the long slender feet lit on the curb's marge
And her moving height went before me,
                    We alone having being.
And all that day, another day:
                    Thin husks I had known as men,
Dry casques of departed locusts
                    speaking a shell of speech...
Propped between chairs and tables...
Words like the locust-shells, moved by no inner being;
                    A dryness calling for death.   (VII/25–26)

Pound places his own appreciation of the "naked beauty" of Nicea (variously identified but certainly in part a reference to Helen of Troy through Poe's "Nicean barks") in the tradition of erotic song from Homer (Helen) through Ovid (the detail of the scarlet curtain comes from Golding's translation of the description of Atalanta's naked beauty as she races Hippomenes) to Arnaut Daniel (whose *"e quel remir"* is from a poem in which he asks to gaze upon his beloved's naked body in the lamplight). In the modern world only the poet and the beautiful Nicea "have being," while the rest of humanity is hollow and desiccated. He has found and can marvel at the "naked beauty" before him, while the husks and shells of what once were men call for death to end their empty existence. Even the words these hollow men speak are only "the shell of speech"; fallen men speak a fallen language. He continues the depiction of this weak and passionless people for most of the rest of the canto, but he is careful to insert a line from Dante that continues his work on the wanderer:

                    The old room of the tawdry class asserts itself;
The young men, never!
                    Only the husk of talk.
O voi che siete in piccioletta barca,
Dido choked up with sobs, for her Sicheus
Lies heavy in my arms, dead weight
Drowning, with tears, new Eros,

And the life goes on, mooning upon bare hills; [...]
Passion to breed a form in shimmer of rain-blur;

But Eros drowned, drowned, heavy-half dead with tears
        For dead Sicheus.   (VII/26–27)

As he calls attention to this partial humanity, he quotes the opening line of *Paradiso* II, in which Dante distinguishes his voyage from Ulysses':

O ye who in a little bark, eager to listen, have followed behind my ship that singing makes her way, turn back to see your shores again; do not put forth on the deep, for, perhaps, losing me, you would be left bewildered. The waters I take were never sailed before. . . .
    Ye other few that reached out early for the angels' bread by which men here live but never come from it satisfied, you may indeed put forth your vessel on the salt depths, holding my furrow before the water turns smooth again. (*Paradiso* II, 1–15)

Like Ulysses, Dante claims to sail waters "never sailed before," and like Ulysses he promises wonderful experience. But unlike Ulysses, who is consigned to hell as a false counsellor for inciting others to follow his dangerous quest, Dante does not seek to seduce so much as to warn. And unlike Ulysses, who drowns in sight of Mount Purgatory, Dante has already undergone purification on that mountain and has begun his ascent through Paradise. Dante calls those few who, like himself, "reached out early for the angels' bread," to follow his "ship that singing makes its way"; the poet's true song, and not Ulysses' false counsel, can lead fellow voyagers safely back to purity and then forward again to blessedness. Pound marks the crucial distinction between Dante's Ulysses and Dante: where the former's wandering is a reckless escape from the oppressive conditions of a corrupt and decadent civilization, Dante's journey is a more deliberate leading of those few who are brave enough to follow a dangerous path toward a new way of being. In this regard, Pound's wanderer is not like Homer's, who simply wants to return to the home he was forced to leave, nor like Dante's Ulysses, who recklessly leads others from home to their destruction, but like Dante himself, whose songs can lead a select few away from the present state of being and toward a new one, away from an inadequate and unsatisfying home toward the lost purity of an original home. The husks and shells of men lack the courage and will to follow Pound's ship that singing makes its way, his "Cantos," but a few people with "inner being" might be able to traverse the dangerous waters to a true home. Pound quotes this moment from *Paradiso* here (and elsewhere) to indicate that his wanderer's vessel sings its way to a new home. This moment establishes that his wanderer is primarily a poet whose song can lead people to a new way of being.

While Cantos IV through VI present a series of troubadour poets whose celebration of eros is relevant to the wanderer's identity, it is Dante who is most important to Pound, for he culminates this tradition by making erotic desire historically significant. The passage that includes the line from *Paradiso II* also refers to *Inferno* V, where Virgil points out Dido who "slew herself for love and broke faith with the ashes of Sichaeus." Pound is following Dante here in presenting a Dido sobbing for Sichaeus, and not for Aeneas who spurned eros for a public destiny as founder of an Empire. Aeneas is not congenial to the poet in his rejection of sexual passion and its utter severance from the public sphere of historical causality. Eros has been drowned, perhaps by the present culture that fears its tremendous potential for destruction. A world that has denied Eros has created a hollow and desiccated humanity not worth ruling over, and Pound, like Dante, wants to make sexual desire once again a factor in the creation of a new and better world.

The first seven cantos form a pattern in their development of a complex figure of an heroic wanderer who desires a movement away from the present order of things and back to an original, lost home that has the potential to become, in turn, the center of a new order. The wit and nostalgia of Homer's Odysseus, the daring and thirst for new experience of Dante's Ulysses, the lyric skill and outlawed religion of the troubadour poets, and above all the example of Dante the pilgrim who successfully negotiates a return to Eden and then leads an elite through the spheres of the blessed: all these qualities are accumulated and added to the character of the poet himself as he creates a composite hero who begins the epic quest for a lost home. These opening cantos establish the palimpsest of an epic tradition over which Pound will attempt to execute a modern epic in the age of the novel. He has developed and begins to deploy an epic wanderer operating within a dense and honored tradition of epic journeys; Pound's poem is indeed nostalgic, not only in the search for a lost home but in the attempt to revitalize an ancient genre. The modern epic begins with an movement "outward and away" from the present, away from "history," seeking the point of origin where the human mind was healthy and whole.

Cantos XIV–XVII

The next set of cantos to continue the development of the
wandering hero is Pound's most explicit, literal, and derivative
borrowing from Dante in the whole of *The Cantos*. In fact, his use
of the Dantesque landscape in this sequence is so obvious that it
would hardly merit examination except that it does advance his
understanding of the problems facing the hero he has established.

Cantos XIV and XV are the famous (or, more properly, infamous) Hell Cantos and one is so repelled by their shrill, strident,
violent tone and language that a comparison to Dante's fuller, richer, and more subtle version always makes Pound's seem wholly
inadequate and unsatisfying. We should try instead to see what element he is working to add to his wanderer theme, not as if this is
his only moment of Dantesque reading and application but merely
as one in a series that continues to the final words of the epic.

The sequence begins with a direct quotation from *Inferno* V,
"Io venni in luogo d'ogni luce muto"—"I came then to a place where
all light is mute." These words announce Dante's entry into the
second circle of hell but the first in which are found active sinners.
While Dante's hell is varied and subtle in presenting human sinfulness, Pound's contains only one type of sinner, the "monopolists,
obstructors of knowledge,/ obstructors of distribution" (XIV/63).
The light of the holy does not shine in the modern world because of
the concerted actions of those who advance the claims of usury, all
those who block the free circulation and just distribution of knowledge and money. Pound rails at profiteers, financiers,

> And the betrayers of language.
>   . . . . . n and the press gang
> And those who had lied for hire;
>   the perverts, the perverters of language,
>   the perverts, who have set money-lust
> Before the pleasures of the senses.   (XIV/61)

The capacity to enjoy the world and possibly see its divine
splendour has been reduced by those who, in obstructing the circulation of wealth, have made us all competitive, aggressive, and
greedy for money. Lust for money has replaced the sensual pleasure that would render the world a delightful place of ease and
comfort, a home. Those who block circulation make what would be
healthy a morass of filth and disease; Pound resorts to the grossest
scatalogical images to indicate that beauty has been covered by the

debased categories and perceptions of a diseased culture. The usurers are seen "plunging jewels in mud,/ and howling to find them unstained" (62); that is, beauty cannot be destroyed but only buried, and we recall Canto VII where Pound himself was making ghostly visits in search of this buried beauty. Beauty can only be hidden under the vulgar bricabrac produced by a decadent culture obsessed with the mass production and uncritical accumulation of material. The poet has identified what he understands as the single major factor in his alienation from the world as a home: the effects of an economic system that hides beauty and distorts a true hierarchy of values.

It is somewhat surprising to notice Pound's claim that he is only following Dante in this. In answering a scholarly quibble about whether Dante meant Plutus or Pluto as the guardian of lower hell, Pound claims for Dante's poem what he will foreground in his own: "Dante meant *plutus,* definitely putting money-power at the root of Evil" (*SL* 255). He seems anxious to find in Dante's poem authority for his own insight:

> One advantage of having [the *Commedia*] in penetrable idiom is that we see more clearly the grading of Dante's values, and especially how the whole of hell reeks with money. The usurers are there as against nature, against the natural increase of agriculture or of any productive work. Deep hell is reached via Geryon (fraud) of the marvellous patterned hide, and for ten cantos thereafter the damned are all of them damned for money. (*LE* 211)

Although this analysis of Dante's scheme is highly questionable and strained, it demonstrates Pound's need to find corroboration of his insight in Dante, who makes visionary capacity the key to one's damnation or salvation. He anxiously claims the security of believing that, even in what might appear highly idiosyncratic, he is only following the master.

After continuing the hysterical indictment of the various personnel in the hire of usury, Canto XV presents a comic escape from hell. Pound's guide, Plotinus, finds a way to make the foul matter into which the two are sinking become solid enough to permit their departure:

> and again Plotinus:
> To the door,
> Keep your eyes on the mirror.

> Prayed we to the Medusa,
>   pertrifying the soil by the shield,
> Holding it downward
>   he hardened the track
> Inch before us, by inch.   (XV/66)

The shield serves as a mirror that reflects Medusa's petrify-
ing gaze onto the ooze of filth, thus hardening the track just
enough so that they make a slow and difficult exit from this foul
place. I want to emphasize the *comic* nature of this escape so we do
not make T. S. Eliot's mistake regarding the intent of these two
cantos. In *After Strange Gods*, Eliot records his famous objection
that "Pound's hell, for all its horror, is a perfectly comfortable one
to contemplate: it is a Hell for *other people,* the people we read
about in the newspapers, not for oneself and one's friends" (47).
Eliot is correct except that he fails to understand that Pound's
point is not to depict the effect of human sinfulness on our eternal
state; rather, he works to expose an economic system that blocks
the light of the holy from our eyes, prevents our seeing true value,
renders us greedy and aggressive in the production and accumulation of material things, and thus has created an ugly and foul culture. Pound has constructed a "comic" hell, a caricature of the
problem because he does not want to frighten the reader but to
show him the problem against which the wanderer must struggle.
In 1920, just about when he is conceiving these cantos, he implies
that the modern poet should not emulate Dante's hell because it
has been used by

> the slaves of usury and an alleged religion which has taught
> that the splendour of the world is not a true splendour, that it
> is not the garment of the gods; and which has glorified the
> vilest of human imaginations, the pit of the seven great
> stenches, and which still teaches the existence of this hell as
> a verity for the sake of scaring little children and stupid
> women and of collecting dues and maintaining its prestige.
> (*LE* 431)

If one wished to apply Harold Bloom's thesis about an Oedipal
struggle between a great precursor poet and his follower, one could
argue that Pound sees the need to "correct" this aspect of Dante's
epic. He transforms Dante's hell into a comic landscape that adds to
the wanderer theme Pound's sense of the economic factors that have
led to the alienation the wandering hero has set out to overcome.

Canto XV ends as Pound's pilgrim emerges from this hell:

Panting like a sick dog, staggered,
Bathed in alkali, and in acid.
[The sun, the sun]
        blind with the sunlight,
Swollen-eyed, rested,
        lids sinking, darkness unconscious.   (XV/67)

Pound even offers a brief comic version of Dante's Purgatory: whereas Dante's eyes are cleansed terrace by terrace of the obfuscating categories of human experience that block the holy light, Pound is bathed in alkali and acid to erode the encrustations of filth that has kept him from seeing the sun's light. The modern version of hell relies on modern science, as Pound replaces the painful discipline required for spiritual purgation with strong corrosives made available by chemical technology; such are the comic fruits of cultural progress. The opening of the next canto continues his depiction of the Dantesque landscape:

And before hell mouth; dry plain
        and two mountains;
On the one mountain, a running form,
        and another
In the turn of the hill; . . .
And the running form, naked, Blake,
Shouting, whirling his arms, the swift limbs,
Howling against the evil.   (XVI/68)

The scene is similar to *Purgatorio* I, where Dante and Virgil emerge from the mouth of hell and lie on the plain before Mount Purgatory. Pound presents two mountains, a small and insignificant adjustment of the Dantesque landscape intended, perhaps, to render his heavy borrowing from Dante more a matter of play than a serious reworking. Dante himself appears—as "Il Fiorentino"—on the "west mountain"; Pound wants us to know that this is Dante's landscape borrowed for his own purposes, namely, to give his own economic theory larger spiritual implications. Canto XVII presents what Pound calls "a sort of paradiso terrestre." It is not, as Terrell says (73), his "first extended vision of Paradise" but of the earthly paradise; it is Pound's first effort to show Dante's achievement of a return to the purity of origins signalled by his entry into the earthly paradise of Eden in *Purgatorio* XXVIII. So Pound manages to escape from "the hell of money" into Purgatory and then to reach the purity of an original consciousness that recognizes the "true splendour of the world." Canto XVII begins "So that the vines burst from my fingers" (76); the last words of Canto I are the opening words here to connect the achievement of this earthly paradise to the wanderer's brave movement "outward and away" that in the opening canto led to the vision of Aphrodite. Pound's "paradiso terrestre" is from the pagan world of Greek mythology. This is another place one could apply Bloom's thesis: Pound must rewrite Dante's version of earthly paradise so it has a distinctly pagan character, for the world of Greek gods and goddesses will be his version of the original consciousness. What Dante's verse has chosen to forget Pound emphasizes: the pagan nature of the original human consciousness.

Canto XX

The next deployment of the wanderer is in Canto XX where Pound invents a song of the lotophagoi—the lotus eaters—who refuse to follow Odysseus on the dangerous journey back home. This has obvious roots in Tennyson, who also depicts their ease and comfort as a foil to the daring and commitment of the brave Ulysses. But Pound places this song in a complex context that deepens its implications concerning the nature of Odysseus's journey.

The canto begins in a way that recalls Canto VII, with another set of fragments that establish a literary tradition of love songs. Pound includes the ringing of wedding bells from Catullus; a line from Bernart de Ventadorn depicting the ideal nature of his love for his lady ("And if I see her not, / No sight is worth the beauty of my thought"); a word from Guido Cavalcanti's Sonnet 35 that blasphemously assigns the miraculous power of a statue of the Virgin to its resemblance to his beloved; a passage from Propertius in which he claims that he will never be able to forget Cynthia's kind nature; and the series ends with the name of Ovid. Such is a series of singers who celebrate erotic love in its potential for divine manifestation. But in the middle of it Pound inserts Homer's description of the sirens' song: "Ligur' aoide"—their "clear sweet song." The songs of erotic love, then, may function like the sirens' song, luring the home-seeking mariner to his destruction.

We then follow a long account of a visit Pound once made to Freiburg to ask the Provençal scholar Emil Levy the meaning of an obscure word in a poem of Arnaut's, *"noigandres."* The poet seems to consider this act of scholarly inquiry a relevant bit of information about what the alienated wanderer must perform to maintain his course: to learn as much as possible about fellow wanderers who have left traces of their journeys in obscure poems in dead languages. He then renders "an ideal landscape" based on Arnaut's poem (Makin 178) that ends with that poet's request to gaze on the almost divine glory of his beloved's naked body: "And the light falls, *remir,* / from her breast to thighs." The implication is that Pound is a wanderer through old texts that contain some potential for danger, texts that may lure him to his destruction.

We then move to a long and confusing sequence of reminiscences that are "jumbled or candied in Nicolo [d'Este]'s delirium" (*SL* 210). After discovering that his young wife Parisina and natural son Ugo have been having an affair, Nicolo has them both executed and enters the delirious state presented. We move from dangerous poems of erotic love to a specific instance in which eros has led to madness. "Nicolo's delirium" resembles strongly Pound's own method in designing a canto, where fact and dream are difficult to distinguish and the references unexplained and hazy. It is as if he presents Nicolo's delirious state as a danger that his own epic quest may fall into: the voyage through the history of Western culture may only end up in such madness and confusion. In a letter to his father, Pound describes this series of confusing juxtapositions of history and fantasy "as a sort of bounding surface from which one gives the main subject of the canto, the lotophagoi: lotus eaters, or respectable dope smokers; and general paradiso." The risk of madness that is part of eros is the "bounding surface" from which the poet turns to the lotophagoi, who avoid this danger by falling into a drug-induced and safe lethargy. These "opium smokers" complain about the fate of those who follow Odysseus:

> "What gain with Odysseus,
> "They that died in the whirlpool
> "And after many vain labours,
> "Living by stolen meat, chained to the rowingbench,
> "That he should have great fame
> > "And lie by night with the goddess? [. . .]
> "Nor had they Circe to couch-mate, Circe Titania,
> "Nor had they meats of Kalüpso
> "Or her silk skirts brushing their thighs.
> "Give! What were they given?
> > > Ear-wax.
> "Poison and ear-wax,
> > > and a salt grave by the bull-field,

"*neson amumona,* their heads like sea crows in the foam,
"Black splotches, sea-weed under lightning;
"Canned beef of Apollo, ten cans for a boat load."
Ligur' aoide.   (XX/93–94)

Pound invents this song of complaint that details "the resumé of Odyssey" (*SL* 210). These "suave, quite, scornful" lotus eaters speak in "voce-profondo" as they consider the difference between Odysseus's adventures and the fate of his crew. As in Tennyson's poem, an ambiguous contrast is established between the heroic vigor and commitment to action of Odysseus and the comfortable ease of the speakers. Hugh Kenner describes this speech as "the drone of blighted voices without being, betrayed not by personal accident or heroic necessity but by an inner saplessness of will" (*Poetry* 278). This description implies a connection between the lotus eaters and the "husks of men" who speak the "shell of speech" in Canto VII. From this perspective, Pound can be regarded as developing his characterization of modern humanity: deficient in will, they refuse to follow the strong-willed and heroic Odysseus and choose instead to enjoy the slothful ease available in an enervated culture, forever cut off from their true home.

Donald Davie challenges Kenner's negative assessment of the lotophagoi: "one can only be astonished at the impression the passage gives, which Pound's letter to his father confirms, that the lotus eaters are offered naively to be admired by the reader as having attained one stage toward an all-important illumination" (134). Davie alerts us to the ambiguous presentation of these comfortable figures that has precedent in Tennyson. While Pound seldom has kind words for "dope smokers," these are "respectable." The letter suggests that these lotus eaters are on the way to a "general paradiso," and the canto does proceed immediately from their complaint to a lovely scene that might merit that label. But we do not have to choose between these two eminent Poundians: Kenner is correct in that the lotophagoi are not exerting their will properly, and Davie is correct in that they have attained "one stage" on the way to transcendence. For Pound has presented the situation of these dope smokers in such a way that it resembles one Dante faces in *Purgatorio* II.

Having just emerged from "hell mouth," Dante meets a friend of his, the musician Casella, and asks:

'If a new law does not take from thee memory or practice of the songs of love which used to quiet all my longings, may it

please thee to refresh my soul with them for a while, which is
so spent coming here with my body.' (*Purgatorio* II, 107–11)

Like the lotus eaters, Dante and the other penitents are weary
of their journey and wish rest from labor. Love songs provide Dante
with the ease and comfort that the lotophagoi derive from the lotus.
When we recall that Pound's Canto XX begins with the series of
singers of love songs and the poet's own devotion to the troubadour
tradition, we may infer that the lotus eaters present Pound's
awareness that his own delight in song may function in the same
way as Casella's song here. For Cato, the guardian of the island of
Purgatory, does not permit an indulgence in the song; he sharply
rebukes their slothful ease and rouses them to continue their journey up the mountain and toward the earthly paradise of Eden:

> 'What is this, laggard spirits? What negligence, what delay is
> this? Haste to the mountain to strip you of the slough that
> allows not God to be manifest to you. (lines 120–123)

"A new law" does render this rest an offense. The penitents
are not yet allowed to rest but are encouraged to continue their
journey that will result in the manifestation of God. Similarly,
Pound's lotus eaters enjoy a false rest, a dangerous ease: for their
comfort prevents them from working toward a purity that would
let gods and goddesses be manifest to them. As Kenner asserts,
they need their wills strengthened so they can continue their journey; and as Davie suggests, they have reached the shores of Mount
Purgatory and are on their way towards Edenic purity. Pound has
conflated the Homeric episode with a Dantesque scene to issue a
warning about the lures of love song and the wanderer's need both
to listen and continue his journey.[6]

This brings us back to the obscure phrase from Arnaut.
Makin argues that Pound follows Professor Levy's solution and
emends "di noigandres" to "d'enoi ganres," which can mean, among
other things, "protection from distress" or "wards off boredom."
The phrase comes from a passage in which Arnaut establishes the
properties of a marvellous flower, "whose seed is joy, its fruit love,
and its scent the protection from distress" (Makin 179). Pound borrows Arnaut's flower and makes it into the lotus that soothes the
pain of those who indulge in it. He even presents "an ideal landscape" (Makin 178) based on this phrase:

> You would be happy for the smell of that place
> And never tired of being there, either alone

Or accompanied. [. . .]
The smell of that place—*d'enoi ganres.*
Air moving under the boughs,
The cedars there in the sun,
Hay new cut on hill slope,
And the water there in the cut
Between the two lower meadows.   (90)

This landscape of pleasant ease and comfort could be the
place the lotus eaters dwell in their drugged lethargy. Arnaut's
flower and the lotus are both beneficial in their power to free us
from the hellish pain and annoyance that would prevent us from
ever reaching blessedness. But the lotus eaters do not proceed to
the love and joy that Arnaut's flower also provides: they remain
only in the state of comfort, free from distress or boredom or pain
but not strong enough to continue on the way to positive delights.

Pound ends the lotus eaters' song with Homer's description of
the Sirens' song, *"Ligur' aoide."* Love songs are doubly dangerous:
they can lead one to embrace the delights of erotic love that can
lead to madness; and they are dangerous in their capacity to comfort and console so effectively that one might abandon the wandering to a true home. Delight in such songs can inspire one to the
heights of heaven but a too heavy indulgence in that delight might
be as destructive as the Sirens' song. Following Dante, Pound
knows that the journey to origins can be destructive (for he has
pondered Ulysses' fate, and Nicolo's delirium can be read as a version of that *"folle vole,"* that "mad flight") and that finding rest
anywhere within the present state of culture is equally dangerous
in losing the opportunity for a new way of being. Canto XX marks
the poet's awareness of the double danger inherent in his craft.

Canto XXXIX

Observing that the erotic aspects of Ulysses' career did not become
a dominant theme until late in the nineteenth century, Stanford
claims that "Joyce makes as much of this erotic element as any
writer before or after him" (217). Once again, Stanford ignores
Pound, who makes the wanderer's sexual adventures central, even
pivotal, to the quest for home. In Canto XXXVI, which focuses on
Pound's translation of Guido Cavalcanti's "Canzone d'Amore," the
poet cries out, "sacrum, sacrum, illumatio coitu"—"sacred, sacred,
the light in coition." It is crucial to note that he emphasizes

coition, the physical act of sexual union, as a source of this holy light he will associate with Eleusis: "The sacrament is coition, and not the going to the fat-buttocked priest or registry official" (*SL* 303). Pound's work on the troubadours of Provence and Tuscany has prepared him to rewrite Dante's journey to purity and blessedness. The modern poet returns Dante's glorification of Beatrice and the Blessed Virgin Mary to its source in sexual passion and the physical act of sexual union. Pound restores the relation between Amor and Eros in Canto XXXIX.

As we have seen, Pound understands that Dante culminates the troubadour tradition of reverence for the ideal lady. As Peter Dronke explains, "the lover has an ideal image of the beloved within him, which is the perfect expression of his own love; but in the outer world, he is shamefast and can express his own love only imperfectly. He cannot wholly attain his ideal beloved" (152). Dronke insists upon a distinction between inside and outside, between the ideal held within the mind and the "real" lady existing in the world. A gap exists between the woman as she is in the flesh and as she comes to exist in the mind of the beloved. Bernart de Ventadorn's line quoted at the beginning of Canto XX, "And if I see her not, No sight is worth the beauty of my thought," expresses the passionate interiorization of the woman into the ideal lady, the lady who exists primarily as a beautiful idea in the lover's mind. As Pound comes to formulate his theory on the dynamics of and possibilities within human sexuality, he sends his wandering Odysseus back to Circe's bed to redress the dissociation between the physical and ideal worlds that is most extreme in Dante's work.

Stuart McDougal demonstrates that "Pound's initial interest in early Tuscan love poetry was precisely in those poems which developed the qualities of the ideal lady surrounded by a brilliant light symbolizing her virtù" (72). McDougal cites an authority whom Pound knew and respected, H. J. Chaytor, on the development of the ideal lady in the troubadour tradition:

> the later troubadours gradually dissociated their love from the object that had aroused it; among them, love is no longer sexual passion; it is rather the motive to great works, to self-surrender, to the winning an honourable name as courtier and poet. (71)

McDougal believes that Pound knew of Chaytor's work describing the troubadour's lady as a product of sexual passion from which it is gradually separated. This dissociation, especially in Dante, can be considered sublimation, for the energy of sexual passion is directed toward higher and nobler ends, in Dante the highest goal imaginable, union with God. Pound comes to reject the idea that beatitude is reached by means of sublimation. He had begun his poetic career, however, by following the traditional version of this ideal. McDougal rightly claims that in the poet's early work in troubadour lyric, "the woman becomes increasingly idealized. . . . There is a noticeable lack of sexuality in these poems" (88). In "The Flame," for instance, the transcendent experience is wholly dissociated from its source in sexual passion:

> We who are wise beyond your dreams of wisdom,
> Drink our immortal moments; we "pass through."
> We have gone forth beyond your bonds and borders,
> Provence knew;
> And all the tales of Oisin say but this:
> That man doth pass the net of days and hours.
>
> Where time is shrivelled down to time's seed corn
> We of the Ever-living, in that light
> Meet through our veils and whisper, and of love. . . .
>
> If I have merged my soul, or utterly
> Am solved and bound in, through aught here on earth,
> There thou canst find me, O thou anxious thou,
> Who call'st about my gates for some lost me;
> I say my soul flowed back, became translucent.
>
> Search not my lips, O Love, let go my hands,
> This thing that moves as man is no mere mortal.   (*P* 50–51)

The focus here is on the transcendent experience without any sense of how the experience came about. The most he can say is that he has "passed through" our "bonds and borders," "through aught here on earth"; maybe it was something on earth that served as a vehicle for this movement outward and away from the mortal world bound by space and time, but we do not get anything more precise as explanation. He asks his beloved to "search not my lips" and to "let go my hands"; as McDougal says about a different early poem in the same manner, "there is a complete absence of sexual contact. Not only are the two separated, but the speaker shows no longing for the physical presence of his beloved" (86). Even the rhythm of the lines suggests a dreaminess rather than an energy and passion. In "The House of Splendour," Pound presents an almost wholly ethereal lady:

> And I have seen my lady in the sun,
> Her hair spread about, a sheaf of wings,
> And red the sunlight was, behind it all.   (*P* 49)

As her hair becomes wings, this lady becomes a radiant angel referred to as an "it" by her lover; she is no longer flesh and blood but a Pre-Raphaelite spirit who can lead her lover "somewhere beyond the worldly ways." In these poems can be detected a shimmering radiance and dreaminess that recall Swinburne, Rossetti, and the early Yeats. In his comment on these very lines, Louis Martz calls the woman "a vision out of Cavalcanti and his peers, through Rossetti" (*CEP* xviii). Pound's early version of the ideal lady dissociates her from sexuality, as an ethereal lady leads a lover to a lethargic repose reminiscent of the drugged state of the lotus eaters in Canto XX. "Pound knew that the power of the masters, Rossetti and Swinburne, had been diluted and enervated by the languid eroticism, the misty landscapes, the melancholy dreams, and the pallid archaisms of their followers" (*CEP* ix). That canto was meant to distance the poet from this version of transcendence that is really only a slothful ease and enervated comfort, not an ecstasy.

Pound's inheritance of a Pre-Raphaelite sensibility led him to these dreamy love songs, and his first study of the Tuscan poets and their ideal love was through Rossetti's translations. He continued the study and translation of troubadour song throughout his years of work on *The Cantos* until he could break out of the sensibility that obscures the way to the transcendence he seeks. As early as 1912, when he was just beginning to develop a harder line and metric largely as a result of his translations of Guido's poems, he was already suggesting that Dante's Amor had a place in the pagan tradition he was tracing in the troubadours:

> The rise of Mariolotry, its pagan lineage, the romance of it, find modes of expression which verge over-easily into the speech and casuistry of Our Lady of Cyprus, as we may see in Arnaut, as we see so splendidly in Giudo's "Una figura della donna miae." And there is the consummation of it all in Dante's glorification of Beatrice. There is the inexplicable address to the lady in the masculine. There is the final evolution of Amor by Guido and Dante, a new and paganish god, neither Eros nor an angel of the Talmud. (*SR* 91–92)

He assigns to the veneration and worship of the Blessed Virgin Mary a "pagan lineage" that finds expression in troubadour song. He alludes to a song of Arnaut's in which the lover claims that his own love for his lady exceeds that of God for Mary and to Guido's Sonnet 35 in which the miraculous powers credited to a statue of the Blessed Virgin are due to the "face of my lady" on whom the statue was modelled. Both poems verge on blasphemy as they render the worship of Mary a product of their sexual passion for their own beloved ladies. This "blasphemy" has its "consummation . . . in Dante's glorification of Beatrice." The *Vita Nuova* tells the story about how Dante's youthful passion for Beatrice becomes love for "the now glorious lady of my mind." Eros becomes Amor, as Beatrice becomes idealized and leads him through Paradise and to the final vision of God that ends the pilgrim's journey. Pound is trying to understand Dante's Amor, which is "neither Eros nor an angel from the Talmud"; that is, neither erotic desire in itself nor some disembodied ethereal being. He is reading the troubadour tradition of love song to understand the way to this "new and paganish god."

About Beatrice, Charles Singleton comments:

> To be sure, she was a woman of flesh and blood, a creature, and mortal even as death had shown. But by this very fact was the greater miracle: that mortal creature, woman, could be the bearer of a beatitude reaching beyond the bounds of nature, reaching back to Heaven because it had come from Heaven. (6)

Singleton notes the wonder of this miracle but Pound wants to know *how* a mortal creature of flesh and blood leads her lover to beatitude; he wants to understand more precisely the process by which a woman becomes the bearer of beatitude. It frustrates Pound that Dante worked hard and well to dissociate Beatrice from any sexual nexus. Francis Fergusson records the legend that Dante "had the reputation for being incontinent," of "thinking too vilely," and of leading "a vile life, usually supposed to refer to his erotic life" (44). Fergusson reads in *Convivio* Dante's attempt to defend his reputation against such charges: "He planned, as he tells us (I,ii) to 'reveal the true meaning' of all his poems, in order to show that 'not passion but virtue was the motivating cause'" (41). *Convivio*, read this way, marks Dante's anxiety about the sexual source of the transcendent experience in his love poetry.

Inferno V records a crucial moment in Dante's complicated

relation to sexual passion (see Mazzotta 165–69). In this lovely but sober canto, he meets the lovers Paolo and Francesca, consigned to hell for subjecting reason to desire. Francesca speaks just like the courtly lovers she and Paolo were reading when they sinned; the very fabric of her speech is textual, derived from books that advance a sensibility and a code of ethics contrary to orthodox Catholicism. Francesca's speech is so firmly grounded in the courtly tradition that we are actually witnessing a sin of misreading, or overreading, in her complete identification with the text. Accordingly, she blames a book and its author for her fate ("A Galeotto was the book and he who wrote it"), at which point Dante "drops as a dead body drops." Many commentators have seen this fainting spell as a sign of Dante's tremendous sympathy for, perhaps identification with, their sin; but Giuseppe Mazzotta offers a more poignant motive, the sense of Dante's possible complicity in their doom as the author of powerful and unorthodox love lyrics. Hearing Francesca's borrowed language and acquired sensibility, he recognizes the texture of his own early work, a recognition that overwhelms him with guilt and anxiety. Even though Francesca is wrong to blame a book for the failure of her own will, Dante would like to dissociate himself from any such complicity in their sin. His fainting spell at the very moment of her accusation is his tacit acknowledgement of the true source of the lyrical power of his early poetry, an acknowledgement so tacit it goes easily unnoticed. Similarly in *Purgatorio* XXVI, he meets Guido Guinicelli and Arnaut Daniel on the last purgatorial terrace which purifies the spirit of lust. In placing his poetic fathers there, he again acknowledges the source of his poetics even as he attempts to distance himself from it as he passes through this terrace and reaches a purity he denies his forebears. Dante is concerned to make clear that he has sublimated the sexual passion that marked his earlier life and gave power to his earlier work.

Pound uses a similar method of placing himself in relation to poetic precursors. As we have seen, Canto VII placed Henry James in a position similar to Guinicelli's and Arnaut Daniel's, as a poetic father the poet surpasses in his quest for and achievement of home; and in Canto XX the entire love song tradition from Homer through Guido Cavalcanti is exposed as potentially dangerous in the ease and comfort it might encourage. But while Dante wanted to distance himself from the sexual source of his transcendent experience, Pound works to bring that source back into clear and precise relation to the experience he is seeking. It is Dante's tendency to conceal the sexual source of the ideal lady that causes

Pound to praise Guido Cavalcanti at Dante's expense: Guido
"shows himself more 'modern' than his young friend Dante
Alighieri, qui étatit diablement dans less idées reçues, and whose
shock is probably recorded in the passage of *Inferno* X" (*LE* 149).
The modern poet translates Guido's "Canzone d'Amore" in Canto
XXXVI as a corrective to what he perceives as Dante's failure to
confront orthodox Catholicism concerning the ideal lady's true
nature and source of her power. Guido emphasizes the danger
involved in love and the relation between eros and amore. For
Guido the "heretic," amore is a "wild affect" that "cometh of Mars."
As the male principle who is the god of war, Mars is the proper
parent of a passion that is potentially violent and destructive. In
Guido's poem, at least in Pound's translation, sexual passion is at
war with reason:

> Beyond salvation, holdeth his judging force
> Deeming intention to be reason's peer and mate,
> Poor in discernment, being thus weakness' friend
> Often his power cometh on death in the end,
> Be it withstayed
> and so swinging counterweight.   (XXXVI/178)

Pound devotes almost an entire canto to Guido's lyric exposi-
tion of amore's power because he considers Dante too eager to pass
over this aspect as he distances himself from sexual passion in the
Commedia. Pound wants to foreground Guido's insight that love
"can unbalance judgment and make will prevail over reason"
(Dronke 159). While Dante does note this in *Inferno* V, Pound
includes Guido's poem as a more daring treatment of love's danger,
more daring because it does not separate the poet from the possible destruction inherent in love. But as soon as Pound's translation ends, the poet constructs a series of fragments that begins
with an image that suggests Dante's *Paradiso*:

> "Called thrones, balascio or topaze"
> Eriugina was not understood in his time
> "which explains, perhaps, the delay in condemning him"
> And they went looking for Manicheans
> And found, so far as I can make out, no Manicheans
> So they dug for, and damned Scotus Eriugina
> "Authority comes from right reason,
> never the other way on"
> Hence the delay in condemning him

Aquinas head down in a vacuum,
      Aristotle which way in a vacuum?
Sacrum, sacrum, inluminatio coitu.
Lo Sordels si fo di Mantovana
      of a castle named Goito.   (XXXVI/179–80)

The poet turns to Dante, Eriugina, and Sordello to indicate Guido's ultimate insufficiency as a model; after all, he is destined for the circle of heretics because of his inability to make amore yield what Dante sees in it, the potential for beatitude. Pound alludes to Dante's "thrones" on which good rulers sit as they dispense heavenly justice. The minds of the just rulers operate according to "right reason" only when their judgments are based on amore. Aquinas and Aristotle, Dante's professed masters also approved by the orthodoxy, are "upside down in vacuum" because their notions of justice are not based on the amore that Guido celebrates and articulates. Dante's thrones are based not on the tradition Dante acknowledges but on the troubadour tradition Guido brings to his young friend. Pound uses Guido's poem to mark the path to the thrones of divine justice, the path Dante has obscured out of fear of condemnation by the orthodoxy that condemns Eriugina and Guido.

The highly erotic Canto XXXIX is Pound's attempt to redress the separation of the ideal lady of the mind from her source in sexual passion. To do so, he returns to the locus of Canto I: we are back on Circe's island, and Pound quotes in the original Circe's advice to Odysseus about how to reach the underworld. At the end of that first canto, Odysseus returns to Circe who becomes, as if by magic, the goddess of love Aphrodite. The present canto furthers an understanding of this transformation. It opens with a description of vulgar sexuality:

Fat panther lay by me
Girls talked there of fucking, beasts talked there of eating,
All heavy with sleep, fucked girls and fat leopards,
Lions loggy with Circe's tisane,
Girls leery with Circe's tisane.   (XXXIX/193)

Circe's charms have the potential to transform Odysseus's men into swine; Pound's version of the Homeric story describes the potential of sexuality to make us less than human, to reduce us to the level of beasts indulging in coarse pleasure. But Odysseus is able to enjoy Circe's beauty and remain fully human. The hero is he who can engage in the physical act of sexual union, maintain

his human qualities, and reach a consciousness of great intensity
and delight in the world. Indeed, at the end of the canto the couple
engage in what can only be called "holy sexuality":

> Beaten from flesh into light
> Hath swallowed the fire-ball
> A traverso le foglie
> His rod hath made god in my belly
>   Sic loquitur nupta
> Cantat sic nupta
>
> Dark shoulders have stirred the lightning
> A girls's arms have nested the fire,
> Not I but the handmaid kindled
>   Cantat sic nupta
> I have eaten the flame.   (196)

The sexual act is not, as it was in the Homeric story, a temptation that impedes our journey back home but the pivotal act that
can either turn us into beasts or open our eyes to the fire and light
of the holy. The woman's "dark shoulders stir the lightning"; a mortal woman has the capacity to awaken our eyes to the bursting light
seen by our original consciousness. Her arms "nest the fire"; her
delicate limbs bring fire down from heaven and make a secure home
for it. She is called "the handmaid" to recall Mary's response to the
angel when invited to become the Mother of God; she feels the "god
in my belly" to further this association with Mary. This is Pound's
effort to place this mortal woman who bears beatitude in the
troubadour tradition of the ideal lady of the mind that culminates in
the worship of the Blessed Virgin Mary. The girl who nests the fire
is in the position of Mary who bridges the natural and supernatural
orders, through whom the holy enters the human world.[7]
    In this regard, Pound deftly injects three moments from *Par-
adiso* in the middle of this erotic canto; he places his Odysseus in
an explicitly Dantesque context:

> When Hathor was bound in that box
>   afloat on the sea wave
> Came Mava swimming with light hand lifted in overstroke
> sea blossom wreathed in her locks,
> "What are you box?"
>   "I am Hathor."
> Che mai da me non si parte il diletto

Fulvida di folgore
Came here with Glaucus unnoticed, nec ivi in harum
Nec in harum in gressus sum.
      Discuss this in bed said the lady.   (194)

Dante's heaven flashes forth in the middle of Odysseus's sexual adventures. *"Che mai da me non si parte il diletto"*—"so that never will the delight pass from me"—records Dante's joyous response in *Paradiso* XXII to a hymn sung by the blessed in praise of the Queen of Heaven. Mary is implicated in the pagan tradition which includes an Egyptian fertility goddess (Hathor) and the enticing Homeric witch. *"Fulvida di folgore"*—I saw the light in the form of a river *"pouring its splendour"*—is just one of the many beautiful moments in heaven (here, from *Paradiso* XXX, 62) in which the divine light pours through the universe. And the speaker has arrived in Dante's heaven "with Glaucus unnoticed"; it is almost as if this Odysseus has managed to sneak into heaven, with only Pound noting his entry. The poet recalls with this line how Dante compares his entry into heaven with Glaucus's metamorphosis into a sea god: "I was changed within, as was Glaucus when he tasted of the herb that made him one of the gods of the sea. The passing beyond humanity cannot be set forth in words" (*Paradiso* I, 67–71). Dante resorts to the story of Glaucus's metamorphosis to suggest what it is to "pass beyond humanity," what it is to transcend the conditions that define and construct our human nature. Pound has high praise for these lines: "Nowhere is the nature of mystic ecstasy so well described as here" (*SR* 141). The inclusion of these three moments from Dante's *Paradiso,* each an image of divine sensual delight enjoyed by those who have transcended human limits, serves to extend the significance of Odysseus's sexual encounter with Circe. Pound borrows the plot and characters from Homer, and gives them a Dantesque destination as they achieve a consciousness of the holy by means of sexual activity. For Pound's Odysseus has not fallen into the pigsty (*"nec ivi in haram,"*) but has arrived in heaven, "with Glaucus unnoticed."

Pound's purpose in Canto XXXIX is to bring the ideal lady back to her source in the passion associated with the physical act of sexual union. Indeed, the central section of this canto represents and mimes this physical act:

      Betuene Aprile and Merche
            with sap new in the bough
      With plum flowers above them
            with almond on the black bough

> With jasmine and olive leaf,
> To the beat of the measure
> From star up to the half-dark
> From half-dark to half-dark
>   Unceasing the measure
> Flank by flank on the headland
>   with the Goddess' eyes to seaward
> By Circeo, by Terracina, with the stone eyes
>   white toward the sea
> With one measure, unceasing:
>   "Fac deum!" "Est factus."
> Ver novum!
>   ver novum!
> Thus made the spring.   (195)

The quiet surge of desire, the slow buildup of enthusiasm, the rocking repetition of cadence and phrasing, the swaying that the spacing of the words on the page suggests, the sudden ejaculation that God is made—Pound manages to make the style mime the content as the sexual act that leads to the evocation of the holy is presented. The moment of vision is not enervated and misty, as were his earlier attempts to describe the experience; it bursts out of a steady rhythm with the flash of surprise and delight. The human couple—Odysseus and Circe—make love under the trees at dusk as the human and the natural orders are made one and their union gives birth to the manifestation of the divine. The couple bring about "ver novum," a "new spring," as their physical act renews their participation in the natural order and brings the supernatural lightning and fire into the world for the wanderer to see. The human act of sexual union, if understood properly as the physical enjoyment of the ideal lady, can bring the human world back into the natural order, overcoming our alienation from nature and bringing the human consciousness back to its perception of the divine principle at work in the world. As his understanding of the way back to an original consciousness grew more concrete, he wrote another canto sending Odysseus on a more clearly defined journey than the one described in Canto I. The new direction for the poem is announced by continuing and developing the Odyssean journey.

Canto XL

The very next canto explicitly defines the centrifugal journey as the attempt to escape the conditions that have formed a corrupt culture, to break free of the confines of the present time and place, to transcend the limitations of history. The first half of this canto focuses on the economic factors that have contributed to the corruption of Western civilization, the factors that have created the gap between the natural and human orders that the sexual act of the previous canto bridged: Adam Smith's observation about the tendency of groups to conspire against the general public for their own private gain; Mr. D'Arcy's permit "for 50 years to dig up the subsoil of Persia" to find oil, a permit that gives him sole rights over whatever oil is found in that region; and most especially, Mr. Morgan's "Taking advantage of emergency (that is war)" to make huge profits from the sale of arms. This half of the canto ends with a description of a corrupt civilization:

> With our eyes on the new gothic residence, with our
> eyes on Palladio, with a desire for seignieurial splendours
> (ÀGALMA, haberdashery, clocks, ormouiu, brocatelli,
> tapestries, unreadable volumes bound in tree-calf,
> half-morocco, morocco, tooled edges, green ribbons,
> flaps, farthingales, fichus, cuties, shorties, pinkies
> et cetera
> Out of which things seeking an exit   (XL/198–199)

According to Kenner, this passage depicts a "pseudocivilization" whose "tokens are things, 'clutter, the bane of men moving'; its touchstone is the multiplication of things" (*Gnomon* 275). Kenner alludes to an Australian myth told by the anthropologist D. C. Fox about Wanjina, a god who created the world by saying the names of things and who would have continued producing material if his father Ungar had not closed his mouth. For this action Ungar is venerated, for if he "had not very wisely done as he did, then the blackfellow would have been burdened with all the glittering claptrap of the white man's culture and would not have been able to devote himself properly to the important things of life" (Terrell 365). For Pound, the modern world created by the bourgeois mentality is characterized by the mass production of vulgar and ornate goods that prevent people from reaching a deeper, more satisfying relation to the natural world of beauty that, seen properly, is the "garment of the gods." The description above centers on the mass production of different kinds of elaborate covers for books to indicate that the bourgeois obsession with ornament hides what real value a culture might contain: the bourgeois mind values the book only as another ornate possession and never penetrates to the insights and truths the "unreadable" volumes set forth within their gaudy covers. It is "out of these *things* seeking an exit," away "from a Victorian suburbia Pound has imagined for him" (Makin 57) that another centrifugal wanderer, Hanno the Carthegenian general, undertakes his periplum:

PLEASING TO CARTHEGENIANS: HANNO
that he ply beyond the pillars of Herakles
60 ships of armada to lay out Phoenecian cities
to each ship 50 oars, in all
30 thousand aboard them with water, wheat in provision.
Two days beyond Gibel Tara [Gibraltar] layed in the wide
    plain
Thumiatehyon, went westward to Solois.   (XL/199)

Like Dante's Ulysses, Hanno "went westward" "beyond the pillars of Herakles" to move away the unsatisfying culture that is his present home. In Pound's hands, the Carthagenian's motive for exploration is the desire to find an exit from a corrupt culture whose modern version is the decadent suburban civilization that values only the accumulation and possession of vulgarly ornate matter. This canto clearly establishes the wanderer's desire to leave the conditions of the present and sail westward, out into the unknown that offers at least the hope of new experience. The second half of Canto XL is another translation of a text that recounts a wanderer's centrifugal movements; and, as in Canto I, Pound is a faithful translator until the final six lines:

Went no further that voyage,
          as were at end of provisions.
          [The translation ends here.]
Out of which things seeking an exit
To the high air, to the stratosphere, to the imperial
calm, to the empyrean, to the baily of the four towers
the NOUS, the ineffable crystal.   (201)

What we discover in Pound's addendum to the translation is that Hanno really seeks a way "to the empyrean," "to the imperial calm" of the heavenly city with "the baily of the four towers" where Dante climaxes his journey out of corruption. Hanno's periplum, his careful navigation around coastlines in waters previously untested and unmarked, suddenly seeks to go up "to the stratosphere." Peter Makin argues that Pound is choosing Hanno's example over and against Dante's; for Makin, Dante's geography that takes its measure from the fixed point of an eternal God is not relevant to Pound's sense of himself as a modern explorer, and so this depiction of Hanno indicates the poet's rejection of the Dantesque model (58–60). It seems to me rather that Pound subordinates Hanno's method—the Ulyssean movement beyond the Pillars of Hercules—to Dante's goal, the achievement of citizenship in the imperial city of heaven. "Going westward" beyond Gibraltar is defined as an attempt to reach blessedness, a state that cannot be attained by remaining within the present culture. Again, Pound takes pains to rewrite the centrifugal voyage so that its ultimate destination is the attainment of a divine consciousness. As in Canto XXXIX, he alludes to Dante's *Paradiso* to indicate the goal of his wanderer, the kind of home sought by his nostalgic hero, a consciousness of the divine operating with the natural order. As he gradually comes to understand his goal more clearly, the poet devises another "wanderer" canto to shape the poem's direction and purpose.

Canto XLVII

Pound's wanderer has chosen to leave the present state of culture in which humanity is alienated and has been seeking a way to return to an original sense of the world as our home. What we learn from an examination of Canto XXXIX is that sexual coupling with a woman who embodies the ideal lady of one's mind can bring the human world into intimate contact with the natural order. This sexual encounter is capable of closing the gap separating the human and natural orders and so lessens our sense of alienation. Canto XLVII continues Odysseus's wandering as it presents Pound's sexual version of the Eleusinian mysteries in which Odysseus finally finds the way back home. The first goal of the epic, the return home, is achieved in this canto.

The poet notes in an essay from the winter of 1931–32, a time which corresponds to the composition of Canto XXXIX, that "unity with nature" is a central concern of the modern artist: "The modern author can write 'aim the union with nature' or 'consciousness of the unity of nature.' This is at the root of any mystery" (*SP* 59). This goal places Pound's modernism in a romantic tradition,[8] for his "unity with nature" has strong affinities with Wordsworth's marriage of the mind of man and nature. But Pound's emphasis is on the "mystery" of this union, the secret and outlawed wisdom about the way to such union. In the same essay, he advances his understanding of the troubadours to its fullest development as he argues that they were initiates in a secret cult with roots in the Eleusinian mysteries and were considered heretics[9] and outlaws by the orthodox Christian Church: "the cult of Eleusis will explain not only general phenomena but particular beauties in Arnaut Daniel or in Guido Cavalcanti.... I suggest that students trying to understand the poesy of southern Europe from 1050 to 1400 should try to open it with this key" (*SP* 59). In a short piece from 1930 called "Credo," Pound connects these singers with the pagan mystery cult: "I believe that a light from Eleusis persisted throughout the middle ages and set beauty in the song of Provence and of Italy" (*SP* 53). He has been reading these singers for years, has associated his wanderer with their songs, and now is ready to formulate his own version of the Eleusinian mysteries that has been the secret source of their power. Pound's "modernism" differs from Wordsworthian "romanticism" most sharply in the more developed role assigned to "history" in *The Cantos*: Pound's wanderer cannot find "unity with nature" simply by strolling in the present but must embark on a journey back through history to the last moment with discernible ties to a pagan tradition of the immanent divine.

Frazer gives a succinct account of the Eleusinian story. As the youthful Persephone was gathering flowers, the earth opened up and Pluto, lord of the dead, carried her off to his abode to be his bride and queen. Her sorrowing mother Demeter searched the world over for her daughter and, when she learned Persephone's fate, she suffered not the seed to grow in the earth and the corn not to sprout until her lost daughter was restored. Zeus intervened and commanded Pluto to return Persephone, who obeyed but not before he gave her a pomegranate seed to eat, which ensured that she would return to him. Zeus worked out an agreement, that Persephone would spend two thirds of every year with her mother and one third with her husband. Demeter was delighted to have her daughter back and made the earth flower once again. In her joy she then revealed to various princes her rites and mysteries (Frazer 456–57). One might already see the appropriateness of this myth to Pound's efforts to return the exile to his lost home, for these mysteries celebrate the renewal of the earth's fertility and growth as it becomes a home to humanity again. It is a story about loss and restoration.

But as Karoly Kerenyi demonstrates in his study of these rites, no one has ever been able to piece together the exact nature

of the ceremony; we merely hear the claim of the ancients that
these mysteries are "a key to unlock the gates of Paradise" (Frazer
462). I shall demonstrate that there persists one legend from Eleusis that Pound adopts as the basis of his own ritual, the legend
that the mother and daughter goddesses are in fact "an insepara-
ble unity" (Kerenyi 32). Frazer was also struck by

> the substantial unity of mother and daughter . . . borne out by
> their portraits in Greek art, which are often so alike as to be
> indistinguishable. . . . The essential unity of mother and
> daughter is suggested . . . also by the official title of "the Two
> Goddesses" which was regularly applied to them in the great
> sanctuary at Eleusis without any specification of their indi-
> vidual attributes and titles, as if their separate individualites
> had almost merged in a single divine essence. (461–62)

Pound responds to this aspect of what is known of the mysteries and creates his own sexual Eleusis. Canto XLVII is his most
original addition yet to the wanderer theme, but he is still careful
to indicate the tradition he draws upon and to compare his wanderer's return home to Dante's.

As Canto XLVII opens, we are back on Circe's island as
Pound once again and for the last time presents Odysseus taking
his leave from Circe and embarking on his descent to the underworld:

> Who even dead, yet hath his mind entire!
> > This sound came in the dark
> > First must thou go the road
> > > to hell
> And to the bower of Ceres' daughter Proscrpine,
> Through overhanging dark, to see Tiresias.   (XLVII/236)

This time, Pound specifies that Odysseus must descend "to
the bower of Ceres' daughter Proserpine" in order to hear Tiresias's counsel about the way back home. The journey "after knowledge" has taken a different direction as he descends not to a bleak
Homeric underworld as in Canto I but to participation in the
Eleusinian mysteries established by Demeter (Ceres) in commemo-
ration of her daughter Persephone's return. After some lines
depicting rituals to Adonis (Tamuz) and various peasant customs
with roots in ancient fertility myths,[10] some of which Pound witnessed during his years in Italy, the poet turns to present oblique-

ly his own ritual, an arcane sexual encounter in which the "wiles"
of the female "call" the male wanderer to her "cave":

> Two span, two span to a woman,
> Beyond that she believes not. Nothing is of any importance.
> To that is she bent, her intention
> To that art thou are called ever turning intention,
> Whether by night the owl-call, whether by sap in shoot,
> Never idle, by no means by no wiles intermittent
> Moth is called over mountain
> The bull runs blind on the sword, *naturans*
> To the cave art thou called, Odysseus,
> By Molü hast thou respite for a little,
> By Molü art thou freed from the one bed
>   that thou may'st return to another.   (237)

Like the moth and the bull who are lured by powerful natural
forces, Odysseus is drawn to the darkness of these mysteries
wherein lies the woman whose only "intention" is to "call" the man
and couple with him. Molü, which in Homer is a plant that pro-
tects Odysseus from Circe's transformative power, here offers
respite to the wanderer; it frees him from "the one bed" so he can
"return to another." One may suppose, along with Daniel Pearlman (180), that he is freed from Circe's bed so he can return to the
bed he has long been absent from, Penelope's. If so, Pound has
drastically rethought the nature of Odysseus's journey and has
transformed the centrifugal wanderer back into the Homeric
home-seeker.

But as the canto continues we note that the bed he returns to
is certainly not Penelope's. Pound moves from Odysseus's encounter
with the woman to an adaptation of Hesiod's *Works and Days:*

> Begin thy plowing
> When the Pleiades go down to their rest,
> Begin thy plowing
> 40 days are they under seabord,
> Thus do in fields by seabord
> And in valleys winding down toward the sea.
> When the cranes fly high
>   think of plowing.   (237)

This seems quite an abrupt jump, from Odysseus's sexual
adventure to an ancient Greek treatise on agriculture, but the

transition is significant. First, we are meant to see that human sexuality is a force of nature similar to the phenomenon of vegetable growth; the man is lured to the woman as the moth and bull move, *"naturans"*—meaning obeying or following one's nature. The passage from Hesiod describes how a keen observation of events—the position of the stars or migration of cranes—can reveal natural rhythms in which agricultural patterns, and by implication human sexuality, fit. So once again Pound is trying to include the human world in the rhythms of the natural order. But even more pointedly, the Hesiod passage links agricultural plowing and the sexual act in such a way that we begin to get a sense of the identity of the woman with whom Odysseus lies:

> So light is thy weight on Tellus
> Thy notch no deeper indented
> Thy weight less than the shadow
> Yet has thou gnawed through the mountain,
>   Scylla's white teeth less sharp.
> Hast thou found a nest softer than cunnus
> Or hast thou found better rest
> Hast'ou a deeper planting, doth thy death year
> Bring swifter shoot?
> Hast thou entered more deeply the mountain?   (238)

The weight of his body is hardly felt by Tellus, for she is both the body of the earth and the woman who has become the goddess of fertility and vegetable growth. Pound blurs the distinction between the earth's body and the woman's, for he wants to suggest that Odysseus's sexual partner in these mysteries is not Circe nor Penelope but the mother goddess of the earth. Molü has freed him from the bed of the woman so that he can return to the bed of the mother. Pound shifts the woman's identity from one aspect of "the Two Goddesses" to the other, as the woman-as-daughter becomes the woman-as-mother. The wanderer imaginatively transforms the woman into the great mother as he lies with her and so performs the one act prohibited by all cultures, by all civilizations. Pound's hero dares to break the primary law of his civilization, a law massively protected by taboo, guilt, and punishment. The only way to move fully "outward and away" from the present civilization is to challenge the law upon which the entire culture rests. Breaking this first and fundamental law is Pound's version of passing beyond the Pillars of Hercules, passing beyond the assigned limits of lawful human experience into the unknown.

Only this lawbreaker, only this outlaw, can achieve the return to the original human consciousness:

> The light has entered the cave. Io! Io!
> The light has gone down into the cave,
> Splendour on splendour!
> By prong have I entered these hills:
> That the grass grow from my body,
> That I hear the roots speaking together,
> The air is new on my leaf,
> The forked boughs shake with the wind.
> Is Zephyrus more light on the bough, Apeliota
> more light on the almond branch?
> By this door have I entered the hill.   (238)

By breaking the primary law of his culture, Pound's wanderer has managed to return to an original human consciousness in which he feels one with the external world. "Io" is both Greek for "hail" and Italian for the first person pronoun: a new identity has been constructed, an "I" that hails the light of the holy. This new self "has entered the hills"; he becomes one with the natural order as he feels the wind on the leaves and hears the language of the roots that nourish vegetable growth. Pound's Eleusis maintains its nature as a fertility ritual, for the human world becomes part of the natural order that grows and increases. The arcane and outlawed sexual act of Pound's Eleusis has returned the wanderer to a consciousness that feels truly "at home" in the world. Though he resembles Dante in his attainment of an original consciousness that allows for true rest, he still resembles Dante's Ulysses strongly in his reckless daring and thirst for forbidden experience. The centrifugal impulse of the one has been reconciled with the centripetal impulse of the other as the exile finally returns to his lost home.

Pound's Eleusis is a way to again possess the mother, the original, forbidden, and lost object of desire. In setting his wandering hero against this "universal taboo," Pound takes issue with the Freudian theory of human nature.[11] According to him, Freud "erects pathology into a system" (*SP* 154), whereas the poet believes in a natural and original health for humanity: "That one's roots are not a disease but parts of a vital organism is worth feeling" (*GK* 244). In *Civilization and its Discontents,* Freud claims that "the inclination to aggression is an original, self-subsisting, instinctual disposition in man" (69) and that there is "an inborn human inclination to 'badness,' to aggressiveness and destructiveness, and so to cruelty as well" (67). What Pound criticizes in Freud is that, in looking at diseased humanity, he posits disease as human essence. For it is possible to read into Freud's theory of the mind, as I think Pound does, the assumption that alienation from the world is a natural and inevitable development that cannot be reversed.

According to psychoanalytic theory as advanced by Freud, the earliest stage of our psychic experience is marked by a "unity of being" in which the world is one, no break having as yet sundered the infant from the world. This sense of vital unity with the world arises from the infant's complete possession of and union with the mother: "An infant at the breast does not yet distinguish his ego from the external world as the source of the sensations flowing in upon him" (14–15). At first there is no differentiation between subject and object: "originally the ego includes everything, later it separates off an external world from itself. Our present ego-feeling is, therefore, only a shrunken residue of a much more inclusive—indeed, an all-embracing—feeling which corresponded to a more intimate bond between the ego and the world about it" (15). In this analysis, the human self begins in a complete immersion in a sea of being, unified and whole.

The child gradually learns that he is not one with the mother and the world; as he is weaned from the breast and becomes somewhat autonomous in the world, he begins to recognize that it is a world of difference and not identity, a world of separation and not of union. He is alienated from the external world, exiled from the intimate union that is "home." He learns that he is a subject in relation to a world of objects that are different, both from himself and each other. With his newly acquired "I," the child must renounce his claim on the mother, the first object of desire, a desire that begins only at the moment of loss. He enters civilization, the world of organized structures and relations, as he relinquishes the mother and seeks after other objects to fulfill his desire, substitutes for the outlawed initial object of desire. In the psychoanalytic formulation, the subject is forever cut off from union because only a return to the mother could satisfy it, and that return is prohibited by the Law of the Father who threatens castration if one attempts to lie with the mother and guilt merely for the desire. We are forever denied fullness and satisfaction, forever to be tormented by a desire that can never find its object. We then become aggressive as we compete to appropriate objects that we hope can end the restless dance of desire, but acquisition only marks our frustration more strongly.

One can see how Pound's Eleusis provides a point of attack against this possible formulation of Freudian theory. If "the Two Goddesses" are really different aspects of a "fundamental unity" of the female, then the woman who calls Odysseus to the sexual ritual can become the mother if the wanderer dares to cross the barrier that separates the mother from the daughter. As the troubadours transform a real woman into the ideal lady of the mind who is closely (and, in certain poems, blasphemously) associated with the Virgin Mother, so Pound's wanderer dares to transform the daughter one is allowed into the mother one has been forbidden. He firmly declares in a letter to Harriet Monroe, "I refuse to accept ANY monotheistic taboo whatsoever" (*SL* 183). By daring to transform the daughter who substitutes for the mother back into the lost object of desire, he is seeking to return to the very source of desire and end it utterly. Such a return, Pound implies, requires tremendous will and bravery, crossing the massively protected barrier between mother and daughter, between first object of desire and its substitutes. Early in the canto, "Scilla's dogs snarl at the cliff's base,/ The white teeth gnaw in under the crag" (236). These female teeth indicate Pound's awareness of the castration the father threatens, the castration that is the fate of the husks and shells from Canto VII and of the lotophagoi of Canto XX. Alan Durant notes Pound's preoccupation with castration throughout *The Cantos* (134 ff.), a preoccupation that indicates the poet's conviction that all humanity is castrated under the present system. As Odysseus persists in his perilous sexual voyage and bravely crosses the barrier, "Scylla's white teeth" become "less sharp." The law of the father has been all bluff, and the brave wanderer has overcome its intimidation and its negative effect of alienation. He has found the way to receive "the gift of healing" (239), the gift that heals the split between the human and natural orders.

In this imaginative transformation of the woman/daughter/ substitute, Pound has extended his application of Dante's "the now glorious lady of my mind." For as Canto XXXIX demonstrated, the ideal lady, held firmly in the mind, can transform any woman into the handmaid who stirs the fire and nests the lightning. Canto XLVII takes this imaginative transformation one step further, as the ideal lady becomes the lost mother. Dante's work even provides the model for this. The *Vita Nuova* tells the story of Dante's first meeting with Beatrice, her elevation into the ideal lady, and then his backsliding after her death. In his climb toward the purity of human origins, Dante's purgation is complete only when Beatrice accuses him of having given up the ideal:

For a time I sustained him with my countenance. Showing him my youthful eyes I brought him with me, bound on the right way. As soon as I was on the threshold of my second age and I changed life he took himself from me and gave himself to another. When I had risen from the flesh to spirit and beauty and virtue had increased in me I was less dear to him and less welcome and he bent his steps in a way not true, following after images of good which fulfill no promise.... (*Purgatorio* XXX, 121–32)

The ideal lady was the way to reach the transcendent experience, but as we learn in *Inferno* I, he had lost the true way. *Purgatorio* records Dante's purgation of false desire until he can see the ideal once again. But Beatrice is not the woman who brings him to God. In the highest heaven, she is replaced by Saint Bernard, who explains, "To terminate your desire Beatrice urged me from my place" (*Paradiso* XXXI, 65–66). *Paradiso* XXXIII opens with the mystic saint's prayer to Mary that she grant Dante the vision of God that culminates the *Commedia;* he addresses her as *"Virgine Madre"*—"Virgin Mother." Only through the intercession of the mother can Dante achieve the beatific vision that is union with God; only through the mother can desire be halted. Immediately before his vision, he compares his state to an infant's: "Now my speech will fall short in respect to that which I remember than of an infant who still bathes his tongue at the breast" (XXXIII, 106–08). To express the nature of the experience that terminates the torment of desire, Dante uses this analogy to an infant's prelinguistic union with the mother, an original state he regains as his journey comes to an end.

But Pound considers the return to the mother the way not to heavenly beatitude but back to the original health and purity of human origins. He does not follow Dante to heaven but instead conflates the earthly paradise with Dante's paradise: at our origins we see the gods; in union with the world we see the holy light enter the cave. Pound indicates subtly that this canto functions as his version of the earthly paradise Dante finally reaches after a long and painful climb up Mount Purgatory. First of all, Pound's wanderer achieves his return to origins on a mountain that suggests Dante's purgatorial mountain on top of which lies Eden. There, Matelda calls the earthly paradise "this place set apart to the human kind for its nest" and "this place for earnest of eternal peace" (*Purgatorio* XXVIII, 77–78 and 92–93). Surely Pound is thinking of this description when, just before climax, he asks:

> Has thou found a nest softer than cunnus
> Or hast thou found better rest?

Unlike the false rest of the lotophagoi in Canto XX, the wanderer has found a true and satisfying rest; he has reached the
"nest" from which humanity originally sprung. Pound has high
praise for Dante's description of the earthly paradise (*SR* 138) and
compares it to the work of Wordsworth: "Wordsworth is, we may
say, the orthodox sign for the comprehension of nature, yet where
has Wordsworth written lines more instinct with 'nature-feeling'
than those in the twenty-eight of the *Purgatorio*" (SR 154). Canto
XLVII is Pound's attempt to write lines of "nature-feeling," as the
wanderer becomes part of the vegetable world and feels all it feels.
He has created his own version of an original consciousness that
stands before humanity's fall into the historical process. By following and rewriting certain aspects of Dante's journey, Pound has
achieved the first goal of his epic, the healing of the split between
the human and natural orders that is alienation. The exile has
returned home.

What we have followed in this chapter is the movement of a
wandering hero alienated both from nature and humanity as he
seeks a return to an original consciousness that feels "at home" in
the world, a consciousness of the divine given shape in the poem
by consistent references to Dante's *Paradiso*. But he has not
bridged the gap between himself and his fellows: his return is a
lonely one in that he enjoys a wholly private imaginative relation
to the world as "home." He has left the present state of Western
culture—what everyone else still calls home—by returning to
what the poet considers the original moment in human history.
But Pound has not forgotten his fellows and has also been developing in the poem a politics based on the fruits of this personal imaginative return to origins. We are now ready to watch the political
implications of this ultimately successful private journey.

2 ❧ The Wanderer as Fascist:
Mussolini, Confucius, and America

Pound's politics—namely, his admiration for and advocacy of Italian Fascism—has been the obstacle to many readers' appreciation of the poetry. All too many critics have attempted to address this issue by separating the two, whereas Pound's project becomes explicitly a search for a way for literature to confront, include, and master the political and the historical. I shall argue that Pound's enthusiasm for Italian Fascism springs from decisions first made and poses first struck in the poetry; his continuing development and deployment of the wandering hero is in preparation for his reception of Mussolini and for his own role as Fascist poet.

The Odysseus he developed as the organizing principle of *The Cantos* comes to operate as the model with which he investigates the activities of "real" people as they affect what we call "history." Thus a further dimension to Pound's wandering hero operates in the first fifty-one cantos, a complementary impulse to the exilic search for home: as early as Canto VIII the wanderer gives way to the political figure, not searching for the lost consciousness that makes the world home for the private individual, but working in the fallen world of political action to create the conditions that would make the world a home for everyone. Pound's political heroes can be placed within a paradigm shaped by the wandering Odysseus: those who have transcended the conditions of history that have created the present alienated state of humanity returned "home" to an original consciousness, and from this perspective struggle to impose a new direction for the course of events toward a public home. This aspect becomes more dominant over the course of years until, in the 1930s, the wanderer comes to be associated with Mussolini himself.

This chapter will once again examine the first fifty-one cantos, this time describing the political figures Pound assembles and how they relate to the exiled wanderer seeking home. The two

67

impulses—the lonely exile seeking his own private return home and the political figure who seeks to construct a new order—finally come together, first in the figure of Mussolini in Canto XLI and then in the "no man" of Canto XLIX. This reconciliation is the first major accomplishment of Pound's epic, and he is free in the next set of cantos (the Chinese History Cantos and the Adams Cantos) to embark in a radically new direction and with a new purpose.

Cantos VIII–XI

In 1938, with the first fifty-one cantos in print, Pound looks back on the earliest public figure presented in the epic and judges him from his present "Fascist" perspective: "the Malatesta cantos . . . are openly volitionist, establishing, I think clearly, the effect of the factive personality, Sigismundo, an entire man" (*GK* 194). Cantos VIII through XI can be read as an extension of or addition to the wandering hero's journey established in the first seven cantos. As Makin notes, "Sigismundo Malatesta is an Odysseus with a constructive element superadded" (*Cantos* 137). We need to examine exactly how the "factive personality"—the man who makes beautiful and good things—develops out of the exilic search for a lost home.

The first seven cantos presented the ideogram of an outlawed wanderer searching for an original consciousness that makes the world seem a true and satisfying home. Twice in these cantos Pound borrows from Dante's *Paradiso* the image of the "ciocco"— the burning log from which sparks fly upward—to which are compared the souls of those who worked for justice. In Canto VII this line culminates a literary tradition of erotic love and martial valor, implying that Dante's heavenly vision of the great eagle formed by these ascending souls reconciles the impulse to love passionately with the courage to act heroically. After Dante, no such vision appears again; instead, Pound turns to Flaubert and James as the bearers of the great prose tradition that diagnoses the disease of the modern world that fails to fuse eros and courage. He presents himself as a seeker after beauty in a debased and vulgar world, and as the only live man among a bunch of husks and shells. At this point, Pound quotes the opening line of *Paradiso* II to warn his readers that they are now coursing through treacherous waters similar to Dante's heaven. We must be careful to follow in his wake as he seeks to achieve and lead us to the vision of the "ciocco," a visionary appreciation of those whose work on earth was directed towards justice. The canto includes the entire Dantesque landscape: the diseased modern world cut off from the visionary is infernal, his own effort to uncover buried beauty is purgatorial, and now he leads us in his ship that singing makes its way to the visionary experience of ideal justice. In a late interview, Pound tells Donald Hall that his investigation of history had been based on the Dantesque divisons:

> I have made the division between people dominated by emotion, people struggling upwards, and those who have some part of the divine vision. The thrones in Dante's *Paradiso* are for the spirits of the people who have been responsible for good government. The thrones in the *Cantos* are an attempt to move out from egoism and to establish some definition of an order possible or at any rate conceivable on earth. [. . .] *Thrones* concerns the states of mind of people responsible for something more than their personal conduct. (Hall 58)

This is more than he knew when he was composing the Malatesta Cantos, but I think the shape of Canto VII allows us to apply this passage to the historical method Pound begins to employ in the first fifty-one cantos. In Dante's heaven one meets the souls of those who acted according to the health of their original nature and not according to debased tendencies of the majority of humankind; in the early cantos Pound is searching for men who have worked against the system and have aimed at "orders possible" on earth, at the construction of the good and beautiful in the external world. At this point in his epic he begins to conceive of history as a field of action preserved textually wherein we can find examples of hellish, purgatorial, and paradisal behavior, a space wherein we meet people dominated by the emotions and values of the present culture, those struggling for a vision of other healthier possibilities, and those, grounded in such a vision, actively working toward a new order.

Pound's daughter records a remark that demonstrates that, in choosing Malatesta as his first "historical" case for study, he was thinking of Dante's analyses of human activity: "Dante has said everything there is to be said, so I start with Malatesta" (*DISC.* 159). His praise for this man is for a figure who struggles against the present culture:

> In a Europe not YET rotted by usury, but outside the then system, and pretty much against the power that was, and in any case without great material resources, Sigismundo cut his notch. He registered a state of mind, of sensibility, of all-

roundness and awareness. . . . all that a single man could,
Malatesta managed *against* the current of power. (*GK* 159)

The movement "outward and away" from the present current
we traced in Canto I is here complemented by a movement "against"
the political system; Malatesta enacts no return to origins but
instead acts in the time and place he happens to occupy "against the
current of power."[1] The Malatesta Cantos mark the beginning of
Pound's extension of the wanderer's journey toward a political goal.
The journey of imagination back to a lost consciousness described in
chapter I is complemented by a journey of action toward the construction of beauty in the public sphere. One man with little material resource and working against the system cannot accomplish the
building of a new order, a new home; but Malatesta did achieve
some permanent good by registering a "state of mind" that sees
beauty and an "awareness" of the possibilities of something better
than the present culture can offer. His achievement, according to
Pound, is the production of a public monument registering the kind
of consciousness his wanderer searches for on his private journey.

Pound's treatment of Malatesta centers on his effort to erect
the Tempio at Rimini, his monument to beauty and to his love for
his mistress, despite the obstacles set against him by an economic
system becoming increasingly tainted and corrupted by usury. One
of the first things we learn about Malatesta is his desire to subsi-
dize the talents of the artist:

But I want it to be quite clear, that until the chapels are ready
I will arrange for him to paint something else
So that both he and I shall
Get as much enjoyment as possible from it,
And in order that he may enter my service
And also because you write me that he needs cash,
I want to arrange with him to give him so much per year
And to assure him that he will get the sum agreed on. [. . .]
And for this I mean to make due provision,
So that he can work as he likes,
Or waste his time as he likes.   (VIII/29)

Pound chooses to make this aspect of Malatesta's work significant because it shows the practical knowledge about the artistic
process a cultural hero must possess. Not every patron offers to
pay a person of creative talent a set sum regardless of production,
nor would every patron go to such pains to assure the artisan or

artist employed of his economic security. Malatesta knows that the artist must have freedom from anxiety and plenty of leisure to produce first-rate work. He also knows that the end of art is pleasure: he hopes that they both "get as much enjoyment as possible from" their working relationship. We gain a further sense of Malatesta's values when, in the midst of his military and economic wars with neighboring city-states, Pound includes a translation of a poem Malatesta composed in honor of his lady Isotta, whom he compares to Helen of Troy; and an account of his relationship with Gemisthus Plethon, a Neoplatonist philosopher whose aim was to provide a pagan mythical dimension to Christianity. Pound places Malatesta in artistic and philosophical traditions with pagan bases, thus connecting him to the wandering figure of the first seven cantos. He is an outgrowth of Pound's presentation of himself in Canto VII as the seeker after buried beauty: that hero works to reveal the beauty buried by the debased consciousness of the modern bourgeois while Malatesta works to construct something beautiful that everyone can perceive despite the obstacles set against him by the forces that determine the debased culture.

As the canto ends, the emphasis surely is on effort and action in the external world of public concerns:

> With the church against him,
> With the Medici bank for itself,
> With wattle Sforza against him
> Sforza Francesco, wattle-nose,
> Who married him (Sigismundo) his (Francesco's)
> Daughter in September,
> Who stole Pèsaro in October (as Broglio says *"bestialmente"*),
> Who stood with the Venetians in November,
> With the Milanese in December,
> Sold Milan in November, stole Milan in December
> Or something of that sort,
> Commanded the Milanese in the spring,
> the Venetians at midsummer,
> The Milanese in the autumn,
> And was Naples' ally in October,
>   He, Sigismundo, *templum ædificavit*
> In Romagna, teeming with cattle thieves [...]   (VIII/32)

Pound presents the complex landscape of Renaissance Italian politics: the religious power of the church and the economic power of the Medici bank set against Malatesta; the unstable, ever-shift-

ing alliances among city-states that render the political scene
treacherous and confusing. As Makin says, "[t]he whole organisation of the Malatesta Cantos is to present difficulty" (*Cantos* 141).
In the midst of this account of Malatesta's political problems,
Pound injects the sudden exclamation that this hero built a temple: "He, Sigismundo, *templum œdificavit*"; against all this, he
erected "'a temple ... full of pagan works'" (IX/41), a place dedicated to the pagan worship of the immanent divine. The surprised
admiration that such depiction is meant to evoke is the appropriate emotion that an epic works to establish: "admiration for the
potential accomplishments of human will, rather than pity and
fear for mankind's inherent limitations, must dominate the epic"
(Bernstein 51–52). We are meant to marvel at the feat of construction, to admire the achievement of a strong man's will.

Pound calls the first eleven cantos "preparation of the
palette" containing "all the colours or elements I want for the
poem" (*SL* 180). In them he registers the various aspects of the
modern epic's understanding of heroic action. I want to isolate two
strands that go into the composition of the Poundian hero: the exilic wanderer who bravely searches for the lost consciousness that
united him to the world and the "factive personality" who uses
whatever material he can find (and Pound notes that Malatesta
even resorted to theft to obtain the marble to build the Tempio) to
create something that makes the world more beautiful and so
more like a home. Peter Nicholls claims that the Tempio is the
"historical emblem" for the calm of contemplation suggested by the
earthly paradise of Canto XVII (37). Malatesta's pagan temple
stands as a physical and enduring monument to the effort of a
man who had a vision of the pagan beauty that is our "home"; the
reader is led to infer that Malatesta's work is based on his visionary capacity. The wanderer of the first seven cantos who struggles
for the visionary experience of our lost consciousness that is culminated finally in Canto XLVII meets his counterpart in Canto VIII
in this man of action who works inside the present system to make
a home. The full reconciliation of these two aspects of heroic action
will be the focus of much of Pound's work in the twenties and thirties, and will receive explicit attention in the figure of Mussolini.

Cantos XVII–XXX

The Malatesta in these early cantos is not, however, sufficient as a
model for the "Fascist hero" Pound will describe and deploy in the

thirties, mainly because his constructive effort lacks an ethical dimension. Malatesta seeks to create beauty but does not aim at social order; he struggles heroically against the present social order but only to register his own personality and greatness. He may be "struggling upwards" and may even have glimpsed the vision of a new order, but his effort is limited largely to personal gratification. He is like Homer's Odysseus, whose self-reliance and wit serve only his individual or private interests. As the poet witnesses the Fascist Revolution, his understanding of heroism undergoes a subtle but significant shift. In the next set of cantos to be published as a unit, Cantos XVII through XXX, Pound returns to the political intrigues of the Italian Renaissance, this time including a sense of public responsibility in some of the heroes he chooses to depict.

Peter Makin notes this addition:

Medici and Este in these cantos add social constructivity and economic/political *savoir faire*, to the ideogram of the achieving man already set up in Odysseus, the tempter of fate, and Malatesta, the temple-builder. (*Cantos* 161)

Makin is right to regard Medici and Este as powerful figures working for social order, but their contribution lies in more than mere superior wit and know-how in the sphere of economics. We must analyze with rigor and close attention the precise nature of Pound's additions to "the ideogram of the achieving man" to understand how carefully *The Cantos* develops its scope and purpose. For in this set of cantos the poet begins the deployment of what we can call the ethical hero.

I propose the following statement as fundamental to any reading of *The Cantos:* whenever Pound needs a new emphasis or new direction, he is careful to write a canto that explicitly advances the nature of the wanderer and the scope of his journey. Canto XXIII contains several historical and mythical figures arranged in such a way that the model of the wanderer undergoes a significant shift of emphasis. Pound includes a brief reference to Odysseus's feigned madness designed to keep him from going to the war at Troy: "The idiot Odysseus furrowed the sand." This deceptive ruse is a purely self-serving stratagem, which is Pound's way of indicating Odysseus's shortcoming as the model for the hero he is now looking to construct. His effort to return home is purely personal and even selfish; he has no sense of public duty or any larger purpose than the reclamation of his own. Despite its extreme brevity and its inconspicuous position in the canto, I believe that this fragment from the Odysseus story governs the meaning of the entire canto as an ethical sense of public duty is added to the heroic wanderer.

The canto begins with the Neoplatonist Gemisto's wish to "make men of the Greeks." We are given two snippets of his comprehensive plan to reorganize an entire culture: Christianity to be replaced with a religion based on the old polytheism of the early Greeks and Plato; and a wall to be built across the Peloponesus to keep out Turkish and "Eyetalian barbarians." The heir of a Neoplatonic tradition rooted in pagan reverence for the immanent divine, Gemisto works to apply his visionary capacity to certain projects affecting the public sphere. With hardly a break Pound then notes the failed attempt of Domencio Malatesta (Sigismundo's younger brother) to bring Greek books and manuscripts to Italian culture; this effort is typical of "Novvy's" devotion to public works and distinguishes him from his brother's more limited effort. The poet abruptly moves to the heroic adventuring of modern science in the story of Pierre Curie whose dedication to his work and the public welfare led him to risk his own well-being. We may already note a new dimension in Pound's conception of heroic endeavor, as the hero's adventures address public concerns.

To place this new ethical dimension in the framework of the heroic wanderer he has developed, Pound then devises a curious passage that combines elements of Hercules, Odysseus, and Dante's pilgrim. The dominant narrative line describes the tenth labor of Hercules, who sails westward in the sun's boat in search of the cattle of Geryon. The movement westward following the tracks of the sun connects this mythic figure to Dante's Ulysses; but while the one is famous for his reckless daring and excessive thirst for knowledge, the other is famed for his labor, for his heroic effort. Then, somehow, this laboring hero winds up in Dante's "selv' oscura," the dark wood where the pilgrim begins his journey. In the midst of this is the brief account of Odysseus's attempt to avoid public service. What is assembled here is a new element to heroic action, that it be seen as labor, as directed effort to some goal; and Odysseus's self-serving strategem is made to look irresponsible and devoid of any ethical dimension. Lost in the dark wood, one must labor to find and negotiate the path to the earthly paradise.

Pound then turns, for the first time, to the story of Mount Segur, a place increasingly associated in *The Cantos* with the pagan and Eleusinian heresy of Provençal preserved cryptically in troubadour song. Austors de Maesnac, the brother of the troubadour, tells the story of Pieire's adventures with the wife of

Bernart de Tierci, which led to an armed conflict referred to as "Troy in Auvergnat" in Canto V. Pound has this narrator shift his attention to Mount Segur, "after the end of all things"; that is, after the successful crusade that destroyed Provençal civilization. The amorous adventure of the troubadour is connected both to the place that has come to be the symbol of Provençal glory and to the ruthless political and military campaign that ended that glory. Provençal song is given a relation to political events: the pagan tradition stemming from Eleusis threatens the established political order and as a result becomes the victim of a bloody crusade. Implied is the necessity for a commitment to the world of public events on the part of those few endowed with visionary capacity.

The canto ends with an overt reference to the fall of Troy, which now is associated with Mount Segur as another impressive social order destroyed by barbaric hostility; and an implicit reference to the hero who emerges from that destruction, Aeneas. Pound's presentation of the hero from the great Roman epic is strange, for it never mentions Aeneas but instead focuses on Anchises. Aeneas is not, at this point, a figure congenial to Pound because he eschews passion and love in favor of a public mission, a choice this poet does not want to be forced to make. So he presents Anchises at the very moment he recognizes the goddess Aphrodite:

> "King Otreus, of Phrygia,
> "That king is my father."
>   and saw then, as of waves taking form,
> As the sea, hard, a glitter of crystal,
> And the waves rising but formed, holding their form.
> No light reaching through them.   (XXIII/109)

Pound turns to the Homeric "Hymn to Aphrodite" for the story of the goddess' meeting with Anchises. She invents an elaborate disguise, that she is daughter to Otreus and fated by the gods to marry Anchises. He agrees to take her as his wife, brings her to bed, takes off her jewels and beautiful clothes, and makes love with an immortal goddess. The moment of his recognition of her divine nature is given in the description of the ever-flowing waves as they take and hold a form as hard and bright as crystal; the incessant motion of temporal perception is halted for a moment when the immanent divine reveals its eternal and permanent form. Pound focuses on the sexual passion and union of Anchises and Aphrodite because eros is still and ever to be an essential element in his wanderer's quest for home; and also because from their union issues Aeneas, who one day will assume a great role in history. Pound has found a way to allude to Aeneas's self-sacrifice and great public mission indirectly through this story of a mortal who sees and enjoys the beauty of Aphrodite. The vision of Aphrodite that ends Canto I is given a further dimension in this canto's focus on Anchises. Eros and visionary capacity characterizing the father are necessary for the piety and labor of the son. Their act of love results in the conception of Aeneas, who will work diligently to begin the historical process that will end in the establishment of the imperial greatness of Rome.

This canto, then, adds ethical direction and strenuous labor to the ideogram of the wanderer, and Odysseus's attempt to evade public responsibility seems a glaring fault. We must for a moment review the other canto in this group that focuses on Odysseus, Canto XX. In my first chapter, the analysis of this canto focused on the difference between the dangerous ease of the weak-willed lotophagoi and the exiled wanderer's heroic effort to return home, and I do not think what I have just said about Odysseus in Canto XXIII invalidates that argument. While we might now be tempted to sympathize more with the lotus eaters' complaint, agree that no one else gains from Odysseus's adventures, and so condemn him for selfish irresponsibility, I contend that Pound still admires the vigor and determination of his hero to return to his lost home. What we ought to notice in these two cantos are the contrary evaluations of Pound's wanderer: the two impulses he embodies—the private desire to return home at all costs and the public responsibility for the common good—operate side by side, in this sequence perhaps at odds but coming ever closer together, until a reconciliation occurs in Cantos XLI and XLIX.

Canto XXIV is devoted to the Marquis of Ferrara, Niccolo d'Este, whom Pound twice refers to as "ter pacis Italiae auctor," "three times the author of the Italian peace." In this capacity of peacemaker, he provides an example of the ethical dimension that Pound's heroes must now include. But how does the leader of an Italian city-state fit in the overall model of the wandering hero? Pound begins an account of a trip Niccolo made to the Holy Land by overtly placing this public figure in relation to the wandering Odysseus:

> And he in his young youth, in the wake of Odysseus
> To Cithera (a. d. 1413) "dove fu Elena rapta da Paris"
> Dinners in orange groves, prows attended of dolphins,
> Vestige of Rome at Pola, fair wind as far as Naxos [....]
>   (XXIV/111)

I find this placement of Niccolo d'Este in Odysseus's wake quite mechanical, but not clumsy, for Pound deliberately employs such artificial connections as a way to emphasize the surprising yoking of two such disparate figures. Niccolo's complicated struggle to keep the peace (his constant refrain to his son is "Keep the peace, Borso") is explicitly placed in the tradition of wandering heroes that Pound is creating in his epic and is extending in these cantos. The concern for the general welfare of Italy is an ethical goal that advances the nature of the epic journey. In *Jefferson and/or Mussolini*, Pound's treatise on "fascism" as the basic principle of all good government, he notes a conscious and deliberate ethical plan on the part of certain leaders from the Italian Renaissance:

> For if Rome was a conquering Empire, renaissance Italy evolved the doctrine of the balance of power, first for the use inside the penisula. Italy produced notable peacemakers who based their glory on peace tho' it came by the sword, Nic. Este, Cosimo, Lorenzo Medici, even Sforza condottiero, all men standing for order and, when possible, for moderation. (*J/M* 79)

These men used whatever means they found at hand, particularly economic and martial power, to advance peace and establish order. As he did for Malatesta, Pound looks back on previous cantos from his fully formed Fascist understanding of political action to trace the development of his own epic toward the position he takes in the thirties. He tries to establish the unity of *The Cantos* by tracing the development of, and making the necessary adjustments in, the various heroes he has presented.

What distinguishes this set of cantos, then, is the emergence of a code of ethics that from this point on will be constantly elaborated and applied throughout the entire epic. In fact, immediately after the depiction of the ease and delight of an earthly paradise in Canto XVII, Pound begins to present "cases" for us to study and assess. Canto XVIII assembles a group of munitions makers who are adventurous, cunning, and potentially heroic. The first one described, Zenos Metevsky (a pseudonym for Basil Zaharoff), is explicitly compared to another problematic figure from the world of public affairs:

> There was a boy in Constantinople,
> And some britisher kicked his arse.
> "I hate these french," said Napoleon, aged 12,

> To young Bourrienne, "I will do them all the harm
>   that I can."
> In like manner Zenos Metevsky.   (XVIII/80)

As the young Napoleon came to hate the French for the way he was treated as a young boy, so Zaharoff hates the English for the maltreatment he received as a youth at their hands. According to Terrell, Zaharoff had a spotty career but, by extreme cunning, he was able to rebound from all adversity and achieve both power and financial success. Pound's comparison of this influential man to Napoleon, coupled with Terrell's implicit comparison to Odysseus (in the matter of extreme cunning), suggest that this man is an adventurer in the heroic tradition Pound is forging. But Metevsky's cunning has no ethical dimension, no goal that aims at the public good. In Pound's belief, naive perhaps but constant, that among the "known causes of war" are the "[m]anufacture and high pressure salesmanship of munitions, armaments etc." (*SP* 222), Zaharoff figures as an historically significant man but one on the wrong side, one working against "peace" and the interests of humankind in general. Zaharoff as a cunning adventurer with no social responsibility serving only his own private self-interest: he sounds like that "idiot Odysseus" who tried to squirm out of military service. Nicholls argues that Pound's attitude toward business in the first thirty cantos is "somewhat problematic": despite his future hostility against usury, people like Baldy Bacon in Canto XII and Zaharoff here seem admirable as examples of "the romance of business" in their "sheer energy and directedness" (30–32). But I see a significant difference between Pound's understanding of Bacon and Zaharoff: he had not yet seen the crucial place of ethical design in his hero's wandering when he told the story of Baldy Bacon, and in the next set of cantos begins to form ethical judgments concerning various adventurers as they wander through history.

At the end of Canto XVIII Pound makes his first explicit statement in the poem of the basis for his ethical judgment that indicts the various adventurers presented in the canto. But first we should briefly look at some other "heroes" contained herein. There is a Mr. Giddings who tells the story of his daring strategy in selling torpedo boats to a Russian prince. When the prince ruined one of the boats in a test run, Giddings had the presence of mind to shrug off the loss, hoping for the prince's gratitude and respect; which he gets, along with a significant sale. But again, such cunning serves no ethical purpose. Near the end of the canto appears a different type of businessman in Hamish and Dave, who use technology in a constructive and publicly beneficial manner to help the Ethiopian emperor Menelik make better use of his land. The last words of the canto advance a maxim by which such activity can be judged:

> War, one war after another,
> Men start 'em who couldn't put up a good hen-roost.
>
> (XVIII/83)

Some men display the constructive impulse, while others could not build the most rudimentary shelter. Munitions makers only destroy, while others delight in building all sorts of things that benefit humanity. Pound recognizes here the potential (even his own) for misreading the Malatesta Cantos: Malatesta was presented mainly as an adventurer with a perception of beauty and a desire for the imposition of his own personality on the world. These cantos offer a corrective, in that the ethical nature and public benefit of the constructive act are emphasized. In this regard Pound refers three times (XXI/97, XXII/101, XVIII/138) to someone of his own family, his grandfather Thaddeus Coleman Pound, who exemplified the joy in constructing characteristic of the ethical hero:

> An' that man sweat blood
>   to put through that railway,
>   And what he ever got out of it?   (XXII/101)

Pound admires his grandfather's enterprising adventure to build a railway through Wisconsin against the obstacles of nature and corrupt economic practice and uses it as the occasion to discuss the nature of the constructive man:

> Over a decade ago, Major Douglas admitted that I had made a contribution to the subject [of economics] when I pointed out that my grandfather had built a railroad probably less from a desire to make money or an illusion that he could make more that way than some other, than from inherent activity, artist's desire to MAKE something, the fun of constructing and the play of outwitting and overcoming obstruction. (*SP* 239)

Pound's grandfather was motivated not by greed but by the "fun" of creating, the form of "play" that is construction. The spirit of adventure, then, is not necessarily good but must be directed at construction of something that benefits the public good. Those who make and sell munitions might be adventurers, but their destructive or obstructive work renders them ethically suspect and generally dangerous. The play of construction, the fun of making, is itself a fundamental ethical category for Pound. These cantos establish this impulse as the basis of Pound's ethics and of his ethical hero.

The poet also continues the meditation on his own potential as hero for the epic. Canto XXII begins with Pound's grandfather, the type of the constructive man, offered as a contrast to "the other type" of businessman, Warenhauser, who used his economic power to drive off all competitors. Such monopolizing only leads to a decrease in quality and an increase in cost, both detrimental to the public good. In contrast to Pound's grandfather, his motive is not to build for the people but to achieve financial success. After this comes an anecdote about a man who still cares about quality in the machine and assembly-line age, and who must either reduce his standards or lose contracts. Such is the context for Pound's next presentation of himself in his poem:

And C. H. [Douglas] said to the renowned Mr. Bukos:
                    [a pseudonym for Maynard Keynes]:
"What is the cause of the H. C. L. [high cost of living]?"
                              and Mr. Bukos,
The economist consulted of nations, said:
                    "Lack of labour."
And there were two millions of men out of work.
And C. H. shut up, he said
He would save his breath to cool his own porridge,
But I didn't, and I went on plaguing Mr. Bukos
Who said finally: "I am an orthodox
"Economist."
          Jesu Christo!
Standu nel paradiso terrestre
Pensando come si fesse compagna d'Adamo!!
          [Jesus Christ!
Standing in the earthly paradise
Thinking how to make a companion for Adam!!]
                                        (XXII/101–02)

Part of the poet's own responsibility as he sets out to write his epic is to seek out the knowledge he needs from various "experts." Here, he and Major Douglas, the founder of Social Credit, interview the leading economist of the day, John Maynard Keynes, and ask what is perhaps the central question for political economics to address, the cause of inflation. Pound is exasperated by what he considers Keynes's inept if not unethical response, and presents the ground on which he bases his own quest for knowledge: he is standing in the earthly paradise thinking about the way to make humanity fit companions for Adam. His own position is firmly grounded in a vision of an Edenic world, and his own goal now is to find a way to bring all humankind to the condition of innocence and original happiness. While he is still embarking on his lonely private journey to the lost home, he registers the complementary impulse, the desire to make a new humanity. It is important to recall that this set of cantos opens with Pound's first extended vision of the earthly paradise: it is this vision that provides the ground on which he stands as he works for the construction of a new home. Pound's goal as a poet is not just to make beautiful objects but, by means of his poetic talent, to make companions for purified man. His understanding of the poet's role undergoes a crucial swing as he assumes this public responsibility. Pound provides the poet's search for buried beauty with a larger, socially responsible, and politically significant aim. The role of the poet in the composition of the epic hero is moving closer to the world of politics.

The conviction that one can indeed transform a corrupt humanity into companions for Adam becomes increasingly clear and emphatic in the prewar years, especially as Pound embraces and includes Confucius in his epic.[2] Pound looks at previous attempts to accomplish this metamorphosis in Canto XXVII. It begins with a quotation from Guido Cavalcanti's Ballata 12, "Formando di disio nuova persona"—Love "fashions a new person from desire." This ballad describes the miracle Love performs in one weighed down by distress and grief, that it can fashion a new person, one who can feel joy and delight, from desire. The poet's new goal, the formation of a new humanity, is asserted at the start of a canto that records an actual moment from history when a new people acted with the instinct toward the construction of something beautiful and harmonious:

> Sed et universus quoque ecclesie populus,
> [And all the people of the church],
> All rushed out and built the duomo,
> Went as one man without leaders
> And the perfect measure took form.   (XXVII/130)

Pound finds a moment when "the people" were so energized and organized toward construction that "the perfect measure took form." This moment is unusual in the history of humankind, when various individuals have been organized to will the effort that results in the making of a beautiful object; but they only seem "one man without leaders." The poet indicates that the perfect measure does not take place without leadership, as the canto suddenly shifts to a lengthy depiction of an energized people who are left to act without the constructive impulse of good leadership:

> These are the labours of tovarisch,
> That tovarisch wrecked the house of the tyrants,
> And rose, and talked folly on folly,
> And walked forth and lay in the earth
>   And the Xarites bent over tovarisch.
>
> And that tovarisch cursed and blessed without aim,
>   These are the labours of tovarisch,
> Saying: [. . .]
> I neither build nor reap.   (XXVII/131–32)

The "tovarisch" (Russian for comrade, suggesting revolutionary man) has the power to destroy the house of the tyrant but lacks the knowledge of whom to curse and whom to bless. Unlike the shells and husks of men in Canto VII and the lotophagoi from Canto XX, revolutionary man has been sufficiently energized but his energy, when released, is destructive only: he neither builds nor reaps, lays "never stone upon stone." Pound uses the failed revolutions of France and Russia to indicate that there have been times in history when a people have displayed the energy to create a new world but lacked the leadership to do so. The failure of a tovarisch either to build or reap demonstrates the need for effective leadership if any sustained and beneficial change is to take place. This canto develops Pound's conception of the epic hero: now he must be able to lead an energized people to the earthly paradise, where they become fit companions for Adam. This set of cantos extends the journey of Pound's wanderer to a public dimension not seen in the very first cantos, as he assumes a public responsibility even as he seeks his private return to the lost home.

Eleven New Cantos

The next set of cantos was published in October 1934, as the Western world was undergoing a severe and prolonged financial crisis that some, including Pound, saw as a sure sign that the present usurious system of exchange had failed. Living in Italy for a decade, he gradually became an admirer of Mussolini and an advocate for Italian Fascism, which, he thought, contained the principle crucial in solving the world's economic ills. While Cantos XVII–XXX advanced the importance of ethical direction and leadership as components of the epic hero, *Eleven New Cantos* works to present a particular figure currently active in the political sphere as the leader who can reform and redeem the world. He finds himself in an awkward position: while he still considers himself primarily an American poet addressing his homeland as its most eminent citizen, he begins to see Mussolini as the emerging hero of the modern world. The work of this set of cantos is, first, to establish a connection between America and Italy and, second, to present Mussolini as a present and active example of the wandering hero his epic has developed. He works to provide a way for America to receive the lessons of Italian Fascism and to make Mussolini a figure in the poem. *Eleven New Cantos* is the most ambitious set of cantos thus far undertaken, committing Pound to a political figure whose future is as open and unsettled as the poem itself.

In Cantos XXXI through XXXIV, Pound presents fragments from the letters and diaries of Thomas Jefferson, James Madison, John Adams, and John Quincy Adams as he establishes the kind of intelligence and will that went into the formation of the healthy and sane civilization of America's first fifty years. In both the prose and poetry he writes at this time, it is Jefferson's curiosity, competence, and agility in diverse matters that seem most important in bringing civilization to the as yet uncivilized new world:

> Jefferson was all over the shop, discursive, interested in everything; to such an extent that he even wrote a long rambling essay on metric. He was trying to set up a civilization in the wilderness, he measured the Maison Carrée, sent over Houdin to America, and thought it would be better not to sculpt Washington in fancy dress costume. (*J/M* 66)

Pound uses the trope that Perry Miller isolated and elevated to a position of eminence in understanding early America, that of an "errand into the wilderness," in assessing Jefferson's ambitions and achievements.[3] A tremendous amount of activity that may appear discursive and rambling actually was directed toward a noble and highly ethical end, the erection of an untainted civilization in the radically open conditions of the wilderness. If the metaphor of "the

wilderness" suggests a state of nature as yet free from the transformative power of human labor, then Jefferson has the chance to
impose new conditions for the creation of a new kind of person, perhaps a companion for Adam. The cantos devoted to Jefferson exhibit
the wide range of interests that Pound saw as essential to this task:

> When the nit-wits complained of Jefferson's superficiality it
> merely amounted to their non-perception of the multitude of
> elements needed to start any decent civilization in the Ameri-
> can wilderness: learning, architecture, art that registered
> contemporary phenomena instead of merely distorting them
> into received convention, seed of the right sort, transporta-
> tion, responsibility, resilience in the individual and in the
> local group. [...]
> Jefferson was *polumetis,* many-minded [...]. (*J/M* 88–89)

Like Odysseus, Jefferson was "many-minded," curious about
many things and quick to see the need to bring various elements
into play to start the process of construction.[4] Among other things,
Pound states that Jefferson desired an art that does not distort
experience by forcing it into received conventions; he sees the
opportunity for new categories that would go into the establishment of a new world, and all his efforts are geared to that ambition. It is Jefferson's understanding and seizing of the opportunity
before him, to avoid the mistakes of the old world and to make a
new one based on a new set of fundamental principles, that Pound
records with admiration:

> Jefferson found himself in a condition of things that had no
> precedent in any remembered world. He saw like a shot that
> a new system and new mechanisms MUST come into being to
> meet it. (*J/M* 62)

Perhaps an "unremembered world" provides precedent for the
opportunity Jefferson has to erect a new system; Pound's language
here hints that the wilderness of America may be something like
the original world humanity first confronted and transformed by
its labor. The challenge before him was to impose his will and
intelligence on the unformed continent and establish the various
elements that would transform the wilderness into a garden.

At the end of Canto XXXII Pound compares Jefferson's
watchful guidance of the early years of the American nation to
Sordello's role in *Purgatorio* VI:

a guisa de leon
The cannibals of Europe are eating one another again
quando si posa.   (159)

These lines come at the end of Jefferson's disparaging remarks about the various kings, queens, and emperors that were ruling Europe in his time. Sordello's watchful vigilance over the valley of Princes in ante-Purgatory is like Jefferson's over the affairs of Europe: just as the troubadour functions in *Purgatorio* as "the scourge of princes" (see Makin, *Provence*, ch. 9), so Jefferson expresses his scorn of European princes to discourage and prevent the importation of the old world's ways to America. We can carry the comparison even further: as Sordello leads Dante and Virgil away from the valley of misguided and irresponsible princes to the portals of Purgatory proper where Dante will begin his purgation, so Jefferson can be our guide away from the corruption of present American leadership and toward the place where responsible leadership is working to renew the earthly paradise that is the culmination of the purgative process. Pound seems to imply that Jefferson's work in early America functions as a guide to the poet's own understanding of the kind of political action that can renew the promise of early America.

The battle against the forces that opposed and eventually destroyed the American promise is presented in Canto XXXVII as part of Jefferson's influence and heritage. Old World conventions and categories block the effort to build a healthy civilization, and Pound devotes this canto to the war against the Second Bank of the United States led by Andrew Jackson and carried on by Martin Van Buren. The problem with the Bank, in Pound's estimation, is that it came to exert almost total control of the national economy without regard to national interests but solely for its own private benefit (Makin, *Cantos* 191–92). Why should a private corporation such as this Bank, which has no wealth of its own and is intended merely to facilitate the exchange of the wealth that is the nation's, control that wealth? The government is the disinterested mechanism designed and established to control the exchange of wealth; the duty of a good government is to ensure that its wealth circulates freely so it is distributed evenly to all the people. The National Bank is one of those "received conventions" that Jefferson and his followers oppose; its precedent is the Bank of England against which, in Canto XLVI, Pound provides evidence testifying to its harmful nature. The American cantos in this group, Cantos XXXI through XXXIV and XXXVII, present the effort of good leadership stemming from Jeffersonian principles, to establish a new system in a new world that might transform the wilderness into an earthly paradise.

In *Jefferson and/or Mussolini,* his most important and sustained presentation of political convictions in prose, Pound claims that this heritage is not at present to be found in America but is active in Fascist Italy:

> The heritage of Jefferson, Quincy Adams, old John Adams, Jackson, Van Buren is HERE, NOW *in the Italian penisula* at the beginning of the Fascist second decennio, not in Massachusetts or Delaware. (12)

The challenge of Mussolini to America is simply:

> *Do the driving ideas of Jefferson, Quincy Adams, Van Buren, or whoever else there is in the creditable pages of our history, FUNCTION actually in the America of this decade to the extent that they function in Italy under the DUCE?* (104)

This is Pound's most original contribution to the discussion of Italian Fascism, that it is based on the same "driving ideas" and "cultural heritage" as the American nation under Jefferson's leadership. He claims that America under Jefferson and Italy under Mussolini exhibit the same fundamental effort as the respective leaders work to drive out corrupt conventions and categories and impose new ones that can lead to a healthy civilization: "I insist on the identity of our American Revolution of 1776 with your Fascist Revolution" (*SP* 313). This thesis allows Pound to make use of Mussolini as he maintains his epic purpose of educating America. The American nation can return to the principles that made it great by understanding modern Italy's emergence under Mussolini.

It is still to America that Pound looks for his epic's audience. In an essay from 1937, he considers the Jefferson-Adams letters a monument to a lost American greatness that can be recaptured:

> The possibilities of revival, starting perhaps with a valorisation of our cultural heritage, not merely as something lost in dim retrospect, a tombstone, tastily carved, whereon to shed dry tears or upon which to lay a few withered violets, in the manner of, let us say, the late Henry (aforementioned) Adams. The query being: should we lose or go on losing our own revolution (of 1776–1830) by whoring after exotics, Muscovite or European? (*SP* 147)

This passage testifies to Pound's conviction that a revival of American civilization is possible if the nation returns to the revolutionary impulses that guided its development from 1776 through 1830.[5] The revolution was not merely the war for independence but something more far-reaching, a revolution in the form of government that was abandoned gradually during the years after Jefferson's influence ended. Pound hopes to "valorise" the American heritage that these letters contain, and that is certainly what the American cantos in this set attempt. The real challenge is to make the principles of Jeffersonian democracy applicable to the present: "you must distinguish between 1820 and 1930, you must bring your Jefferson up to date" (*SP* 243). Mussolini is the figure who brings Jefferson's principles to the modern world. One studies early American history to prepare for a study of Mussolini, and one studies Mussolini to understand how to revitalize America.

But America cannot naively import the "exotic" Italian Fascist Revolution in its external or accidental forms in an effort to return to the principles that guided its revolution. This question arises: How does Italian Fascism as it takes shape under Mussolini in the twenties and thirties resemble—or, more pointedly, *continue*—the American Revolution of 1776 through 1830? Pound does not look to ideology or party platform for the resemblance; he cares little for the specific details of Italian Fascism because they are merely local "accidents" of a more fundamental reality, "the cupolas and gables of fascism" (*J/M* v). On the surface, no two men could appear less similar than Jefferson and Mussolini, but that is because the geographical and political situations they find themselves in differ so drastically. On a more fundamental level, they are both men who get things done. About Jefferson he says: "I am concerned with what he actually did, with what his mind did when faced with a particular problem *in* a particular geography" (11). "No man in history had ever *done* more and done it with less violence and with less needless expenditure of energy" (15). What interests Pound is the "essence" of fascism, the role of a great leader as he seeks to impose his will on a particular place and time and divert the course of history. What he admires in *Jefferson and/or Mussolini* is their recognition of the opportunities for this kind of far-reaching change before them:

> There is opportunism and opportunism. The word has a bad meaning in a world of Metternichs, and Talleyrands it means doing the other guy the minute you get the chance.
> There is also the opportunism of the artist, who has a defi-

nite aim, and creates out of the materials present. The greater
the artist the more permanent his creation. And this is a matter of WILL.

It is also a matter of the DIRECTION OF THE WILL. And
if the reader will blow the fog off his brain and think for a few
minutes or a few stray half-hours he will find this phrase
brings us ultimately both to Confucius and Dante.

The whole of the *Divina Commedia* is a study of the "direc-
tio voluntatis" (direction of the will). (*J/M* 15–17)

The "Fascist hero" is the artist who directs his will toward a
visionary goal and uses whatever materials he finds at hand to
drive a new set of conditions through a firmly entrenched present.
Pound reads Dante as a political study in verse recording how the
will can be redirected toward goals very different from those of the
present culture, goals based on an original health and visionary
capacity.[6] The hero is the person who has broken free of a decadent
present and wills a new world into being. The local details, of early
America and modern Italy, are important insofar as they reveal
how the hero's mind works, how he wills and aims at a better order
in a particular place and time. The essence of the actions taken by
Jefferson and Mussolini is the same, in that they are men who take
advantage of the given opportunity to impose, by the sheer power of
will, new conditions that might lead to a healthy civilization.

The obstacles against which the modern leader struggles to
impose a new set of conditions are more powerful than those faced
by the American. Pound describes the geographical and cultural
differences between early America and modern Italy that render
Mussolini's task more difficult than Jefferson's: while Jefferson had
the unprecedented opportunity of imposing a new system in a
wilderness, Mussolini finds himself in a more entrenched and tradi-
tion-laden culture. There is no more frontier where a leader has the
opportunity to create a new world from as yet uncorrupted material. Mussolini is faced "with a crusted conservatism that no untrav-
elled American can even suspect of existing" (23), with traditions
and habits "milleniar, forgotten, stuck anywhere from the time of
Odysseus to the time of St. Dominic" (25). "All of 'em carved in
stone, carpentered and varnished into shape, built in stucco, or
organic in the mind of the people" (32). How can sweeping change
be implemented in a world of cultural traditions so powerful that
they have been forgotten as parts of tradition, that they have
become unconscious and "organic in the mind of the people"? "It
takes a genius charged with some form of dynamite, mental or

material, to blast [the people] out of [their] preconceptions" (26). What Pound admires in Mussolini is his capacity to effect funda- mental and far-reaching change in a country deeply conditioned by centuries of conservatism. While Jefferson merely had to watch out for the importation of corrupt ways from the old world, Mussolini has to blast away the deeply ingrained traditions that prevent the imposition of a new system leading to a new way of being.

Pound's fascism, which is really a sophisticated and elaborate form of "hero-worship," takes its character from his attempt to execute a poem in the epic mode which traditionally features the role of heroic will in the realm of public affairs. The epic poet does not regard history as a process in which economic and other cul- tural conditions determine all possible responses for effective action; instead, the heroic individual rises above all such considerations and makes a crucial difference in the course of events. Pound's subscription to the Fascist cult of the great man is a result of his working as a poet in an epic tradition, in this regard especially the classical epic, where an Achilles changes the for- tunes of war simply by showing himself to the enemy, or where an Aeneas can carry the entire destiny of the Roman Empire in his person. So in *Eleven New Cantos* Pound creates a hero in Mussoli- ni who has assumed the task and burden of changing the course of history: "Italy had a risorgimento, a shaking from lethargy, a par- tial unification, then a forty-year sleep, from which the next heave has been the work of one man, pre-eminently, with only here and there a notable, perhaps a very temporary, assistance" (*J/M* 89). As he contemplates the epic tradition, Pound works to create a hero who can transcend the given conditions that have determined the shape of the modern world and who can impose his own intel- lect and will to alter these conditions. The wanderer who works to free himself of all cultural constraints in his centrifugal movement away from home can become the Fascist hero who works to impose new conditions for a new home.

In the complex international structures of an advanced capi- talistic economy, such belief in one man's will seems hopelessly naive and nostalgic. Pound rescues his poem from such dismissal by creating a new kind of hero for a modern epic, the bureaucratic hero. In this regard it is worth noting Nicholls's assertion that Pound is less a revolutionary than he is a reformer (49). Pound does not see the need to change the entire system, as a revolutionary would; rather, he believes that a leader can take whatever system, whatever machine of exchange, he finds at his disposal and make it run efficiently and toward justice. Nicholls notes Pound's interest in various "devices" that the poet believes can procure a share of justice (53–54). His advocacy of Gesell's "stamp scrip" is perhaps the most famous of these "tricks": Gesell invented "counter-usury" when he proposed the issuance of "paper money which requires the affixation of a monthly stamp to maintain its par value. . . . Thus taxation was fixed on the money itself, and accelerated the circulation of this money" (*SP* 276). Nothing "revolutionary" is attempted; rather, simply by this "trick" of affixing a monthly stamp, the current system of exchange is made to run more equitably as hoarding is discouraged and the circulation of money and the goods it can purchase is encouraged. Indeed, Pound's entire attitude toward money rests on his belief that money is merely a device to facilitate exchange. While analyzing the various schemes, tricks, and devices he advocates, we should note first and foremost that a belief in such gimmicks indicates his politics. In Pound's estimation, government is simply a machine that can run toward justice or toward inequal distribution, depending only upon who is running the machine. The bureaucratic hero is the strong man who can take the machine of exchange currently in place and tinker with it until it runs toward an equitable distribution of wealth thoughout the nation:

> Mussolini may at any moment find out that some laboured and ingenious device for securing a fair amount of justice in some anterior period and under earlier states of society NO LONGER works, or is no longer capable of giving as much justice as some new rule made to fit the facts of the year ELEVEN, facts, i.e. that have been facts for a short time only. (*J/M* 77)

The leader dismantles old devices and invents new ones while leaving the present capitalistic machine in place; he constantly tinkers and reforms the workings of the machine in his work toward "economic justice, which latter is no more impossible or inconceivable than the just functioning of machines in a power-house" (*J/M* 123). The metaphor is telling: the state is a machine whose function is to keep all things moving evenly and smoothly so the entire people can use and enjoy the wealth of the nation. "The entire function of the state is to facilitate the traffic, i.e. the circulation of goods, air, water, heat, coal (black or white), power, and even thought" (*SP* 213). One man can effect drastic and far-reaching change by taking charge of the complex bureaucracy through which circulates the wealth of the nation, by redirecting the mechanisms of exchange so that they run toward justice.

It is, I am suggesting, primarily because of his work as an epic poet that Pound formulates and advocates what he calls a "volitionist economics." This theory of economics rests on his belief that economic justice can be achieved only by the directed will of a powerful leader: "The science of economics will not get very far until it grants the existence of will as a component; i.e. will toward order, will toward 'justice' or fairness, desire for civilisation, amenities included. The intensity of that will is definitely a component in any solution" (*SP* 240). While assuming that economics is a science, he does not advocate any specific economic system but the basing of the system in place on a strong man's will: "I am trying to base a system on will" (*SP* 238). "The science of economics" must learn how to include and calculate the effect of human will in the various mechanisms of exchange. In this regard Pound cites Mussolini's dictum, "Discipline the economic forces and equate them to the needs of the nation" (*SP* 298). Whatever "economic forces" happen to be operating can be disciplined to a new end, that of the good of the entire nation. The bureaucratic hero cannot invent new forces but he can impose his will on those that exist and direct their running toward justice.

The wandering of Hanno in Canto XL provides the context for the introduction of Mussolini into the epic. Pound is careful to establish the centrifugal wanderer who reaches, or at least glimpses and aims for, Dantesque heights as the model for our understanding of the achievements of the political hero. As we saw in the previous chapter, the first half of Canto XL focuses on the economic factors that have contributed to the corruption of the Western world. It documents the concerted efforts on the part of businessmen and bankers to advance their own interests ahead of, and sometimes even against, those of the nation. Pound's source for most of the details, Lewis Corey's *The House of Morgan*, describes how a powerful man can take advantage of various national emergencies to amass huge profits at the expense of the nation's welfare. Against this background emerges the Carthagenian general Hanno. The way the canto slides from its documentation of Morgan's villainous opportunism to Hanno's periplum invites us to conclude that Hanno's voyage of discovery out into the unknown is motivated by the desire to leave corrupt economic conditions. We note that Hanno's journey is an economic mission:

Out of which things seeking an exit

PLEASING TO CARTHEGENIANS: HANNO

that he ply beyond pillars of Herakles
60 ships of armada to lay out Phoenician cities
to each ship 50 oars, in all
30 thousand aboard them with water, wheat in provision.
Two days beyond Gibel Tara [Gibraltar] layed in the wide
    plain   [....]

So laid we house: Karikon, Gutta, Akra, Meli, Arambo
These are the cities, then Lixos.   (199)

Unlike Dante's Ulysses, this centrifugal wanderer does not drown but instead sails safely beyond the Pillars of Herakles; and unlike Ulysses, his goal is not to satisfy his thirst for new personal experience but to found trading cities on the Atlantic coast of Africa. By bravely breaking the confines of his culture, Hanno is able to open new possibilities for the exchange of wealth by founding new centers for trade. He is an heroic wanderer for breaking culturally imposed limits and finding a way to create new conditions that advance the prosperity of his state. Carthage achieves its greatness due to such heroic adventuring. Morgan stands for the kind of selfish adventuring that creates the corrupt economic conditions that stifle a nation's growth; and Hanno for the kind of political action that challenges these conditions and opens new avenues for the circulation of wealth for the good of the state. The journey "outward and away" is given an ethical and public dimension. The wanderer who defies cultural limitations in his search for home is joined in the figure of Hanno to the responsible man of action working for a new home.

Pound associates this voyage of economic discovery with Dante's *Paradiso* to provide Hanno with a visionary capacity. As we saw in the previous chapter, the account of Hanno's periplum is an accurate translation suddenly halted and supplemented:

Went no further that voyage,
        as were at end of provisions.
        [translation ends here, without a break]
Out of which things seeking an exit
To the high air, to the stratosphere, to the imperial
calm, to the empyrean, to the baily of the four towers
the NOUS, the ineffable crystal   (201)

Hanno's sense of civic duty that led to his daring journey of economic discovery is motivated by this vision of "the imperial

calm" and "the baily of the four towers." Pound suggests with this
addendum that Hanno has glimpsed the greatness of the ideal city
that Dante records in the upper reaches of heaven and that this
vision inspired the economic mission. Hanno is both the wanderer
seeking an exit from the present state of things and a return to the
original human consciousness that is one's private home; and the
man of action dedicated to the construction of a public home based
on the visionary grandeur of the heavenly city. The exile becomes
the center of a new order. In Canto XL Pound brings the twin
impulses of his wandering hero together as the context and model
for his understanding of Mussolini as the Fascist hero in Canto XLI.

He examines the present historical figure as a possible
embodiment of the prototypical epic hero. The movement of these
two cantos, from Hanno to Mussolini, implies that the Fascist
leader's efforts are in the form of the wanderer who bravely breaks
the confines and conventions of his culture and works from a
visionary experience of an ideal city. After following the Carthagenian's periplum in search of new trading centers, the poet begins
the next canto (and the last in the sequence) with *il Duce's* efforts
to open new possibilities for expanding the wealth of Italy:

> Ma questo"
>   said the Boss, "e divertente."
> catching the point before the aesthetes had got there;
> Having drained off the muck by Vada
> From the marshes, by Circeo, where no one else wd. have
>   drained it.
> Waited 2000 years, ate grain from the marshes;
> Water supply for ten million, another one million *"vani"*
> that is rooms for people to live in.
>   XI of our era.   (XLI/202)

In twentieth-century Europe it is more difficult to find new
sources of wealth than it was for Hanno or, for that matter, Jefferson. Hanno had the opportunity of breaking the assigned limits of
his culture beyond which lay new sources of wealth and new centers for the circulation of existing wealth; as a result, Carthage
became a great city. Jefferson had an entire continent before him
rich in resources of all sorts; his chief accomplishment was the
purchase of the Louisiana territory from the French which allowed
the American nation to expand and find new sources for wealth.
But in twentieth-century Italy, operating in a culture dominated
by the greedy businessmen and monopolistic bankers epitomized

by Morgan, how does one expand wealth and find new ways to cir-
culate and distribute it? The lines that open this canto record
Pound's admiration for Mussolini's discovery of a way to reclaim
the natural abundance of the land. As the exilic wanderer in Canto
XLVII "enters the hills" to establish a new consciousness and a
new identity rooted in veneration of the earth and its fertility, so
the Fascist leader is working here to reclaim the earth as the
source of all value. With the closure of all frontiers for expansion
and discovery of new markets, Mussolini imposes his new sense of
values on Italy and finds ways to make the land yield new wealth:
grain, homes, and water from land unuseable for centuries. By the
strength of will he has opened new possibilities for wealth in what
had seemed a closed system.

It is as an example of Mussolini's will to discipline the economic forces that the poet then relates an anecdote concerning the
Boss's efforts to wrest control of the machine of economic exchange
from greedy and selfish profiteers:

> That they were to have a consortium
> and one of the potbellies says:
>   will come in for 12 million"
> And another: three millyum for my cut;
> And another: we will take eight;
> And the Boss said: but what will you
>   DO with that money?"
> "But! but! signore, you do not ask a man
> what he will *do* with his money.
> That is a personal matter.
> And the Boss said: but what will you do?
> You won't really need all that money
> because you are all for the *confine*."   (202)

The profiteers try to invalidate Mussolini's question about
their need for all that money by appealing to the practices and
ethics of a liberal state: "that is a personal matter." The present system of economic practice is based on the primacy of the individual,
who is conceived of as anterior to and independent of the state.
Mussolini is not blinded by the standards and conditions established and enforced by a usurious economic system: the hero seizes
control of the machine of exchange and distributes these "personal"
profits to the "public." In opposing the values of the liberal state,
Mussolini addresses what Pound considers the central issue of modern politics: "In politics *the* problem of our time is to find the border

between public and private affairs" (*SP* 240). Mussolini persists with his question—"what will you *do* with that money?"—because in the new Fascist order profit is a public and not a private matter. He imposes new terms and conditions for the circulation of wealth. The epic hero is a political figure who has broken free of the conditions that determine the present state of affairs, has achieved a vision of a different social ordering whose highest expression is Dante's heavenly city, and uses the means at his disposal (in Mussolini's case, often military strength) to impose a new set of economic conditions on the Italian nation. He threatens to banish the "potbellies" to the *"confine"*—the "border" or "boundary"—if they do not comply with his will; that is, those who currently occupy the center of the economic system will be thrust by force to the margins by the man who uses his power to assume the position of cultural center. The central become the outlaws and the exiles; and the exiled (that is, the rest of the nation) can begin the movement back home.

What differentiates Mussolini from the profiteers is that he works for the good of the entire nation while they care only for their own private gain. It is, in Pound's estimation, a question of giving economics an ethical basis. The poet advances an aphorism that presents this aspect of his politics and connects these cantos to the previous sequence: "You can not make good economics out of bad ethics" (*SP* 282). The strong leader does not allow ethics and economics to be made separate and distinct. Pound believes that all economic systems have an ethical component; his hero recognizes that the ethics informing usury are bad ethics and that a different economic system based on good ethics is possible. *Eleven New Cantos* advances the previous set of cantos by distinguishing the role of great leadership, as the man strong enough to provide a new ethical direction to the system of economic exchange so that system can be made to work toward justice. These cantos move the epic forward in a more radical way, by committing the poem to a real figure whose career is still open, whose actions are geared to the immediate future.

Peter Nicholls provides a Marxist critique of Pound's economics that needs to be stated, not because it necessarily invalidates Pound's position but because it highlights the very attitudes toward economics and history the poet deliberately challenges. Nicholls accuses Pound "of an explicit recasting of fiscal problems as ethical ones," as if this were an obvious and complete absurdity the poet should have been embarrassed to register so clearly:

> It was this aspect of his thought which was to make so much of his economic theory irretrievably anachronistic, since (it

hardly needs to be said) complex modern economies inevitably comprise areas of ethical 'indifference', and they are for that reason intractable to the kind of simple moral analysis Pound was constantly to advance. His failure to grasp this would later prevent him from seeing that the decline of the medieval doctrine of the 'just price' was less a result of the moral degeneracy of the Church than an inevitable consequence of the rise of a capitalistic economy. (56–57)

Pound's epic hero acts upon an economic theory directly opposite to Nicholls's contention that it is inevitable for some areas of "complex modern economics" to be ethically indifferent. His response to this sort of attack might have been to cite one of his favorite phrases from Mussolini: "The indifferent have never made history" (*J/M* viii). Anyone who has risen to a position where he can "make history" is motivated by some sort of desire and aims at some sort of goal; neither Morgan nor Mussolini is ethically indifferent. Pound would contend that the divorce between ethics and economics is not an obvious and necessary result of "progress" but the deliberate effect of those who want to use the system of exchange for selfish (that is, private) benefit and gain. The theory of economics that Pound develops as he creates a type of epic hero insists on the primacy of an ethical will. If such belief is an error, then it is the error of a poet who studies an epic tradition instead of Marx as he fashions a modern hero.

Nicholls relies on the concept of "necessity" as he accuses Pound of naivete and simplicity: the divorce of ethics from economics that led to the decline of the medieval doctrine of the just price was "an inevitable consequence of the rise of a capitalistic economy." Much of the poet's hostility to the Marxist theory of economic determinism can be attributed to his vehement rejection of Necessity as a force that explains historical events. His epigram to *Jefferson and/or Mussolini*—"NOTHING IS WITHOUT EFFICIENT CAUSE"—marks his understanding of historical causality, that all events are brought about by an identifiable "agent whereby a change or state of rest is first produced."[7] People make decisions and act in the public domain, and not some mysterious force called "necessity." A constant refrain of Pound's in his radio broadcasts is that the Second World War was not necessary; certain people acted—whether consciously or otherwise is another matter—in such a way that the war was brought about. Only those who act against the good of the nation hide behind the concept of inevitability; hence Pound's admiration for Mussolini's phrase: "We are tired of a government in which there is no responsible person having a hind name, a front name and an address" (*SP* 261). Nicholls considers Pound naive in conceiving of economic change "not in terms of the dialectical movement of history but as a moment of rupture within it" (53). Pound regards as criminal the absolution of all political leadership from responsibility by recourse to a mysterious force called "the dialectical movement of history" or "necessity."

Makin asserts that the "epic, as Pound practiced it, sharpens one's perception of what is possible" (*Provence* 254). It is important to remember that for this poet "economic justice . . . is no more impossible or inconceivable than the just functioning of machines in a power-house" (*J/M* 123). The Fascist hero works to open new possibilities in a world that seems to be running according to necessary and inexorable laws. It takes a Hanno or a Mussolini to dare to break the limitations established and enforced by the present usurious system of economic exchange; it takes the daring of the wanderer to sail "outward and away" from the conditions that determine the present state of affairs. What the Fascist hero sees when he passes beyond Gibraltar is a vision of the ideal city. He does not dismiss this vision as impossible or anachronistic but instead thinks about the ways to realize the ideal: "You can quite meritoriously sigh for justice, but Mussolini has been presumably quite right in putting the first emphasis on having a government strong enough to get the said justice" (*J/M* 45). While most of humanity is bound by the iron laws of economic determinism, the Fascist hero rises above them, sees the possibility of justice, and uses whatever means he finds available to bring about a new world, a new home.

The Fifth Decad of Cantos XLII–LI

This set of cantos, published in June 1937, continues and concludes what I consider the first movement of *The Cantos,* as Pound establishes his own potential, as poet, to become the hero of his epic. He puts in the forefront his own sensibility and his unusual gift for recording that sensibility to implicate himself in the movement of public events as their shaper and guiding spirit. The contrary motions of the exile seeking a private return to a lost consciousness and of the active man working in the public domain are reconciled in the figure of "no man" who records in Canto XLIX his private vision of the ideal public order. One major goal of *The*

Cantos is accomplished as the exiled wanderer who returns home in Canto XLVII becomes the poet of a new order in Canto XLIX. The centrifugal becomes the centripetal, the poet as exile becomes the poet as Fascist sage, Odysseus becomes Confucius.

As early as Canto III, Pound understood that his own capacity to experience and record visionary experience might be a component of the modern epic hero, and throughout the early cantos he presents himself in various relations to the heroes he collects. But it is in Canto XLI, "the Mussolini Canto," that he recognizes the full potential of his own poetic gift in the composition of the epic hero. For in that canto the actual Mussolini is transmuted by the power of the poet into a "mythic" figure; the "real" man is turned into a character in a poem. The canto opens with the politician's polite response to the first thirty cantos, a deluxe edition of which Pound sent Mussolini when the latter finally granted the poet an interview:

> Ma questo,"
>   said the Boss, "è divertente."
> catching the point before the aesthetes had got there;
> Having drained off the muck by Vada
> From the marshes, by Circeo.   (202)

The poet takes this vague compliment as evidence that Mussolini has understood the deeper purposes of the epic: to "divert" the course of events called history so that a corrupt culture can return to its original strength and beauty.[8] A relation is suggested between Mussolini's quick and penetrating comprehension of *The Cantos* and his political activity: he understands the poem because of what he has been doing, and he will now be able to continue with deepened awareness his constructive efforts because they match the heroic paradigm this poet is creating. Pound begins this canto with the politician's critical assessment, one, to suggest that "the Boss" is already acting upon the principles the poet has discovered by studying past heroes and, more profoundly, to create the context for the politician's past and continuing actions. These lines suggest that Mussolini acknowledges Pound's role as the visionary poet who grounds healthy and constructive political action. I think we can take this strange moment of delusion—after all, any "sane" person would understand in an instant that Mussolini has not read the poem and is responding as vaguely as one can—as evidence that Pound has come to see his own poetic enterprise as politically powerful. His task as poet is to create a Mussolini that matches the heroic paradigm he has been developing and deploying since 1917. Norman and Torrey have documented fully Pound's grandiose belief in his own public or historical importance that is diagnosed by the psychiatric world as a psychotic delusion.[9] The ambition of the epic poet to be the guiding force behind the political power of Mussolini is "insanity" to one group yet gives *The Cantos* its grandeur and intensity. In a very real sense, Pound comes to see himself as the shaping power behind the different kind of power embodied in the politician. The poet is emerging as the true hero of the poem.

Pound, then, considers the poet essential to the process of historical action in that his visionary gift provides the context and aims for the politician's efforts. *The Fifth Decad of Cantos* opens with the poet's creation of an historical context for the actions of Mussolini and any other political figure who might be convinced by *The Cantos* to follow his lead, the battle against usury undertaken by the Monte dei Paschi, a "damn good bank, in Siena" (XLII/209). The very name of the Bank, "the Mount of the Pastures," indicates that, unlike the banks of usury which have no wealth of their own, this one is founded on the abundance of nature, specifically the grazing pastures surrounding Siena. Unlike the banks that work against the good of the people, this one does not seek to amass profit but to facilitate the circulation of the wealth of all the people. What I wish to add to the existing analyses of these cantos is Pound's subtle focus on his action as tradition-maker: it is the poet who finds and transmits an historical example of the kind of public-minded political action that ought to guide the efforts of modern statesmen. On the first page of this sequence he describes the motives of benevolent rulers: the leaders of Siena acted "'With paternal affection/ justice convenience of the city" in mind. They acted for the advancement of the common good:

> having chief place and desire that the
> citizens get satisfaction (siano soddisfatti) contentment
> and be fully persuaded of what for the common good is here
>   being dealt with.   (XLIII/216)

Such is the proper aim of political leadership, to satisfy its citizens and make them content with their lives. The rather prosaic account of the effort by the Sienese leadership to establish this Bank is juxtaposed to an account of a parade that celebrates its establishment (XLIII/216). Pound joins these two passages with a short but telling phrase, "To the end:"; that the labor of the leaders was directed "to the end" is indicated by the parade, the people's delight in the achievement of a just system of exchange. Canto XLIV, which opens with "this so provident law" enacted by Ferdinando III, grand duke of Tuscany, depicts at some length and with much enthusiasm the people's celebration following a similar securing of justice. An entire month of "unforeseen jubilation" spontaneously ensued after the passing of a law that recognized grain as the basis of the region's wealth. These cantos suggest that "the people" respond with joy and energy at leadership that works for economic justice: "There was the fruit of nature/ there was the whole will of the people" (XLIII/218). Such historical precedents provide Mussolini with a tradition of healthy political action that can be followed and updated for the twentieth century.

Pound is careful to suggest that it is the poet who makes the tradition that guides the modern hero. After his translation of the document that proposes the Bank, he adds what can only be regarded as its lyric or poetic justification:

> wave falls and the hand falls
> Thou shalt not always walk in the sun
> or see weed sprout over cornice
> Thy work in set space of years, not over an hundred.
>   (XLII/210)

The phrasing and rhythm here suggest Ecclesiastes, where the preacher emphasizes the vanity of all projects that do not recognize the absolute limit enforced by the fact of human mortality. Pound inserts his version of this platitude as justification for a Bank that recognizes and is indeed based upon the temporal process and the transciency of wealth. Later in the same canto, another "poetic" moment interrupts the transcription of the prosaic labor that went into the erection of the Bank:

> let all sundry and whoever be
> satisfied that the said MOUNT may be created.
> so that the echo turned back in my mind: Pavia:
> Saw cities move in one figure, Vicenza, as depicted
> San Zeno by Aldige...   (213)

In this passage Pound returns to the phrase that ends Canto I, "So that," to indicate that the founding of the Bank is being brought into relation to the theme of the wandering hero. As he records the words that bring the Bank into existence, the poet hears an echo in his mind, an echo of other ideal cities he has imagined and glimpsed. Not only is Siena now made part of the ideogram of the ideal city, but Pound draws attention to his own mind, as if his sensibility is of historical importance. It is the wanderer who imagines various ideal cities and causes them to "move in one figure"; the poet creates the ideal city from the texts that record the various attempts to realize it throughout history. Even these cantos that seem purely "historical" are now part of the periplum, as the wanderer sorts through documents searching for the material he can fashion into the ideal that guides the political heroes.

In attempting to make the poet's talent the ground of political action, Pound draws aesthetic and economic values into a relation that a Marxist literary critic like Nicholls finds untenable (57). Whether Nicholls is right or not is not my concern; I simply wish to show that the poet is working in these cantos to make the qualitative values of the aesthetic world the basis of the quantitative measuring of the economic. Pound seems to believe that the poet's imagination and talent are the ground of economic justice:

> Pine cuts the sky into three
> Thus BANK of the grassland was raised into Seignory.
> (XLIII/219)

A causal relationship exists between the brief fragment of careful observation of nature that is characteristic of the poet's sensibility and the establishment of the Bank: because the natural world is seen clearly and lovingly, the Monte dei Paschi is created. The cantos devoted to the Bank of Siena are Pound's attempt to create the context and aims for the political hero, and to place his own sensibility and talent at the foundation of all healthy and constructive political action.

The poet, then, has two distinct but complementary roles. His is the talent to appreciate the beauty of the natural order and to record that appreciation in written texts; and, equipped with such talent, he is the most qualified to sort through the texts that record history and distinguish between the healthy and the corrupt, the constructive and the destructive. Canto XLVI opens with the telling juxtaposition of the poet in his twin roles, as recorder of "nature-feeling" and as historical investigator:

> That day there was cloud over Zoagli
> And for three days snow cloud over the sea
> Banked like a line of mountains.

> Snow fell. Or rain fell stolid, a wall of lines
> So that you could see where the air stopped open
> and where the rain fell beside it
> Or the snow fell beside it. Seventeen
> Years on this case, nineteen years, ninety years
>   on this case.   (XLVI/231)

The man who observes nature so closely and can record it so
clearly is also the man "on this case," on the trail of usury. Just as
the appreciation of this meteorological phenomenon shifts into the
resumé of his years on the case, so his role as lyric poet is intimately
bound to his role as reader of history. Only the man who can appreciate nature and record that appreciation can write the epic that
presents the paradigm of action based on nature-feeling. He then
continues the presentation of himself as character in the poem:

> An' the fuzzy bloke sez (legs no pants ever wd. fit) 'IF
> that is so, any government worth a damn can
> pay dividends?'
> The major chewed it a bit and sez: 'Y—es, eh . . .
> You mean instead of collectin' taxes?'
> 'Instead of collecting taxes.' That office?
> Didja see the Decennio?
> ?
> Decennio exposition, reconstructed office of Il Popolo.
>   (231)

He presents his own body, fuzzy and long-legged, because it is
not "the poet," just any poet, who can be trusted to write the epic
that shapes political behavior in the modern era, but the poet who
looks like this, sounds like this, and joins the celebration of the
tenth anniversary of the Fascist regime in Italy. It is this particular poet's understanding of economics—how any good government
can pay dividends instead of collecting taxes—that has the potential to become the guiding force behind political renovation in Italy
and elsewhere. *The Cantos* enacts a subtle refinement of focus, as
Pound presents himself, in his very person, as the poet we ought
to trust as our guide to historical matters. Later in the canto he
offers the "evidence" he thinks will convince the reader of the vil-
lainy of certain men, documents that "prove" how Paterson and
one of the Rothschilds conspire against the public good for personal gain. He enters these documents crucial to his case in this canto
because its explicit and intimate presentation of himself in the act

of historical investigation has, he hopes, earned our trust. He has placed himself so boldly and directly into his epic in an effort to become its dominant and ultimate hero.

It is in the relation between Cantos XLVII and XLIX that the first major movement of *The Cantos* comes to a conclusion, as Pound manages to reconcile his centrifugal thirst for new and exciting experience unavailable anywhere within the confines of the present culture with his devotion to a Fascist regime that demands strict and unwavering adherence to a well-defined social order. He reconciles these apparently contrary impulses in the figure of his wandering Odysseus, who in Canto XLVII overcomes the alienation of the exile and who in Canto XLIX as "no man" becomes the poet of the new Fascist reordering. Canto XLIX opens: "For the seven lakes, and by no man these verses" (244). Pearlman argues that Pound's Odysseus is called "no man" now because he has been "chastened" by his insights from Canto XLVII and here records his "vision of Confucian social order" (193). The Odysseus who has been seeking his lost home finally finds it in Canto XLVII, and he becomes "no man" not because he has been chastened but because he has returned to an original and pure consciousness that is before any particular naming of self, before any individuation into a personality. The wandering Odysseus who regains this lost consciousness common to all humanity at its origin is free to imagine a social order based on this common health. He becomes the Confucian visionary who writes the verses that set the ideal goal for good and benevolent action. The wanderer seeking a private home becomes the poet who inspires and guides the active man working to build a public home.

Canto XLIX is Pound's inspired vision of the kind of social order a benevolent leadership seeks to create. It is his most complete expression of what he thinks "fascism" ought to aim at. The visionary goal here established for Italian Fascism is of "a people of leisure," a people whose freedom from anxiety and aggression allows them to delight in the world:

> Rain; empty river; a voyage,
> Fire from frozen cloud, heavy rain in the twilight
> Under the cabin roof was one lantern.
> The reeds are heavy; bent;
> and the bamboos speak as if weeping.
>
> Autumn moon; hills rise about lakes
> against sunset

> Evening is like a curtain of cloud,
> a blurr above ripples; and through it
> sharp long spikes of the cinnamon,
> a cold tune amid reeds.
> Behind hill the monk's bell
> borne on the wind.
> Sail passed here in April; may return in October
> Boat fades in silver; slowly;
> Sun blaze alone on the river.   (XLIX/244)

The simple joy in perception that these lines record is the chief characteristic of "a people of leisure." Such lines "evoke something one can only call a sense of timeless depth" (Makin, *Cantos* 208); they suggest the ease and comfort of an ancient tradition unchanged in centuries that yet seems new because forgotten. The careful observation of natural detail suggests a consciousness at one with the world and unhurried by any external exigencies. What was accomplished by the daring of the heroic wanderer in Canto XLVII, a return to a consciousness that feels at home in the world, is here projected by the poet "no man" as a goal that can be made available to all the people. The achievement of the heroic individual is now the goal for the whole.

It is fair to say that Pound's fascism consists in large part of his wish to impose his private vision of "home" on the public. But Pound's totalitarian aim is not to use political power to frighten and coerce people into compliance with officially sanctioned forms of behavior but to use available power to amass and distribute goods equitably so that the people are free to enjoy the world. Donald Davie is correct in saying that the avowed end of Pound's ideal civilization is pleasure, and that the mark of the civilized human being is an ability to discriminate among pleasures (100–01). The way to achieve such a social order is, in Pound's estimate, to increase the availability of leisure, which he defines as "spare time *free from anxiety*. Any spare time not absolutely obsessed by worry can be made the means to a 'better life'" (*SP* 243). The person with ample leisure "would get a good deal more out of life.... I know, not from theory but from practice, that you can live infinitely better with a very little money and a lot of spare time, than with more money and less time" (*SP* 241). Pound's version of the ideal Fascist state regulates the machine of exchange in such a way that the citizenry lives free from economic anxiety and so enjoys the world. "A civil society is one where Strength comes with enjoyment" (*GK* 157). The proper and legitimate use of political and military power is to provide the citizenry with the leisure to experience pleasure and joy.[10] An entire people, a whole nation, can be brought to the consciousness of the world as home if the ruling forces free the people from being aggressive and anxious about mere survival and greedy and envious for more. Only "a people of leisure" can fully enjoy the world.

Pound believes that humanity is naturally healthy and has been "driven off the norm by economic pressure of one sort or another" (*GK* 157). He even believes that "the forbidden fruit of hebrew story is a usury parable" (*GK* 42), an economic interpretation of the central Western myth of origins that implies the possibility of a return to Eden. Canto XLIX is Pound's version of an earthly paradise in which the people have been made perfect, presumably by the restoration of economic justice; but "the people of leisure" have no awareness of the causes of their own harmony and joy:

> Sun up; work
> sundown; to rest
> dig well and drink of the water
> dig field; eat of the grain
> Imperial power is? and to us what is it?
>
> The fourth; the dimension of stillness.
> And the power over wild beasts.   (245)

The people spontaneously respond to the natural order, their lives regulated by natural rhythms. In an ideal state the laborer is not alienated from his labor; there is an immediacy to his labor, in that it is directed toward ends that meet his personal needs. As the individual lives this life of harmony with nature, he has no awareness of the leadership that has brought it into being. Such is the Confucian principle, that "the benevolence of the administration should be unnoticeable, or like wind on grass" (Makin, *Cantos* 210). The leadership that managed to construct this healthy version of humanity did not seek to dominate the people but instead organized them into perfection. Pound insists on a sharp distinction between "domination" and "organization":

> The last state of degradation whether of a democratized or of a non-democratized people is that in which they begin to wail to be dominated. DISTINGUISH between fascism which is organization, with the organizer as its head, to whom the power has not been GIVEN, but who has organized the

power, and the state of America, where the press howls that
we should GIVE power to Roosevelt, i.e., to a weak man. . . .
(*J/M* 108)

In Pound's view, fascism is not the "Muscovite tyrannous
man-crushing variety of collectivism" (*Agenda* 17 & 18, p. 74), but
the organization of the power that resides in the people toward a
visionary goal. Pound's fascism does not harm or reduce the individual but rather brings a renewed group of individuals into harmonious relation with others and nature:

A thousand candles together blaze with intense brightness.
No one candle's light damages another's. So is the liberty of
the individual in the ideal and Fascist state. (*SP* 306)

No one's flame is threatened with reduction but encouraged
to blaze to its fullest capacity and then joined to others until the
ideal state shines brilliantly. Pound's "ideal and Fascist state" values the individual because each person's flame adds to the beauty
of the harmonious group.

The poet's fascism avoids the opposite errors made by liberal
democracies and Stalinist tyrannies. The first regards the individual as anterior to and independent of the state, and so does not
aim to direct the various wills of the people into a perfect order
that reaches the dimension of stillness. Instead, the liberal state
allows each person the liberty to pursue his own private desires
and goals, even if these be against the good of the whole. For the
Fascist, a liberal state can only be a chaotic arena in which individual wills compete and conflict.[11] But the Stalinist tyranny
makes the opposite error, in that it desires harmony to the point
that it is willing to crush its people into banal uniformity: "Stalin's
regime considers humanity NOTHING save raw material" and
"treats man as matter" (Doob 49). Pound's version of Italian Fascism hopes to renew each person's original strength and then
arrange the movement of the various individuals into the "perfect
measure" that reaches "the dimension of stillness." Makin reports
that, in an effort to gloss this line, Pound alludes to Dante's cos-
mology in which the stillness of the empyrean is both the cause
and the effect of the perfect motion of the various heavenly
spheres (*Cantos* 208–09); so the stillness of the earthly paradise
depicted in Canto XLIX is created by and creates the perfect
ordering of the movements of the renewed energy of the people.

Pound works to transform the "real" Mussolini into a political hero working for the goals "no man" has recorded. He writes that *Il Duce* does not have a Nietzschean "will to power"; he does not "thirst [...] for power." "The great man is filled with a very different passion, the will to *order*" (*J/M* 99). Pound does not deny the need for military power in the work toward order, but power is the means and not the end. John Espey explains that Pound understands the word "order" as the synthesis of the forces that make Beauty possible (Espey 328). The poet understands the Fascist call for order, then, not as a rigorous enforcement of uniformity but as a political program directed at the creation of a humanity that sees, enjoys, and adds to the beauty of the natural world. The Fascist leader imposes a new set of economic conditions that in turn create nothing less than a renewed and harmonious humanity, fit companions for Adam.[12]

The foregoing indicates how acutely Pound is aware of the potential for a totalitarian state to crush its citizens and extinguish their flame, and he sets for himself the enormous task of guiding Mussolini away from violent domination and toward the proper ends. I propose that it is in the spirit of a Confucian sage who advises the leader that Pound approaches Mussolini; the poet is not working to describe so much as create "Mussolini." Michael Bernstein tells us that we cannot excuse Pound's endorsement of Mussolini as a "'fiction the poem had to create in order to assure its own coherence" because it casts grave doubts on the poet's "instincts" in assessing historical matters (117). But if we regard Pound not as "endorsing" an existing Mussolini but as seeking to gain mastery over an emerging one; if we recognize that Pound is not content merely to watch and celebrate the political hero of his time but works instead to fashion and guide him; if we appreciate the full extent to which the poet is competing with the politician for power; then we begin to understand the enormity of this poet's epic ambitions. The dominant effort of the first fifty-one cantos has been to earn the position Confucius held: "Kung is the master of emperors" (LV/294).

Cantos LII–LXXI: "The Dynasty Cantos"

What I conceive of as the first movement of *The Cantos* has come to a successful conclusion, as the wanderer reaches the lost home in Canto XLVII and asserts his vision of a new home as a general public goal. The next set of cantos, the Chinese History Cantos and the Adams Cantos, exhibits a very different shape and texture because Pound has assumed a new role and consequently has a new purpose. The wanderer has achieved a position of rest from which he can proceed to teach the lessons necessary for the actual achievement of an earthly paradise. These cantos are purely and explicitly didactic, and this radical shift in intention and design is not, as Makin claims (*Cantos* 212), a swerve from his original plan dictated by the pressure from external events but comes primarily and directly out of the shape of the wanderer's journey. What he thinks was accomplished by the first fifty-one cantos allows him now to act as a Confucian sage offering counsel to political leaders. The didactic mode is exactly what the first movement of *The Cantos* was preparing for.

Bernstein argues that the role of "Odysseus the voyager" is "much over-valued as the text's main integrating principle. Surely it is impossible to experience . . . either the Jefferson/Adams sequence or the Chinese History Cantos primarily as the chronicle of two civilizations Pound-Odysseus encounters on his *nostos*" (170). Bernstein assumes that the epic is all *nostos*, whereas I am arguing that the Dynasty Cantos are written from the point of view of the traveller who has reached the lost home and now works in a new guise, as sage and counsellor. The first canto written in the new mode ends with a Chinese ideograph about which Pound says, "there is no more important technical term than this chih(3), the hitching post, position, place one is in and works from" (*Con* 232). Chih³ signifies the wisdom "rooted in coming to rest, being at ease in perfect equity. Know the point of rest and then have an orderly progression" (*Con* 29). He uses this mark at the end of Canto LII to indicate that the wanderer has achieved the point of rest from which he now can work in his new guise.

Bernstein can make the judgment above because he has not recognized how flexible the poet has made his wandering persona. In fact, Pound scatters several hints that it is still his wanderer who is "behind" these cantos guaranteeing their legitimacy. Like Chao-Kong, the wanderer is now "on a journey . . . made for the good of the state" (LIII/269). The nature of the journey has reached an explicitly political intention, but the motif of journey still controls the text's meaning. Only at first glance, then, does it seem odd that Pound waits until these cantos to offer an explicit definition of "periplum, not as land looks on a map/ but as sea bord seen by men sailing" (LIX/324). This strategy, of abruptly breaking a coherent narrative with a fragment patently out of place and apparently irrelevant, is a favorite of Pound's because it allows him to highlight certain ideas and render them dominant to the narrative they interrupt. This fragment of definition is meant to call our attention to the presence of the person recording the historical narrative, that his investigation of history is every bit as much a "periplum" as anything he has attempted before. Pound makes use of this strategy earlier in the sequence, when he brings Homer's Odysseus and Dante into the movement of the historical narrative:

> Yu-chan to pay sycamores
> of this wood are lutes made
> Ringing stones from Se-choui river
> and grass that is called Tsing-mo' or [molü]
> Chun to the spirit Chang Ti, of heaven
> moving the sun and stars   (LIII/263)

Such brief allusions to Homer's and Dante's works only become meaningful in the overall context created throughout the poem by the figure of Pound's wanderer. He associates a Chinese herb "Tsing-mo'" with the magical molü for no other reason that I can discover than to bring Odysseus into play. We recall especially how in Canto XLVII molü frees him from one bed so he can return to another; we recall the daring sexual voyage that results in his return to the earth. Pound then associates Chang Ti with Dante's final line in *Paradiso,* "the love that moves the sun and the other stars." The active divine force that guides the emperor Chun is one with Dante's God that orders the perfect motion of the universe. He calls on the Homeric and Dantesque journeys to identify the sensibility behind these cantos, the wanderer grounded in the original human consciousness with access to the divine principle that gives order to the universe.

The journey of Pound's heroic wanderer has led him to this project, to transmit the Confucian history of China to the West. Nicholls suggests that the Chinese History Cantos contain no heroic elements; that, unlike Western epics, the chronicles of Chinese history which serve as Pound's source do not present a hero for our admiration and emulation (113). My contribution to the study of these cantos is to demonstrate that Pound works to devise an heroic role for himself in relation to America based on the one Confucius had for China.[13] For these cantos do have a hero, though it is not a warrior or man of policy; the hero of Chinese history, as Pound presents it, is Confucius the sage.

Pound begins his translation of *The Great Digest* with a note that indicates the heroic dimension of Confucius's work:

He had two thousand years of documented history behind him
which he condensed so as to render it useful to men in high
official position, not making a mere collection of anecdotes as
did Herodotus. His analysis of why the earlier great emperors
had been able to govern was so sound that every durable
dynasty, since his time, has risen on a Confucian design and
been initiated by a group of Confucians. China was tranquil
when her rulers understood these few pages. When the principles here defined were neglected, dynasties waned and chaos
ensued. The proponents of a world order will neglect at their
peril the study of the only process that has repeatedly proved
its efficiency as social coordinate. (*Con* 19)

The poet advances three separate propositions here that I
would like to isolate and use as the basis of my analysis of his aim
in the Chinese History Cantos. First, Confucius condensed two
thousand years of history for a particular purpose, "to render it
useful to men in high official position." He made a tremendous
amount of textual material manageable and accessible to those
who rule the state. Confucius's greatness lay in his work with textual discourse, in his ability to make his version of the past "true"
and "relevant" to present needs. As Michel Foucault teaches, discourse "poses the question of power; it is an asset that is, by
nature, an object of struggle, a political struggle" (120). Foucault
advances the thesis that "in every society the production of discourse is at once controlled, selected, organised, and redistributed
according to a certain number of procedures" (216). Both Confucius and Pound engage in the political struggle to control the production of discourse, to establish the authority of their own version of the past to those who occupy what are normally regarded
as positions of power. In a particularly telling moment, Confucius
reviews the past to teach the present emperor:

> Honour to Chao-Kong the surveyor.
> > Let his name last 3000 years
> Gave each man land for his labour
> > not by plough-land alone
> But for keeping of silk-worms
> > Reforested the mulberry groves
> > Set periodical markets
> Exchange brought abundance, the prisons were empty.
> 'Yao and Chun have returned'
> > sang the farmers

'Peace and abundance bring virtue.' I am
      'pro-Tcheou' said Confucius five centuries later.
With his mind on this age.   (LII/268)

Confucius looks back five hundred years to counsel the present emperor. He offers a condensed version of the activities of Chao-kong, who was instrumental in providing the foundations for the greatness of the Tcheou dynasty, and then declares that he is "pro-Tcheou in politics"; he wants his version of the past to decide present policy. His "politics" have nothing to do with ideology or party platforms but with the example of great men from the past whose actions led to peace and virtue throughout the land. The sage works to provide the authoritative historical context for the rulers of his own age, in just the same way Pound had looked to Siena to provide a model for Mussolini. They both struggle to produce the discourse that determines the values and aims of the political tradition. One reason for writing the Chinese History Cantos is to provide a precedent for a master of discourse to dominate the political scene. Pound was preparing for a reception of his history similar to that of Confucius's:

> And they received the volumes of history
> with a pee-rade with portable cases like tabernacles
> the dynastic history with solemnity.   (LXI/336)

Pound finds in China a festive and solemn parade like those he presented in the cantos devoted to the Monte dei Paschi, except that this one spontaneously celebrates the delivery of "the dynastic history." It is not discourse that is the hero of *The Cantos*, as Bernstein suggests via Barthes (171); it is the giver of the discourse who attains the position of the true hero of the process called history.

The second proposition to be isolated comes right out of this understanding of the power of discourse, that whenever a group of people came together and applied the principles of good government Confucius described, a dynasty was founded that would last until the principles were abandoned. Confucius is the true hero of the Chinese History Cantos, not only because he was able to produce a powerful discourse but because it "has repeatedly proved" its efficacy in guiding China to peace and virtue. His discourse *worked*. One emperor in particular recognized its power:

> Said TAÏ-TSOU: KUNG is the master of emperors.
> and they brought out Ou-tchao's edition, 953.
>   (LV/294)

This founder of the later Chou dynasty acknowledges Confucius's position of political power, as the sage who guides all benevolent rulers, and permits the printing of the *Shu Ching* (*Book of History*) and the *Shih Ching* (*Book of Odes*). The historical and literary traditions devised by Confucius are disseminated so they can attain the position of prominence they deserve. For "Kung is to China as is water to fishes" (LIV/285); that is, his discourse is the very element that allows China to live. Discourse is not an appendage or embellishment to a state, but the medium in which it exists. As fish can survive only in water, so Confucius's discourse is the element in which a state can flourish.

Thirdly, by referring to "proponents of world order," Pound seems to be addressing Mussolini and even Hitler. Nicholls reviews the passages that might indicate that these cantos "were designed to provide precedents for the Fascist regime, and perhaps even sanctions for Mussolini's seizure of power" (112). Both Nicholls (112) and Makin (212–13) assert that Pound writes these cantos as an urgent and desperate attempt to find a way to intervene directly in the politics of a Europe that was leading the world to war. But Wendy Stallard Flory provides an important qualification to Confucius's career that has serious implications for our understanding of Pound's emerging sense of his own role. She demonstrates that Confucius "was denied the power to act in his own time" (166). He was not a shaping force in his own time but only in subsequent centuries, when his disciples succeeded in circulating his ideas and gaining authority for his discourse. Perhaps Pound uses Confucius partly to soothe his own profound disappointment that nobody in power was following his perceptions. Certainly some of his actions suggest that he did not yet deny the possibility that he might reach an audience prepared and able to implement his ideas; for example, his trip to America in 1939 and the broadcasts over Rome radio were motivated by what the psychiatrists later would call his delusion of grandeur, that he could prevent America's participation in the war and save the West.[14] The virulence, meanness, and hatred so much to be regretted in the broadcasts are signs that he was becoming increasingly desperate to be recognized by the present generation of political leaders as the great sage. But in the more measured tones reserved for *The Cantos*, it is possible to see that he is coming to the realization that the maker of a discourse intended to dominate practical politics is not appreciated in his own time and must discover the patient hope that the future might be inhabited by a handful of people who regard *The Cantos* as "a schoolbook for princes" (LIV/280).

In this light he writes the history of America through the struggle of John Adams to guide the slow growth of an emerging nation by laying its foundation in a profound respect for law. Flory correctly observes that Pound's shift from Jefferson to Adams reflects his growing admiration for the deliberate, patient, plodding work of the man of law rather than the spectacular and immediate gains of the opportunist (174). His choice of Adams fits in with his choice of Confucius, as men who look to provide the stones for a future building:

> These are the stones of foundation
> J. A.'s reply to the Governor
> Impeachment of Oliver
> These stones we built on.   (LXII/343)

Pound is beginning to defer his own ambitions, that he is writing the history lessons for a future he will never see. He must have known that the men whose careers he chose to condense and present to the "proponents of world order" never lived to see their insights applied, that one had to wait for disciples to transmit his teachings until a receptive ruler applied them and that the other laid a foundation that was soon to be betrayed and forgotten. The Adams Cantos are Pound's efforts to restore that tradition and that foundation for a future set of American rulers to apply. His ambition is to be the Confucius of America, an America he has perhaps already despaired of ever seeing. But despair is not the right word: the sage accepts the hard lesson learned from Confucius, that the application of his insights to the political realm is to be deferred.

Pound suspends writing poetry during the war, as if nothing more can be said in verse until the hostilities were over and he could decide on what role he is next to assume in his ongoing epic. He has opened his poem to the pressure of current events and allows them to determine his own aims and ambitions. The death of Mussolini and his own arrest and internment call a sudden and dramatic halt to the didactic mode of the Dynasty Cantos and provide the setting for his greatest achievement.

3 ❧ The Wanderer as Prophet:
Aeneas and the Ideal City

Perhaps the most innovative feature of *The Cantos* as a "poem including history" was its inclusion of Mussolini as a potential embodiment of the epic hero, for his presence opened the poem to the world of historical events in a way that is unprecedented in literary history. Makin notes how important it was for Pound's poem that Mussolini succeed: the poet "had put all his credit as a writer behind Mussolini" (*Cantos* 233). The poet's authority as judge of history and his power as shaper of political destiny are put into serious doubt when the Fascist State falls and Pound is interned in the Pisan D. T. C. *The Pisan Cantos* are his attempt to recuperate his project. His strategy, in part, is to distance himself from Mussolini and establish a new role for himself in the process of history, the role of prophet of the ideal city.

The Pisan sequence signals a drastic shift in intention and method and a marked advance in artistry and brilliance from the Dynasty Cantos. Under arrest for treason, the poet can hardly assume an heroic role for himself and so cannot write purely didactic verse; it seems that he writes his greatest poetry when under the strain of his extraordinary ambition to prove, to himself and his readers, his own epic status.[1] He decides that, to become prophet of the ideal order, he must first purge himself of the distractions and impurities of a personal identity. The work of Canto LXXIV is to overcome nostalgia for his personal past and empty himself of the memories that constitute the identity of the man who finds himself under arrest. To accomplish this, he invokes the pilgrimage of Dante through Purgatory, a journey of purification culminating in the immersion in Lethe. This act of lustration rids the pilgrim of certain aspects of his old self so that he can ascend through Paradise and become the visionary prophet of the heavenly city.

Pound's "passing over Lethe" prepares him to make, in Canto LXXVIII, the startling identification[2] of himself with the hero of the *Aeneid:*

115

    and belt the citye quahr of nobil fame
        the lateyn peopil taken has their name
    bringing his gods into Latium
        saving the bricabrac
    "Ere he his goddis brocht in Latio"   (LXXVIII/478)

While critics have noticed that Aeneas functions as "an analogue of Odysseus, [who] is then an analogue of the poet himself"
(Woodward 52), no one has yet argued that *The Pisan Cantos* take
their shape and meaning from this addition of an Aeneas dimension to Pound's already multi-layered wandering hero, "no man."
This addition allows the poet to maintain his epic project despite
the ignoble end Mussolini meets. Aeneas, fleeing a burning Troy,
does not despair but rather discovers the hope that he is destined
to found Rome; so Pound, imprisoned by his own country for his
efforts on behalf of the now fallen Fascist State, refuses to yield to
despair and comes to see himself as the poet whose vision of the
ideal city is still the true and proper goal of the historical process.

In Canto LXXX, which as Massimo Bacigalupo points out "is as
long and comprehensive as c. 74—a new prelude and summary—...
Pound is now ready for a more intimate journey through his past
and his dream world" (129); that is, after the establishment of the
Aeneas dimension he is ready to confront the personal. But to do so
he makes one final adjustment to his wandering figure, who undergoes a second immersion and reaches the safety of a sanctified self.
The remaining cantos in this sequence depict the prophetic wanderer embarking on a private journey of memory as he tests out his role
under the most trying circumstances. *The Pisan Cantos* are most
often acclaimed for various highly "personal" elements previously
neglected and usually attributed to Pound's sudden awareness of
his own arrogance and fallibility. Flory goes so far to say that the
personal is "clearly the main organizing principle of the sequence"
(182). On the contrary, the personal elements included for the first
time are needed to provide the tension against which this broken
man of sixty struggles to convince himself and his reader of his
transformation by these poems into the prophet who keeps the
dream of ideal justice alive for the rest of humanity.

Canto LXXIV

The Pisan Cantos open with an elegaic lament for the failure of the
Fascist dream of justice, after which Pound immediately resumes
the deployment of his multilayered wanderer:

The enormous tragedy of the dream in the peasant's bent
    shoulders
    Manes! Manes was tanned and stuffed,
    Thus Ben and la Clara *a Milano*
          by the heels at Milano
That maggots shd/ eat the dead bullock
DIGONOS, but the twice crucified
         where in history will you find it?
yet say this to the Possum: a bang, not a whimper,
  with a bang not with a whimper,
To build the city of Dioce whose terraces are the colour of
                    stars.
          (LXXIV/425)

    The opening lines of the Pisan sequence record the poet's sorrowful lament for the passing of Mussolini and his dream of an "ideal and fascist state." The elegaic voice is soon suspended when the speaker asks the reader to convey a message to Eliot, that the world does not end with a whimper but with a bang, a reversal of the ending of "The Hollow Men." Events in history are eruptions not whimpers; sudden and dramatic and contingent, not gradual and subtle and necessary.[3] Elegaic despair is countered by the hope to be wrung from this attitude toward history: if Mussolini's fall is not a whimper at the end of an unavoidable sequence of events but the explosive climax of a strategic alliance designed to destroy the Fascist dream, so with a sudden eruption into the course of events can the dream still be realized, "to build the city of Dioce whose terraces are the colour of stars." Already Pound begins to distance himself from Mussolini: if one man has fallen, another has survived (thus far, at any rate) to record the dream and preserve it for the future.

    Begun in elegaic lament, *The Pisan Cantos* are soon brought securely into the more hopeful mood of the epic[4] as Pound resumes the deployment of his wanderer. First he returns to Confucius:

The suave eyes, quiet, not scornful,
          rain also is of the process.
What you depart from is not the way
and olive tree blown white in the wind
washed in the Kiang and Han
what whiteness will you add to this whiteness,
          what candor?
          (LXXIV/425)

The sage's quiet eyes look with profound understanding upon "the process," "the way," the principle of natural morality that unifies all of one's actions and gives them order (Kenner, *Era* 455–56). In his translation of *Chung Yung: The Unwobbling Pivot* (on which he was also working during his internment), Pound describes what following "the process" entails:

> What heaven has disposed and sealed is called the inborn nature. The realization of this nature is called the process.... You do not depart from the process even for an instant; what you depart from is not the process. Hence the man who keeps rein on himself looks straight into his own heart at the things wherewith there is no trifling; he attends seriously to things unheard. (*Con* 99–101)

"The process" is the "inborn nature" to be found by looking into the heart with sincerity and rigor; and if one finds this "unwobbling pivot" and acts according to it ("realizes" it), one's movements are harmonious and just. Pound recites this Confucian ethic to "keep rein" on himself as he confronts the fear and despair consequent to his arrest and internment. He must overcome scorn—both the scorn of others and self-hatred—and discover how to return to "the process." He calls on Confucius to announce that his own effort in Pisa is to stand firm and remain true to his convictions: "The master man finds the center and does not waver"; his "axis does not wobble" (*Con* 103). It is as Confucian sage searching for the "unwobbling pivot," the principle at the center that orders all movement into harmony, that the wanderer confirms his faith in the "Axis" and resumes his periplum.

Peter Nicholls provides a much-needed corrective to the view that in *The Pisan Cantos* Pound recants his commitment to Italian Fascism and concedes the impossibility of realizing the ideal city on earth (161–163). But we need to recognize further the distance Pound is putting between his enterprise as poet and Mussolini's failed effort as politician. Nicholls argues that in the Confucian passage above "Pound is still thinking in elegaic terms of the Duce" (165). The poet alludes to a discussion which occurred sometime after the death of Confucius. Another man who resembled the sage also dies, and some disciples of Confucius wish to render him the same observances they had rendered the master. But one disciple refuses to go along with them, and asks the question, "what whiteness will you add to this whiteness, what candor?" Nicholls suggests that Pound identifies Mussolini with Confucius and so uses this story to announce his continued devotion to Mussolini. Another explanation seems more plausible. It is Mussolini's recent death that might tempt an admirer to offer the observances accorded Confucius, and it is Mussolini who is refused. Pound has decided to follow the sage and distance himself from the politician.

With the Confucian ethic now governing his movement, Pound brings his present situation into relation with various elements of the wanderer theme from the earlier cantos:

> "the great periplum brings the stars to our shore."
> You who have passed the pillars and outward from Herakles
> when Lucifer fell in N. Carolina.
> if the suave air give way to scirocco
> OY TIΣ, OY TIΣ? Odysseus
> > the name of my family.
> > > (LXXIV/425)

The speaker of the passage addresses the reader ("you") who has, like Pound's centrifugal wanderer, "passed the pillars and outward from Herakles." This movement recalls the very first canto which ends with Odysseus sailing "outward and away"; and it recalls Hanno's periplum, who also "passed beyond the pillars of Herakles" in an effort to found new centers for Carthagenian trade. As "no man" (OY TIΣ), he recorded the vision of "a people of leisure" that was intended to guide the Fascist Revolution. He has not abandoned the organizing principle of his earlier work; rather, he calls on it again as his foundation upon which he can build a new role, as his "pivot" that can guide him back to "the process." Though Mussolini has fallen, he once again asserts the dream of building a visionary city when he claims that "the great periplum brings in the stars to our shore." For the stars suggest the terraces of the city of Dioce, and it is Pound's wanderer who makes the periplum that will bring these stars to the shore, that will realize the dream of the ideal city in history. The wanderer must carry the stars along with him through his exile and bring them to the chosen shore. With this image, Pound begins to prepare for Aeneas's entrance into the poem, for the Roman's task was to bring the city of Ilium to Latium, to bring the brilliance of Troy to Italian shores.

Also in preparation of Aeneas, Pound begins a subtle critique of the Homeric ethic when he incorporates into his wanderer's story a highly ambiguous moment from *Odyssey* IX. Odysseus boasts to the defeated and agonized Cyclops that he has been blinded not by "no man" but by "Odysseus, the conquerer of Troy,

the son of Laertes, whose address is in Ithaca" (Rouse's translation). If Odysseus had refrained from this bravado and remained
"no man," the Cyclops would not have known whose name to put in
the formulaic prayer that he makes to his father Poseidon, who
then would not have tried to prevent Odysseus's return home. The
"no man" who achieved unity with the natural order in Canto
XLVII and wrote the verses of Canto XLIX has been discovered to
have another name, one that happens to be registered as an American citizen who can be accused of treason. Pound accepts full
responsibility for his wartime activities and does not waver in his
beliefs. If Odysseus was foolhardy to brag to Cyclops, Pound might
be accused of the same for the manner in which he reiterates all
his opinions to his captors and interrogators; but to do any less
would be cowardly: "If a man isn't willing to take some risk for his
opinions, either his opinions are no good or he's no good" (*SP* 18).
Douglas Stewart argues that Odysseus errs in the Cyclops episode
by responding to the heroic or epic impulse to give his name and
address; it is part of the epic code for the hero to take credit for his
accomplishments, even if that means (as it does in this case)
endangering oneself (37–38). The morally dubious lesson of the
Odyssey, then, might be that to take responsibility for one's actions
is a mistake, and that one should survive at any cost. Odysseus's
giving of his name is not, for Pound, an error; it is rather a mark of
honor and heroism. He refers to this moment because it is one of
the last times that Odysseus adheres to the epic tradition of
responsible action, the heroic code the poet has made his "unwobbling pivot" in his dire predicament.

Pound's use of the Cyclops episode functions as his announce-
ment that a certain aspect of the *Odyssey* is not adequate as a
model for his wanderer. Stewart provides a reading of the
Odyssey—as a "sequel" to the *Iliad* and as its "counterepic" (21)—
that might help us understand Pound's growing dissatisfaction
with Homer's hero:

> The *Odyssey* fundamentally challenges the social ideology of
> a heroic class, and seems to be struggling to replace it with a
> different ideology, partaking of both peasant and middle-class
> values.... (18–19)

In Stewart's reading, Homer's hero is wily and brave but has
lost his heroic or epic destiny. As we have seen, Pound has already
(in 1938) testified to the nonheroic aspect of the *Odyssey*: "a world
of irresponsible gods, a very high society without recognizable

morals, the individual responsible to himself" (*GK* 38). The poet fastens on the moment in the *Odyssey* that makes the epic act of naming the "efficient cause" of the entire action, as if to call attention to the dangers an heroic destiny necessarily entails. In this way he prepares for Aeneas, a contemporaneous wanderer from Troy who also exhibits courage and tenacity but who subordinates his own personal desire and needs to the good of the people; he is an exile who maintains an heroic destiny, a destiny "no Homeric hero shares with Aeneas" (Eliot, *On Poetry and Poets* 129). This epic act of naming begins the contrast between Aeneas and Odysseus that the sequence will develop, a contrast Stanford puts this way: "Aeneas is less impressive in personality, more impressive in destiny than Ulysses" (136). Pound's needs are different from the early cantos where the impressive personalities of the scheming Odysseus and the daring Ulysses attracted him almost exclusively; in his most trying predicament, he turns to Aeneas as a means of consolation, as an example of a hero consoled by the elimination of the personal and the submission to a larger destiny.

Once he reasserts his intention to retain the epic role of social responsibility, he moves immediately back into the explicitly didactic intentions of the Dynasty cantos:

> and in India the rate down to 18 per hundred
> but the local loan lice provided from imported bankers
> so the total interest sweated out of the Indian farmers
>   rose in Churchillian grandeur
> as when, and plus when, he returned to the putrid gold
>   standard
> as was about 1925   Oh my England   (LXXIV/426)

There is here no demonstrable difference in tone or intention from any earlier passage that explains some "facts" of history. Readers who want to find in this sequence signs of Pound's "abandonment of [his initial] goals" (Bernstein 119) must ignore the persistence of the didactic mode that such passages demonstrate. Lessons are still to be taught, and the poet assumes, for a moment here and there, the role of teacher again as a way to indicate that the political hope of a just government has not been forsaken. The reduced role for the didactic urge in this sequence indicates not abandonment of hope but the need for its renewal; the work to be done in Pisa is for an incarcerated and humiliated sixty-year-old man to maintain his role as the poet who can teach the lessons that can bring the stars to the shore.

Pound continues his reworking of the nature of his wanderer by incorporating a quite unexpected element:

> and Rouse found they spoke of Elias
> in telling the tales of Odysseus   OY TIΣ
>   OY TIΣ
> "I am noman, my name is noman"   (LXXIV/426)

Pound notes W. H. D. Rouse's discovery, that people in the Aegean still tell stories about Odysseus but use the name of the Hebrew prophet Elijah. This information, the first of many references to prophets of the Old Testament,[5] explicitly connects Pound's "noman" with a Hebrew prophet who tells of the coming of a redeemer. Only the place of Aeneas in *The Pisan Cantos* can explain this conflation that seems so odd after the bitter anti-Semitism of the radio broadcasts. As the Hebrew prophets foretell the redemption of humanity by means of a chosen people led by a reluctant leader, so the *Aeneid* tells of the founding of a city whose people have been chosen by the gods to rule the earth and bring peace and stability to the earth, a people led by a man who must be reminded of his destiny several times in the course of his wandering. Aeneas and the prophets have a deeper connection that informs Pound's new stance: the Hebrew prophet is largely ignored and discredited by his own people and must wait for future generations to attend to his message; and Aeneas does manage to get to the shores of Italy where the work toward the founding of the Roman Empire is begun, but he dies with only the promise of the future to comfort him. The "noman" who wrote the verses of Canto XLIX now aspires to a prophetic role, so that his vision of an ideal order can be preserved for the future to find and follow.

Despite his "virulent abuse" of the Old Testament in the past, Pound is able to use this aspect of the Hebrew prophets as preparation for Aeneas. I want to document with three passages the full extent to which Pound relies on the Hebrew prophets:

> 4 giants at the 4 corners
>   three young men at the door
> and they digged a ditch round about me
>   lest the damp gnaw thru my bones
>   to redeem Zion with justice
>   sd/ Isaiah.   (LXXIV/429)

In this passage, Pound makes three distinct references: to the legend of the ideal city of Wagadu, to his own internment in the D.

T. C., and to Isaiah 1:27, "Zion shall be redeemed by justice, and those in her who repent, by righteousness." As he sits a prisoner in his cage, the poet thinks of the ideal city that the four corners of the detention camp merely mock and thinks of himself as a prophet who still insists on the redemption of the city by justice. Later in the same canto he refers to another Hebrew prophet:

> "Thou shalt purchase the field with money."
> signed Jeremiah
> from the tower of Hananel unto Goah
> unto the horse gate $8.50 in Anatoth
> which is in Benjamin, $8.67.   (LXXIV/440)

Pound makes fragmentary references to Jeremiah's prophecies about the founding of Zion, the just city: "Behold, the days are coming, says the Lord, when the city shall be rebuilt for the Lord from the tower of Hananel to the Corner Gate.... It shall not be uprooted or overthrown any more for ever" (Jer. 31:38, 40). The Lord tells Jeremiah to purchase some land to begin the divine work of redemption for the chosen people. Pound must have particularly liked the exact demarcation of the land destined for the city and the precise accounting of "dollars and cents"; this is no heavenly city but one in such and such a place that costs just so much to purchase. The poet uses Jeremiah to give his own voice a deeper resonance, so "noman" can prophesy of the just city to come: "[Y]our work shall be rewarded, says the Lord, and they shall come back from the land of the enemy. There is hope for your future, says the Lord, and your children shall come back their own country" (Jer. 31: 16–17). As this prophet promises heaven's sanction for the work of the people to build a city, so Aeneas inspires his followers to seek their true home. Indeed, Mazzotta demonstrates how for Dante Aeneas is a figure of "salvation history" (99) leading his fellow exiles on a "journey in search of Italy, their true promised land" (29); Trojan exiles led by Aeneas are understood by Dante as the extension of the journey of the Israelites under Moses. Pound is thus following a Dantesque tradition in using certain Hebrew voices as preparation for the inclusion of Aeneas:

> with justice shall be redeemed
> who putteth not out money on interest
>   "in meteyard in weight or in measure"
>   XIX Leviticus or
> First Thessalonians 4, 11

300 years culture at the mercy of a tack hammer
                    thrown thru the roof
Cloud over mountain, mountain over the cloud
I surrender neither the empire nor the temples
                                        plural
nor the constitution nor yet the city of Dioce
each one in his god's name
as by Terracina rose from the sea Zephyr behind her
              and from her manner of walking
                          as had Anchises
    till the shrine be again white with marble
        till the stone eyes look again seaward
                              (LXXIV/434–35)

Leviticus 19:35 instructs the chosen people to be just "in measures of length or weight or quantity," and Pound's juxtaposition of this counsel with Isaiah's prophecy about the redemption of Zion implies that just measure (which is what Pound's crusade for monetary reform was always all about) is the cornerstone to such redemption. "Or" we can turn to the words of St. Paul, "But we exhort you . . . to aspire to live quietly, to mind your own affairs, and to work with your own hands" (I Thes. 4:10–11). Only by devoted labor can the city be redeemed. With the prophetic voice established, Pound swears his faith in and hope for "the city of Dioce." This unequivocal statement of position is followed by a vision of Aphrodite rising from the sea and walking to the poet, who recognizes her by her walk "as had Anchises." "Each one in the name of his god,"[6] and Pound's goddess has always been Aphrodite, whom he saw in Canto I and under whose statue he imagines "holy sexuality" in Canto XXXIX; the sudden disorienting move from the exacting monotheism of the Hebrew world to the relative freedom of the pagan sensibility signals that the Hebrew voice is not meant to gain dominance in the text but to extend the character of Pound's more classical wanderer. As we saw in Canto XXIII, Pound likes to allude to Aeneas through his father so a choice does not have to be made between a delight in pagan eroticism and the grim determination to follow a public destiny. The physical act that leads to Aeneas's conception is suggested more graphically in a later canto: "or Anchises that laid hold of her flanks of air/ drawing her to him" (LXXVI/456). Pound manages to suggest that Aeneas shares with the Hebrew prophets a vision of the just city destined to redeem the world, and yet bring that prophetic function into the composition of a mainly classical wanderer whose character has already been largely developed and who has already brought so much material into the epic.

The opening canto of the Pisan sequence makes one further addition to the figure of the wanderer that, I shall argue, determines the meaning of the canto and the shape of the sequence as a whole. Pound returns to Dante, this time with a focus on the purgatorial dimension of his journey. In the early cantos, Pound was most interested in Dante's vision of an ideal justice that he would append to and include in his wanderer's periplum. Now, the incarcerated poet asserts the need for purgation, not simply to purge himself of the excesses that led to the bitterness and hatred of the Rome radio broadcasts but more pointedly to cleanse himself of the sentimental weakness of nostalgia that prevents him from attaining his epic role as prophet of the ideal city. On the fourth page of the sequence, we find some lines that recall the opening of *Purgatorio* VIII:

> el triste pensier si volge
> > ad Ussel. A Ventadour
> > > va il consire, el tempo rivolge
> and at Limoges the young salesman
> bowed with such french politeness "No that is impossible."
> I have forgotten which city
> But the caverns are less enchanting to the unskilled explorer
> > than the Urochs as shown on the postals,
> we will see those old roads again, question,
> > > > > possibly
> but nothing appears much less likely,
> > > > Mme Pujol,
> and there was a smell of mint under the tent flaps
> especially after the rain
> > > and a white ox on the road toward Pisa
> > > > as if facing the tower.
> > > > > > (LXXIV/428)

The opening lines are Pound's own poetry: "the sad thought turns back/ toward Ussel. To Ventadour/ goes the thought, the time turns back." Compare Dante:

> It was now the hour that turns back the longing of seafarers and melts their hearts the day they have bidden dear friends farewell and pierces the new traveller with love if he hears in the distance the bell that seems to mourn the dying day . . . .
> (*Purgatorio* VIII, 1–6)

Pound manages to suggest a moment in Dante's journey where the pilgrim is stricken with nostalgia. Dante thinks of nostalgia in terms of "seafarers" and "the new traveller" to advance the metaphor of a spiritual journey that should be forward-looking, a journey endangered by excessive longing for the identity that was constituted by one's former role in a system of relations among people and places, an identity that is, to a large extent, what one means by "home." As he is about to embark on the arduous process that purges the spiritual traveller of the sinful aspects of one's personality and leads to a purity on which one erects a new identity, Dante recalls with bittersweet fondness the comforting relations that, along with much less that is not desirable, he left behind. The purgatorial process is painful, and it is "only natural" for the pilgrim to wish he were back home, even if that home was not perfect. But Dante does not change his course and head back home (in a literal sense, he was barred from a return by the threat of execution); he continues his movement ahead through Purgatory in the hope of reaching the Edenic state, the first and pure home for all humanity. Nostalgia can block the movement that cleanses the self of corruption and culminates in the vision of the heavenly city.

Pound calls on this moment from *Purgatorio* to underscore both his own temptation to dwell on the past and the danger attendant to that desire. After citing this warning from Dante, he proceeds to indulge in some memories of the past, which provide some measure of temporary relief to the discomfort and horror of his present placement in a cage in a D. T. C. By remembering scenes from the past he can reconstitute his former identity. But he expresses the doubt that he will ever "see those old roads again" and then moves into a depiction of his placement in the world that precludes a return to the past. The memories that he turns to for solace do not enjoy a merely positive value, for, if the incarcerated poet succumbs to the sentimental weakness of nostalgia, he risks becoming bound by the past to a personal identity that must be cleansed of errors and excesses in order to be raised to epic status. Pound is comforted and sustained by his selected memories, but his allusion to *Purgatorio* VIII constitutes a warning to himself that his goal still lies ahead, that he cannot rest too long in the comfort that thoughts of the past might deliver. Nostalgia for one's former identity can prevent one's attainment of the role of prophet of the ideal city.

Two pages later he includes a word from the opening of *Purgatorio* VIII in a context explicitly about "no man" and the ideal city:

ΟΥ ΤΙΣ
a man on whom the sun has gone down
nor shall diamond die in the avalanche
           be it torn from its setting
first must destroy himself ere others destroy him.
4 times was the city rebuilded, Hooo Fasa
               Gassir, Hooo Fasa   dell' Italia tradita
now in the mind indestructible, Gassir, Hoooo Fasa,
With the four giants at the four corners
and four gates mid-wall Hooo Fasa
and a terrace the colour of stars
pale as the dawn cloud, la luna
               thin as Demeter's hair
Hooo Fasa, and in a dance the renewal
     with two larks in contrappunto
               at sunset
                    ch'intenerisce
a sinistra la Torre   (LXXIV/430–31)

This passage begins with the heroic wanderer as "ΟΥ ΤΙΣ" to
link this moment to the Cyclops story: the man who takes responsibility for his actions can find himself in serious trouble. But
though "the sun has gone down" on him (a recurrent Homeric epi-
thet for Odysseus in time of trouble), he refuses despair and commits himself to the dream of the ideal city. Though "torn from its
setting," the precious dream of the city of Dioce does not "die in the
avalanche." In fact, one might wish to argue that the tremendous
pressure of an avalanche not only cannot crush the diamond, it
makes diamonds. The course of events might crush one particular
effort to realize the ideal city, but this same avalanche provides
the pressure that makes the dream, if it survives at all, "now in
the mind indestructible." The prophet's vision is rendered permanent and inviolable only by the failure of history to realize it; only
a fall creates the conditions that enable the prophetic role to
emerge.[7] In his visionary inviolability, "no man" cannot be
destroyed by others, but only by his own failure to remain stead-
fast to his dream, his failure to remain firm in the middle. To
remain committed after the fall to the vision that inspired the Fascist Revolution means to become its prophet.

Pound then alludes to "Gassire's Lute," the Soninke legend of
the dream city Wagadu that has been rebuilt four times. Terrell
quotes the opening of this legend that recurs frequently throughout the sequence:

> Four times Wagadu stood there in all her splendor. Four
> times Wagadu disappeared and was lost to human sight: once
> through vanity, once through falsehood, once through greed
> and once through dissension. . . . Wagadu is not of stone, not
> of wood, not of earth. Wagadu is the strength which lives in
> the hearts of men and is sometimes visible because eyes see
> her and ears hear the clash of swords and ring of shields, and
> is sometimes invisible because the indomitability of men has
> overtired her, so that she sleeps. . . . Should Wagadu ever be
> found for the fourth [sic] time, then she will live so forcefully
> in the minds of men that she will never be lost again. (370)

By incorporating this legend into *The Pisan Cantos,* Pound
makes some important decisions about the role of the ideal city in
the process of earthly history. A number of critics have found in
The Pisan Cantos generally, and in this passage particularly, what
Kenner calls "the concession that the High City may not be built
on earth: only 'in the mind indestructible'" (cited in Nicholls 161).
Indeed, the legend of Wagadu might at first glance imply as much.
The city is not the material phenomenon but "the strength which
lives in the hearts of men." Pound does seem to consider the city
primarily a mental phenomenon and not an external reality; it is,
at first, an idea that exists only in the mind. But when enough
people see it and hear it (by attending to their own hearts, a Confucian ethic found in an African legend), the city takes on an external form composed of whatever material those who see it have
access to and mastery over. The city must first "live so forcefully
in the minds of men that she will never be lost again"; that is, if people can be made to see the city clearly and powerfully in their
minds, they will work to build it and maintain it. Such an attitude,
that the city is first an image of the mind which inspires historical
action, accords the poet a fundamental role in history, as the man
who records the city to guide the actions of men. Pound has not
given up on the possibility of the realization of the ideal, but
instead works, now that the most recent attempt at Wagadu has
failed ("dell' Italia tradita"—the attempt "of the betrayed Italy"), to
become its prophet and leave a record of the dream.

The passage I have quoted ends with a word from *Puragtorio*
VIII, "ch'intenerisce"—it was now the hour "that melts" the seafarer's hearts with longing for home. Pound incorporates into his
effort to reassert his epic ambition the mood of the Dantesque pilgrim who journeys through Purgatory toward Eden. While "no
man" struggles to retain the hope for the realization of the ideal

city, he thinks of himself as a Dante who must eschew nostalgia for the past and continue to work toward the vision of the ideal city made possible by a return to purity. Now that Italy has fallen, Pound must to a large extent forget what had gone into its making; he cannot remain so absorbed in what he had been working for that he now turn to bitterness and scorn at the betrayal. He must work out his own purgation, regain his status as prophet of the city, and work toward its next incarnation, the next attempt at the renewal of the ideal. This image from *Purgatorio* suggests that the work at Pisa is to forge a new identity based on his visionary capacity, and not to indulge in sorrowful lament for what he had thought was about to take place but failed.

Canto LXXIV ends as Pound explicitly aligns himself with the Dante of *Purgatorio*:

> How soft the wind under Taishan
> > where the sea is remembered
> out of hell, the pit out
> of dust and glare evil
> Zephyrus / Apeliota
> This liquid is certainly a
> > property of the mind
> nec accidens est but an element
> > in the mind's make-up
> est agens and functions   dust to a fountain pan otherwise
> Hast 'ou seen the rose in the steel dust
> > (or swansdown ever?)

> so light is the urging, so ordered the dark petals of iron
> we who have passed over Lethe.   (LXXIV/449)

Pound ends the opening canto of the sequence with images that conflate the beginning and one of the climaxes of Dante's purgative experience. The speaker of these lines has just emerged from hell and finds himself under a mountain, feeling the soft wind of Zephyrus / Apeliota (these winds were also felt in Canto XLVII, where they play upon the vegetable world with which the wanderer has become one). He sits "where the sea is remembered"; caged in a detention center in sight of a mountain, Pound can only remember the sea that Dante has a glimpse of in *Purgatorio* I: "The dawn was overcoming the morning breeze, which fled before it, so that I descried far off the trembling of the sea" (115–17); "we came then on the desert shore that never saw man sail its waters who after had experience of return" (130–32); and, in *Purgatorio* II, "we were still by the sea" (10). In Dante, these references to the sea recall the Ulysses who took an alternate route to the island of Purgatory and drowned just as he sights Mount Purgatory. Pound seems to have taken both courses, for he has just emerged from hell like Dante and remembers the sea which he has been travelling like Ulysses. Perhaps he implies that now he sees the need for a more deliberate purgation than he had recognized earlier; that he is ready to accept his internment and make use of the mountain he sees as the equivalent of Dante's purgative mountain. "The liquid" in question in these lines suggests the waters of Lethe that the canto ends with and that Dante describes in *Purgatorio* XXVIII and passes through in *Purgatorio* XXXI:

> On this side it flows down with virtue which takes from men the memory of sin; on the other it restores that of every good deed; here it is called Lethe and on the other side Eunoe . . . .
> (*Purgatorio* XXVIII, 127–131)

> The fair lady opened her arms, clasped my head, plunged me under, where I must swallow the water; then she took me out and led me bathed into the dance of the four fair ones, and each covered me with her arm. (*Purgatorio* XXXI, 100–105)

Dante describes the effects of this immersion later in the canto:

> O splendour of living light eternal, who has ever grown so pale under Parnassus' shade or drunk so deep of its well that he would not seem to have a mind disabled, trying to render thee as thou appearedst, heaven with its harmonies over-hanging thee, when in the free air thou didst disclose thyself? (139–145)

In a canto that has already called attention to the dangers inherent in excessive attachment to certain images held in memory, this explicit reference to Dante's crossing of Lethe deserves close attention, for it implies that Pound's wanderer has also been immersed in Lethe. Like Dante, he has cleansed certain aspects of himself that have prevented him from returning fully to the purity of an original self. Those who cross Lethe are no longer prone to nostalgia; they have overcome the longing for an old identity and reached the condition that allows for the taking on of a new identity, one that has access to the visionary splendour Dante records at the end of *Purgatorio* and throughout *Paradiso*. The "rose in the steel dust" is Pound's version of the heavenly roses which are, at the upper reaches of paradise, the manifestation of the heavenly community, the heavenly city of ideal justice. Only the person who refuses the sentimental longings of nostalgia and continues ahead with his spiritual quest for a visionary experience of the ideal city can become its prophet.

The critics who see personal memory as the organizing principle of the sequence have missed the implications of the final line of Canto LXXIV. Anthony Woodward asserts that "in the Pisan series the poet by numerous acts of personal memory tries to reconstitute his fractured self, master his past, and attain a contemplative superiority to the flux of time" (68). Flory notes that he spends a great deal of time "on nostalgic reminiscences. These thoughts are not only a distraction from the discomfort and boredom of his present reality, but also a way of preserving his sanity in this frightening predicament. He clearly relies on these moments from the past" (188). Peter Makin argues that "memory becomes the storehouse of real knowledge of things because it retains only the essential shapes imprinted there by love—shapes 'truer' than any literally recorded reality" (*Cantos* 241). All these critics agree on one thing, that personal memory is a central element in the shape and meaning of *The Pisan Cantos,* and to a certain extent they are correct. Only Makin's formulation allows us to advance to an understanding of memory as that which *"becomes* the storehouse of real knowledge" by means of a purgative experience compared to and given shape by Dante's. What Canto LXXIV has been working to establish is the wanderer's purgative journey that empties him of personal memories and prepares him for the new identity which will be made by the addition of Aeneas. The effort to "master his past" is first made by the establishment of an epic persona, after which the wanderer will return to memory and make a more positive use of it. He will go back over his past and "reconstitute his fractured self" only after he has raised himself to epic heights.

The Pisan Cantos are all the more remarkable when we recall that Pound had almost no access to books; that, unlike all of the other cantos, they are written almost solely from memory. By its use of *Purgatorio,* the opening canto focuses on the need for the incarcerated poet to purify and discipline his memory so that he can preserve the documents from the past that can be used to

begin the historical work of building the city of Dioce. If Philip
Furia is at all correct—"To preserve and transmit those documents
[while incarcerated in a D. T. C.] is tantamount to the epic task of
founding and protecting the city" (104)—then it is crucial for
Pound to fortify his memory so that only the good is preserved and
any bitterness and scorn consequent to his own fate be purged
from his transmission. Canto LXXIV announces, especially in its
final lines, that this poet has undergone the purgative process that
has rendered his memory fit for the task ahead, that of becoming
like Aeneas who inspires the actual work of building the city.

The very short canto that follows exchanges the Dantesque
landscape of *Purgatorio* for the classical one from the *Aeneid:*

> Out of Phlegethon!
> > out of Phlegethon,
> > > Gerhart
> > > > art thou come forth out of Phlegethon?
> > > > > (LXXV/450)

In Book VI of the *Aeneid* the hero descends to the underworld
to learn his destiny; while there, he hears the groans of the wicked
souls who are punished for their sins. Phlegethon is the fiery river
that surrounds the infernal city of the wicked. While Canto LXXIV
invokes the Dante who emerges from a Christian hell, this canto
calls on the movement of Aeneas "out of Phlegethon," away from
the wicked city and toward the blessed fields of Elysium. Pound
devotes the rest of the canto to Gerhart Munch's arrangement of
Janequin's "Le Chant des Oiseaux." He praises Munch for tran-
scribing Janequin's song in a way that transmits "the dynamic
form which is like the rose pattern driven into the dead iron-fil-
ings by the magnet" (*GK* 152). Munch's song achieves a perfect
ordering of its material and so leads one "out of Phlegethon" and
toward a blessed state. The end of the previous canto, in which a
Dantesque wanderer emerges from hell toward a visionary experience of "the rose in the steel dust," is given its classical equivalent
through the allusion to the *Aeneid.*

The exchange of the medieval Christian landscape for the
classical one suggests that Pound's wanderer has a secular goal
similar to Aeneas's, that Pound's wanderer aims not at a heavenly
city but at one to be established on earth through human labor. In
both *De Monarchia* and *Paradiso,* Dante relies on the image of a
"threshing-floor"[8] to describe the temporal world: we work on
earth for a just state to earn personal redemption and a place in

the heavenly city. Pound invokes Aeneas because, like Dante, he has a sense of ideal justice guiding his actions; but, unlike Dante, the city is to be built only in this life. Pound invokes Virgil's hero in this canto to "correct" any misreadings the allusion to *Purgatorio* in the previous canto may have occasioned: Pound's wanderer is on a purgatorial journey given shape by Dante's poem; but the end of the purgation is, by this allusion to Virgil's epic, implied to be like that of the classical hero whose vision of the future greatness of Rome inspires future political action.

Canto LXXVIII

In Canto LXXVI Pound presents an image that suggests his sense of a significant place for himself in the historical process:

> As a lone ant from a broken ant-hill
> from the wreckage of Europe, ego scriptor.   (LXXVI/458)

While the image of the "lone ant" might at first indicate a diminishment of stature, the terms of the metaphor suggest otherwise. For the whole of Europe is "a broken ant-hill," reducing the complex scope of Western politics to a simpler, more uniform state; the one who staggers out from the rubble emerges in bold relief from such a background. It is "the writer" who survives, the man fashioning a record for the future who looms so large in the process of history. This attitude toward himself informs his decision to include Aeneas in the composition of his wanderer.

In Canto LXXVIII, Pound makes the crucial addition to his wanderer when he identifies his own journey northward after the fall of the Fascist State in Rome to Aeneas's journey from Troy to Latium:

> "alla" non "della" in il Programma di Verona
>   the old hand as stylist still holding its cunning
> and the water flowing away from that side of the lake
> is silent as never at Sirmio
>   under the arches
> Foresteria, Salò, Gardone
>   to dream the Republic. San Sepolchro
>   the four bishops in metal
> lapped by the flame, amid ruin, la fede—
>   reliquaries seen on the altar.

"Someone to take the blame if we slip up on it"
Goedel's sleek head in the midst of it,
　　　　the man out of Naxos past Fara Sabina
"if you will stay for the night" "it is true there is only one
room for the lot of us"
"money is nothing"
"no, there is nothing to pay for that bread"
　　　　　　　　"nor for the minestra"
"Nothing left here but women"
　　　　　　"Have lugged it this far, will keep it" (il zaino)
　　　　　No, they will do nothing to you.
"Who *says* he is an American"
　　　　　a still form on the branda, Bologna
"Gruss Gott," "Der Herr!" "Tatile is gekommen!"
　　　Slow lift of long banners
　　　　　Roma profugens Sabinorum in terras
and belt the citye quahr of nobil fame
　　the lateyn peopil taken has their name
bringing his gods into Latium
　　　　　saving the bricabrac
"Ere he his goddis brocht in Latio"
　　　"each one in the name"
　　　　　　　　　　　　(LXXVIII/478–79)

In this long fragment, Pound presents himself as the survivor
of the Fascist Revolution whose task is to provide a record of the
vision on which it was based and the effort to which the vision led.
He begins with his appreciation of the verbal precision (the rights
"to" not "of" property) still displayed by Mussolini in "The Program
of Verona," the manifesto written to support the new Italian Social
Republic at Salò. Pound moves from Mussolini's "grasp of the
essential issues of man's right relation to the earth" (Woodward
47) to his own placement beside Lake Garda doing what poets do
best, recording his admiration for the still beauty of the water.
Once again he hints that the poet's lyric talent is the basis for the
politician's healthy action.[9] But something more is being suggested. Both Pound's daughter and a recent biographer testify to
Pound's continued adherence to Mussolini during the brief and ill-
fated Salò Republic: Tytell reports that the poet wrote articles and
pamphlets for the new government and even spoke regularly on
the radio (274–75). Pound puts at the forefront his own presence
beside Lake Garda to suggest that, among all his bustling activity
on behalf of what everyone at the time knew was a desperate and

feeble attempt to sustain Italian Fascism, his work as poet emerges, in retrospect, as Salò's legacy to the world; though the government was soon to fall and Mussolini to die ignominiously, this attempt to maintain the Fascist State at least provided the poet with one last chance to sit by the lake and "dream the Republic." "Amid the ruin, la fede": the poet survives to maintain "the faith" in the Fascist dream.

After the Fall of Rome Pound travelled northward to Gais to visit his daughter Mary. It was there that he heard news of Mussolini's abduction by the Nazis and the establishment of the Salò Republic. It is to this journey that Pound now turns. We hear snatches of conversaton spoken to and by the poet as he makes this difficult trek, and then his reception by Mary's foster mother. This scene is a remarkable exception to most of *The Cantos,* where Pound's personal life and relationships are so seldom recorded or even hinted at. Somehow, his identity as Mary's father is relevant to his role as poet of the dream. The establishment of a personal identity seems, at first sight, to contradict my argument, that he must avoid nostalgia for the past as he aspires to an epic status. But the purpose of this visit was to inform Mary of Dorothy's existence in Rapallo and Omar's in England (*Disc* 187); he made this journey to set things straight, to settle the unfinished business of his "personal life." Tytell calls it an "almost penitent journey" (273); it seems to me a fully penitent, even a purgatorial journey that prepares for the passage from the *Aeneid,* which follows immediately. It was a painful journey: Mary reports that her foster mother did not even recognize as "der Herr" the dirty and tattered man who appeared at her door, and that his feet were full of blisters and his ankles swollen (185). And we can imagine the anxiety and guilt attendant to such a confession. The journey from Rome to Gais is placed at this point in the sequence to function as a purgatorial journey enabling the poet to go beyond a purely personal identity and claim kinship with Aeneas.

The hero of the Roman epic is the appropriate example for Pound only now (in the D. T. C. and cut off from all comforts and pleasures), for Aeneas is marked by an ability to eschew the good of the private life well lived and devote himself fully to a public destiny. Earlier in *The Cantos* Pound worked to avoid the division between his own search for personal fulfillment and his public-minded goal of an earthly paradise; now, with no prospects for personal happiness, he turns to the "man apart, devoted to his mission (*Aeneid* I), the man for whom "the mission is everything" (Eliot *On Poetry and Poets* 128). Pound turns from a reliance on

Homer's Odysseus as the chief model for his own journey for, while that hero is more attractive to Pound as a personality, it is Aeneas who is able to sacrifice all for a commitment to a vague and distant destiny. We recall Stanford's phrase, "Aeneas is less impressive in personality, more impressive in destiny than Ulysses" (136). Book IV of the *Aeneid*, which tells of Aeneas's reluctant but complete rejection of Dido in favor of a commitment to further wandering toward an unknown coast where he will lay a foundation for a city and empire he will never see, distinguishes him from Odysseus, who manages to get back home, reclaim and enjoy all that he regards as his; and it distinguishes him from Dante, who manages to achieve a place in the heavenly city.

T. S. Eliot notes this aspect of Aeneas:

> Aeneas is himself, from first to last, a 'man in fate', a man who is neither an adventurer nor a schemer, neither a vagabond nor a careerist, a man fulfilling his destiny, not under compulsion or arbitrary decree, and certainly from no stimulus to glory, but by surrendering his will to a higher power behind the gods who would thwart or direct him. He would have preferred to stop in Troy, but he becomes an exile, and something greater and more significant than any exile; he is exiled for a purpose greater than he can know, but which he recognizes; and he is not, in a human sense, a happy or successful man. (*Selected Prose*, "What is a Classic" 128)

In his own misery and loss, Pound calls on Aeneas to provide solace and to register his determination to overcome the desire for personal happiness. Similarly, he is an involuntary exile who comes to surrender his will to destiny; he seeks to be comforted, like Aeneas, by the purely public hope that the process of history will reach the end he has envisioned. As Rome will, at long last and only after a complex and violent chain of events, renew the greatness of Troy, so Pound hopes that his record of the dream-city of perfect justice will inspire the action that will result in its eventual realization "in history." Aeneas's example teaches that history is a state of exile between an original fullness and the eventual establishment of the ideal city that will renew the splendor of those origins:

> To stop at Rome is thus a meditation on hope, a belief in God's promise and the recognition by Aeneas that he is subject to the contingent order of history, that he is between the

"no longer" at Troy and the "not yet" of the fulfillment: he follows the sun but stops and waits. (Mazzotta 100)

Pound appends Aeneas to his wanderer to indicate that he
too does not abandon history. The poet has chosen against an
Odysseus who returns home to a purely personal and immediate
triumph; and against a Ulysses who never waits but instead continually follows the sun's tracks to his doom. And his use of Dante
in this sequence renders the pilgrim's purgation a necessary but
preliminary stage on the way to the establishment of an epic status. In Pisa he has chosen to follow Aeneas, for the journey of
Pound's wanderer is now one of waiting, "in history," for the fulfillment of the vision of the ideal city he has been granted.

I shall pass over a brief memory of pre-W. W. I London, where
the poet sat with friends such as Gaudier, Lewis, and Hulme; and a
depiction of those in whose company he finds himself in the D. T. C.,
Steele, Blood, and Slaughter. Such a contrast might lead another
poet to admit a great falling off and to blame his private misfortune
on the duplicity of the Fascist cause. But with Aeneas in mind, he
overcomes any temptation to recrimination and despair and
describes what a poet in the modern world can do to imitate Aeneas:

> "definition can not be shut down under a box lid"
> but if the gelatine be effaced whereon is the record?
> "wherein is no responsible person
>   having a front name, a hind name and an address"
> "not a right but a duty"
>   those words still stand uncancelled.
> "Presente!"
>   and merrda for the monopolists [. . .]
>   (LXXVIII/479)

Philip Furia's study provides the proper orientation to a passage such as this, for this critic examines Pound's use of documents
and his hope to preserve those that are essential to the construction
of a good and healthy state. Pound worries that the "historical
black-out"[10] that attempts to keep certain documents out of circulation will "efface the gelatin" on which Mussolini wrote fascism; the
poet's job is to carve these Fascist slogans more deeply and perma-
nently so that they remain intact and available for a future generation to read and receive. Mussolini wrote the words and tried to put
them into action, but his effort failed; the poet has survived the
débacle and takes up the politically significant task of preserving
the crucial documents. In Pisa, without access to any texts, the poet

can preserve the records necessary for the eventual realization of the ideal state only by the powers of his purified and disciplined memory. He had to purge his memory of its personal elements (for a while, at any rate) so it could function as the storehouse for "public" memories, for memories drawn from the political and cultural spheres, for memories that must be recorded if the hope for the ideal state is to be preserved against the forces that have destroyed the most recent attempt to realize it. It is as Aeneas bringing his gods to Latium that he attempts this task of preservation. Like the wanderer who saved the "bricabrac" that preserved the traces of Troy that can inspire others to work toward its renewal as Rome, Pound carves the traces of Italian Fascism for the future.

In this way, the poet has succeeded the politician as the man of power, and in this spirit he examines Mussolini's actions. In the preceeding canto (p. 470), he accuses Mussolini of "losing the law of Chung Ni [Confucius]," a law Pound was trying to provide the politician as a guide to his actions. Pound juxtaposes to this indictment a story of the Tyrolese placing a valise next to a statue in Brunik "to remind the Italians it was time to pack up and leave" (*Disc* 194). Because Mussolini did not follow the law of Confucius, the people turned against him. In Canto LXXVIII, two pages after the long passage we have been reading, Pound remembers his interview with Mussolini:

> "No longer necessary," taxes are no longer necessary
> in the old way if it (money) be based on work done
> > inside a system and measured and gauged to human
> > > > > requirements
> inside the nation or system
> and cancelled in proportion
> > > to what is used and worn out
> à la Wörgl. Sd/ one wd/ have to think about that
> but was hang'd dead by the heels before his thought in
> > > > > proposito
> > came into action efficiently.　　　(LXXVIII/481–82)

The same image that inspired elegaic lament at the very opening of *The Pisan Cantos* now seems bitter regret that Mussolini did not attend to the poet's advice about taxation. Elegy has turned into political analysis as the poet criticizes the politician for failing to adhere to the proper advisor, the Confucian poet who wrote the Dynasty Cantos. The "process" ideogram is included in this analysis to indicate that Mussolini distanced himself from the

Confucian principle that provides balance and direction to public action. The same complaint is registered even when Pound seems to be exonerating Mussolini:

> and as to poor old Benito
>   one had a safety-pin
> one had a bit of string, one had a button
>   all of them so far beneath him
> half-baked and amateur
>   or mere scoundrels
> To sell their country for half a million
>   hoping to cheat more out of the people
> bought the place from the concierge
>   who could not deliver
> but on the other hand   emphasis
>   an error or excess of
>   emphasis   (LXXX/495–96)

While this passage seems to focus on the inadequacy of Mussolini's advisors rather than on Mussolini himself, one ought to note, first, that the tone established by the opening phrase—"poor old Benito"—is one of condescending pity not admiring praise. Second, given the context of Pound's ambition to play sage to the ruler, the mediocrity of those Mussolini chose as advisors ultimately reflects *il Duce*'s own poor judgment in failing to recognize in Pound the poet who could guide his revolution. Lastly, the passage concludes with a repetition of Pound's final judgment, that Mussolini did not find the "unwobbling pivot" that could have given him balance but instead exhibited certain excesses that led to his downfall. We recall Kung from Canto XIII:

> "Anyone can run to excesses,
> It is easy to shoot past the mark,
> It is hard to stand firm in the middle."   (XIII/59)

It is thus that Pound provides a certain distance between Mussolini and himself in his present role as prophet: not by renouncing and rejecting his former devotion to the Fascist State but by noting Mussolini's failure to accept him as Confucian sage. He adds Aeneas to his wanderer to announce that, after the fall, the bricabrac of Italian Fascism can be preserved only by the poet. Pound expects that these cantos establish him as the true and lasting hero of the historical process, as the survivor of the Fascist experiment who can maintain the vision that inspires political action.

Canto LXXX

While it is difficult to discern and demonstrate the organizing principle of *The Pisan Cantos,* the sheer length of Canto LXXX tends to confirm Bacigalupo's assessment that it functions as the point of transition in the sequence from the public to the private (129). While Canto LXXIV established the need to purge and fortify memory so that it can preserve the dream that had prompted Italian Fascism, this canto begins the shift back to personal memory. It seems that even the prophet of the ideal city cannot deny the claims of the personal. To enact this crucial transition, Pound writes two passages that prepare the wanderer for the more personal journey through memory. A second immersion takes place, and I shall argue that, whereas Canto LXXIV culminated in the crossing of the river Lethe "which takes from men the memory of sin," the immersion in this canto is in water that, like Eunoë in *Purgatorio,* "restores [the memory] of every good deed" (*Purgatorio* XXVIII, 128–29).

The explicit recuperation of memory begins much earlier in the sequence, when Pound recalls a line from Guido's "Donna mi priegha":

> nothing matters but the quality
>   of the affection—
> in the end—that has carved the trace in the mind
> dove sta memoria [the place where memory lives]
>   (LXXVI/457)

These lines are not meant to suggest that memory contains only traces of what has been loved, as if by its own nature ultimately only the good remains. "What matters" is that memory be disciplined sufficiently that it comes under the mastery of the individual, so that "in the end" it records the beloved and the beautiful. The wanderer has crossed over Lethe, and these lines begin the process of recuperation culminating in the second immersion of Canto LXXX that restores to memory the good of its agency.

Pound must travel through a more personal past because even the prophet of the ideal city is but a man, even the epic hero has a personal dimension to his identity. In this particular instance the man is under the extraordinary pressure of humiliation and possible execution for treason. The establishment of the epic dimension to his identity has had a residual benefit, that it now enables the prophet to face his past and accept the fate that

being an American citizen named Ezra Pound has landed him. E.
Fuller Torrey reports that, after two weeks in the cage, Pound suffered what amounts to a nervous breakdown. One camp psychia-
trist noted at this time a "loss of personality resilience." But the
records indicate that the poet soon recovered and spent most of his
internment "in excellent spirits" (Torrey 7–9). It seems likely that
the writing of *The Pisan Cantos* did in fact provide Pound with the
strength and hope needed to sustain him through the difficult
times ahead. His work to establish an epic grandeur to his predicament enables the man to reassert his personality and identity,
which the last cantos in the sequence reassemble.

It is as the epic wanderer that Pound enacts the journey
through his personal past:

> following the Battle Hymn of the Republic
>> where the honey-wagon cease from stinking
>>> and the nose be at peace
> "mi-hine eyes hev"
>> well yes they *have*
> seen a good deal of it
>> there is a good deal to be seen
> fairly tough and unblastable
>> and the hymn . . . . .
> well in contrast to the *god*-damned crooning
>> put me down for temporis acti
>> ΟΥ ΤΙΣ
>> [no time]
> now there are no more days
>> [no man]
>> [no time]   (LXXX/498–99)

First the poet records his response to the rendition of "The
Battle Hymn of the Republic" he hears played over the camp loud-
speaker, which prompts him to assert his own visionary capacity:
his eyes have also seen the coming of the Lord. The song celebrates
the apocalyptic vision from *Revelation* of the final days when the
Lord establishes the millenium, and Pound is quick to refer to his
own prophetic vision of the ideal city he has seen, a vision that is
"tough and unblastable." No matter what they do to him, the vision
remains to sustain him. From this consideration he turns to register his preference for "temporis acti," for bygone days. This preference is understandable, for in memory can be preserved traces of
the past that are far more satisfying to contemplate than the "*god-*

damned crooning." But he is quick to indicate that it is as "ΟΥ ΤΙΣ"
that he will finally yield to nostalgia, that only as the epic wanderer
is he able to move over the past in which his more personal identity
as Ezra Pound was created and lies waiting for him.

Asserting his epic status, he is now "no man" wandering
through "no time." Pound understands memory as a power that
obliterates temporal relations for, in the mind under the sway of
memory, traces of the past exist side by side with scenes from the
present and intimations, either hopeful or anxious, of future
prospects. For the memory-traveler, "there are no more days"; a
journey through memory brings one to a timeless realm in which
one is free to select and arrange moments from the past into new
relations to each other and to the present so that a new self is constituted. "No man" is ready to embark on a journey through the
poet's personal past in the effort to create a personal identity that
can support his heroic status. It is only now that Pound is ready
"by numerous acts of personal memory to reconstitute his fractured self" (Woodward 68).

Later in this canto the wanderer is called upon once again
(and for the last time in the sequence) to demonstrate that the
poet has disciplined his memory and has reached the safety of a
sanctified self:

> care and craft in forming leagues and alliances
>   that avail nothing against the decree
> the folly of attacking that island
>   and of the force [beyond what is destined]
>
> with a mind like that he is one of us
>   Favonus, vento benigno
>   Je suis au bout de mes forces/
> That from the gates of death,
>   that from the gates of death: Whitman or Lovelace
>   found on the jo-house seat at that
> in a cheap edition! [and thanks to Professor Speare]
> hast'ou swum in a sea of air strip
>   through an aeon of nothingness,
> when the raft broke and the waters went over me,
>
> Immaculata, Introibo
>   for those who drink of the bitterness
> Perpetua, Agatha, Anastasia
>   saeculorum

repos donnez à cils
    senza termine funge Immaculata Regina
      Les larmes que j'ai creées m'inondent
Tard, très tard je t'ai connue, la Tristesse,
I have been hard as youth sixty years   (LXXX/512–13)

Pound opens this last explicit deployment of the wanderer in the Pisan sequence with a reference to Odysseus's "folly of attacking that island"; in Canto LXXIX he made more explicit reference to this brief episode from *Odyssey* IX: "no sooner out of Troas/ than the damn fools attacked Ismarus of the Cicones" (p. 485). Pound chooses to focus on an unusual moment for Homer's hero, an unprovoked, unnecessary, and brutal attack: "From Ilion the wind carried me to Ismaros of the Ciconians. There I destroyed the city and killed the men" (Rouse's translation). In the passage above, the effort to form alliances among nations is compared to Odysseus's pointless attack: both "avail nothing" and work against destiny. Pound's own attack on the Western alliance that crushed the Fascist State is implicitly condemned as also fruitless and against the forces that are beyond fate; he did not attend to "the process" when he took to the airwaves in bitterness and hatred. "No man" must refrain from such folly and learn to follow the destined course; in this admission of error and call for discipline Pound's wanderer resembles the pious Aeneas.

    The next segment begins with Pound's own pithy translation of Zeus's comment on Odysseus, "with a mind like that he is one of us"; that is, his mind is of divine quickness and splendour. The poet reasserts his admiration for the wit and intelligence that had originally prompted his decision to employ Odysseus as the model of the epic hero. The errors and excesses committed in his name do not invalidate the good accomplished and registered on the journey. The poet then speaks the Latin for "west wind," the Italian for "with kindly breeze," and the French for "I am at the end of my tether." Pound expresses his own very personal plight (for might he not soon be at the end of a rope?) through the filter of a dense cosmopolitan consciousness: the whole of Europe has gone into the making of the epic voice that speaks his personal crisis. "[F]rom the gates of death" the wanderer now swims "in a sea of air strip," which sounds like Dante's voyage through the various spheres of heaven toward the city of God; he travels through the liquid air seen only by those with the visionary capacity.[11] But instead of alluding to a relevant moment from *Paradiso* where Dante feels overwhelmed by this voyage, he includes a scene from *Odyssey* V in which Odysseus is thrown from his raft and almost drowned. That he is saved from destruction by the pity of the sea-nymph Leucothea suggests that the wanderer is secured by supernatural grace. On the land he prays the opening words from the Catholic Mass, "Immaculate, I shall enter." He has emerged from his second immersion in water onto the shore of a purified self.[12]

The last segment quoted above is a confessional outburst: "The tears I have created flood me / Late, very late have I come to know you, Sadness, / I have been hard as youth sixty years." It was in the water of his own tears that he almost drowned and from which he emerges purified and sanctified; his own sorrow is the element that almost destroys him but ultimately purifies him. His daughter testifies to the dramatic shift in focus made by these lines: "Until then the attitude towards personal feelings had been somewhat Henry Jamesian: feelings were things other people have. One never spoke of them or showed them" (*Disc* 258). He confesses hardness and error in order to emerge onto sanctified ground from which he can range safely over the past and reassemble his personal identity. This lustration is patterned after Dante's immersion in the river Eunoë at the very conclusion of *Purgatorio:* "From the most holy waters I came forth again remade, even as new plants renewed with new leaves, pure and ready to mount to the stars" (XXXIII, 142–45). Only now is Pound's wanderer fully prepared to remake himself; only after this second immersion does he achieve a purified self ready to remember the good he has done and create an identity based on those memories. I suggest that all the reminiscences of a personal nature recorded in *The Pisan Cantos* are governed by the acts of lustration patterned after the twin immersions of Dante's *Purgatorio.*

But why does Pound insist on using Odysseus in the Dantesque context? He still does not like Aeneas or admire his personal characteristics; it is still Homer's wily, scheming, versatile, and adaptable hero whose personality appeals to the poet. When he returns to reassert the claims of the personal, he does so through Dante's acts of purification but as Odysseus, the hero Stanford calls "impressive in personality."

Cantos LXXXI–LXXXIV

The Pisan Cantos are structured upon a distinction between the public and the private, between an epic status as prophet of the ideal city and the man who aspires to that role. Pound makes memory central to these cantos, as an agent to be purged and disciplined so it can perform its twin functions: to perform its epic function as the storehouse of images that preserve the dream of the ideal state and to perform its lyrical function as the timeless realm where one can recreate one's identity. These cantos establish a tension between his public role and private identity: the prophet is also a man accused of treason and threatened with execution as a traitor. The last cantos in the sequence each end with a depiction of the sixty-year-old man who struggles to maintain hope and strength despite the ignominy and anxiety of his plight. These cantos test whether the private man can live up to his task.

Canto LXXXI contains what is perhaps the most famous passage in the entire sequence, one that describes the legacy of a memory properly employed:

> What thou lovest well remains,
>   the rest is dross
> What thou lov'st well shall not be reft from thee
> What thou lov'st well is thy true heritage
> Whose world, or mine or theirs
>   or is it of none?
> First came the seen, then thus the palpable
>   Elysium, though it were in the halls of hell,
> What thou lovest well is thy true heritage
> What thou lov'st well shall not be reft from thee
>   (LXXXI/520–21)

The man who speaks these lines is no longer haunted by the memory of his errors, nor is he prey to the despair that memories of former happiness cause in those suffering in the present a miserable fate with no happy resolution in sight. Memory purified and fortified enables the wanderer to travel throughout the past and select only the good, only what he has truly loved. Only after the establishment of the epic persona and the purgation of the errors made under its influence is Pound free to roam over the space created by memory and find the beloved and the good stored there. *The Pisan Cantos* are the manifestation of the "will to remember," a memory made good enough to build a self able to face the horror of his present predicament. He is strong enough only now to claim the ability to assemble selected images carved in memory and form from them a personal heritage that cannot be destroyed by any force, by any set of circumstances: "Amo ergo sum, and in just that proportion" (LXXX/493)—I love; therefore, I am. Flory seems puzzled by Pound's "stoic attitude toward the prospect of facing his own dangerous personal predicament" evident in the last cantos of the sequence (227), but it becomes the dominant purpose of *The Pisan Cantos* to prepare a self able to withstand whatever fate may have in store, to create an identity with both public and private dimensions that has risen above circumstance.

After registering this meditation on the power of memory to ground one's identity in a heritage of love, Pound moves to a consideration of the peculiar position his epic journey has brought him to:

> Pull down thy vanity
> 　　　　　　How mean thy hates
> Fostered in falsity,
> 　　　　　　Pull down thy vanity,
> Rathe to destroy, niggard in charity,
> Pull down thy vanity,
> 　　　　　　I say pull down.
>
> But to have done instead of not doing
> 　　　　　　this is not vanity
> To have, with decency, knocked
> That a Blunt should open
> 　　　　　　to have gathered from the air a live tradition
> or from a fine old eye the unconquered flame
> This is not vanity.
> 　　Here error is all in the not done,
> all in the diffidence that faltered . . .　　(LXXXI/521–22)

Only the desire to have the treasonous poet publicly acknowledge his arrogance could have led to the belief that this passage is Pound's apology for his wartime actions, a reading that both syntax and tone belie. There is no indication that the poet includes himself in the call for humility; the language and tone are those of a prophet castigating the people who have failed to live according to the heritage of love. This passage is not confessional but its opposite, an affirmation of the course of action that he took and that landed him in the Pisan camp. At least he acted, at least he gathered a tradition of living song, at least he did not falter due to lack of confidence in his insight and authority. Error lies not in choosing the wrong side in a conflict but in not caring enough to act. One may ask, from what place is he speaking, to what place does he call attention to by saying, "*Here* error is all in the not done"? It seems to me that he speaks this defense from a place of his own making, from what we can call an "epic space" that he has come to inhabit. For the charge he defends himself from is vanity, which is not the charge he faces at the hands of the Justice Department of the United States; "vanity" is an ethical charge that, in his eyes and from his placement, matters more dearly than the charge of treason, which is merely political. The man who speaks as prophet is not affected by accusations of treason, which is merely a local and partisan description of his actions; he can only be charged with "vanity," a charge of larger, maybe cosmic criminality. Of this he says quite clearly, "Not guilty."

The following canto recalls the immersion of Canto LXXX and moves directly into the starkest depiction of the anxiety of the poet's position:

> fluid ΧΘΟΝΟΣ o'erflowed me
>> lay in the fluid ΧΘΟΝΟΣ;
>>> that lie
> under the air's solidity
>> drunk with ΊΧΩΡ of ΧΘΟΝΙΟΣ
>>> fluid ΧΘΟΝΟΣ, strong as the undertow
>> of the wave receding
> but that a man should live in that further terror, and live
>> the loneliness of death came upon me
>>> (at 3 P.M., for an instant)
> three solemn half notes
>>> their white downy chests black-rimmed
> on the middle wire
>>> periplum   (LXXXII/526–27)

As in Canto LXXX, the wanderer is overwhelmed by water, now the fluid "of the earth," and made drunk with the ichor, "strong as the undertow of the wave receding." But this time, he emerges from the fluid to find himself not on sanctified ground but a prisoner in a detention camp under threat of execution; after all, it was as a consequence of his epic ambitions that he finds himself in such a predicament. He experiences moments of extreme terror and great loneliness, which last but "for an instant"; he pulls himself out of the horror by watching the birds whose various position upon the wires over the camp remind him of musical notation, which in turn recalls Janequin's "Le Chant des Oiseaux." It was that song that in Canto LXXV provides a way "out of Phlegethon." Pound attributes his resiliency in the face of death to the virtue of the wanderer on his "periplum." The man who for a moment suc-

cumbs to terror and loneliness regains courage by asserting his
epic status and continuing the journey.

At the end of Canto LXXXIII Pound registers the weary and
exasperated mood of one who has seen his efforts come to nothing:

> and in my mother's time it was respectable,
> it was social, apparently,
> > > to sit in the Senate gallery
> or even in that of the House
> > to hear the fire-works of the senators
> (and possibly representatives)
> as was still done in Westminster in my time
> and a very poor show from the once I saw it)
>
> but if Senator Edwards cd/ speak
> and have his tropes stay in the memory 40 years, 60 years?
> in short / the descent
> has not been of advantage either
> > to the Senate or to "society"
> > > or to the people
> > The States have passed thru a
> > > dam'd supercilious era
> Down, Derry-down /
> > Oh let an old man rest.   (LXXXIII/535–36)

At one point in United States history senators spoke with
such vigor that their "tropes [would] stay in the memory" for
years; their speech was part of the national heritage and was
stored in the collective memory of the nation. But that state of
affairs has passed away and the poet laments the decline in
rhetorical power heard in the senate. He has been trying to
redress the problem by creating the "tribal encyclopedia" (see
Bernstein) that records for the nation its most noteworthy tropes,
ideas, facts. The lament for the passing of a healthy tradition is
part of the prophet's role, and he has been playing it when he
makes a most personal plea to be left alone. After all, the poet is
an old man who cannot be expected, especially under the present
circumstances, to maintain the intensity and confidence required
for epic judgment. Woodward points to this passage as a sign of
Pound's "disillusion with worldly action and politics" (89), and of
course it is that. But this moment seems to emphasize less disillusion than exhausation due to age: he is an old man under tremendous pressure who asks to be left alone, who needs some rest from

the strain of the epic ambition. We hear an intimate and quiet plea
for some respite from the man who has been trying to preserve the
dream that could redeem the world.

As Flory has noted, the final canto of the Pisan sequence
includes many references to "lost causes" (227–28), coming to focus
closely on figures from the lost cause to which Pound had committed himself, "heroes" of the Axis. He hails Alessandro Pavolini
(secretary of the Fascist Republican party of the Salò government), Fernando Mezzasoma (minister of popular culture at Salò),
il Capo (the head of government, Mussolini), Pierre Laval (premier
of Vichy France), Vidkun Quisling (Nazi collaborator who became
head of the Norwegian government under the German conquest),
and Phillipe Henriot (French Fascist journalist). At the end of this
list he misremembers the words spoken by Arnaut Daniel at the
end of *Purgatorio* XXVI: "quand vos venetz al som de l'escali-
na"—"when you reach the summit of the stairway." I want to quote
Arnaut's speech in full to mark the position Pound takes at the
end of *The Pisan Cantos:*

> 'I am Arnaut, who weep and sing as I go. I see with grief past
> follies and see, rejoicing, the day I hope for before me. Now I
> beg of you, by that goodness which guides you to the summit
> of the stairway, to take thought in due time for my pain.'
> Then he hid himself in the fire that refines them. (*Purgatorio*
> XXVI, 142–48)

Pound hails other men who had also been committed to the
Axis cause and who had met or were presently in danger of meeting death as a result of their convictions; and then associates himself with Arnaut Daniel, whom in his early days he took great
pains to understand and translate and to whom his friend Eliot
compared him in the dedication of *The Waste Land.* He salutes
those who took the same risks as he to confirm that he has not
recanted his commitment to and work for Mussolini, and then
speaks to us as Arnaut, suffering because of his earthly excesses
and asking for our prayers on his behalf. In this way Pound asks
his reader for pity and pardon, but also places himself on the final
terrace of Purgatory from which he will soon emerge into the purity of his Edenic state and thence ascend to heaven. Even as he
asks for pardon, he makes sure we realize that he admits no fundamental error and aspires to the heavenly vision of the ideal city
to which he has elsewhere testified. He acknowledges past follies
but insists that the day he has been hoping for is at hand.

The Pisan Cantos end with a couplet that is entirely personal to the man who writes it:

If the hoar frost grip thy tent
Thou wilt give thanks when night is spent.   (LXXXIV/540)

While these lines seem to offer the reader a chance to identify with the poet's plight, they actually mark the distance between the reader (who is, in all likelihood, in the relative safety of his study) and the man incarcerated in a Pisan D. T. C. Few readers of the sequence have ever been forced to spend chilly nights in a tent. Pound chooses to end this sequence, which for all he knew might have been his last, with lines that can refer only to his unusual plight because his fate as an individual is crucial to the historical process that he has sought to master. The address to the nonexistent second person is made in archaic language ("thy" and "thou") to suggest again a Biblical resonance and prophetic tone that do not include the reader but rather strongly and deliberately mark the gap between poet and audience. The man who gives thanks for making it through another frosty night (and it is worth noting that he is speaking as a survivor) is not merely the American citizen who broadcast for the Fascist State but the great epic wanderer who can direct our progress toward the city of Dioce. For one of the very few times in the history of literature (with the possible exception of Dante), the actual circumstances of the writing are crucial to the poetry in question. His idiosyncratic situation is presented in this last couplet to underscore the extraordinary nature of the poetry we are reading: this old man forced to sleep in a tent on cold autumn nights is the one with the tremendous ambition to speak as the prophet of the ideal city. He is, like Arnaut Daniel, presently suffering but with his eyes fixed on the glory still to come.

The final cantos of the Pisan sequence challenge the poet's assertion that he is a man who has achieved epic status as prophet of an ideal order still possible. The extreme danger of the situation challenges Pound to give up his epic journey and acknowledge his error, but instead he continues the periplum by adding a further dimension to his already multilayered wanderer, the sacrifice and devotion to the future characteristic of Aeneas. *The Pisan Cantos* are organized around a tension generated by the contrast between a broken sixty-year-old man under arrest for treason and a poet who aspires to the epic status of prophet. Nowhere in *The Cantos* do we come to know Pound's personal life—both from the past and in the precarious present—as we do in this sequence; not as an appeal to the readers' sympathy for his personal plight but as a way to convince us that this very man, in these unusual circumstances, has sought and achieved the status of epic hero. *The Pisan Cantos* are organized and informed by the extraordinary ambition of a broken man whose cause has been defeated to assert his own unbroken faith in the continued possibility of the vision he has been granted.

4 ❧ The Wanderer as Historian:
Writing Paradise

Before beginning an examination of *Section: Rock-Drill* and *Thrones de los Cantares,* it is worth noting that both sequences were fully conceived and for the most part executed while Pound was confined to Saint Elizabeths Hospital in Washington as mentally incompetent to stand trial for treason. Such placement renders the ambitions of these sequences all the more extraordinary, for the man who might be well excused for entertaining doubts about his authority on matters of history maintains the stance he feels he earned in and by *The Pisan Cantos;* that is, he continues his journey through Western culture, a journey of and through texts containing historical data, a master of history who now sees in the multitude of detail the material out of which paradise can be made. He ignores the implications of his confinement and continues his wandering, seeking to bring his epic to a close by writing paradise.[1] It is to *Rock-Drill* and *Thrones* that Pound refers in one of the final fragments: "I have tried to write Paradise" (Notes for CXVII/802).

The two sections can be considered together because, in both, Pound examines the same kind of material using the same radically innovative technique.[2] These cantos are made up of fragments drawn from various texts, always broken off in a way to prevent any sense of narrative logic from allowing easy connections to be made and often juxtaposed to other fragments culled from other texts. The dizzying speed with which the fragments are presented give to these sections a kind of difficulty not yet encountered in the poem. It is part of the critic's job to account for this new technique, which I will argue is best approached as the poet's attempt to create a paradise that can bring the epic to a close. In fact, in these cantos Pound is working most independently and originally to create a distinctly new kind of journey for the epic wanderer. For now he embarks upon a journey through a sea of texts which, if understood and organized properly, becomes the liquid light of heavenly vision.

153

Still, even in this most idiosyncratic effort, Pound takes pains to mark his wanderer with characteristics drawn from the tradition. As he works to "write [a] Paradise" that is purely his own addition to the epic tradition, he calls upon Dante's progression through paradise to mark certain far-reaching changes in direction for the journey of *The Cantos*. For now the wanderer is moving toward a transcendence of the human condition described and claimed by Dante. By reading Dante's *Paradiso*, Pound comes to a radical revision of his understanding of the purpose of human action. As with Dante, knowledge of human history is not rejected as a value but made subordinate to the higher end of achieving beatitude. In *Rock-Drill* and *Thrones*, though the nature of the journey is radically new, Pound relies more than ever on Dante to establish its goal and conclusion. Through his understanding of Dante's heavenly attitude toward history, he can maintain the continuity and integrity of his "long poem including history" by using historical data in a radically new way: as the raw material of text with which he can "write the Paradise" that will, he hopes, end the poem.

Rock-Drill

While earlier in *The Cantos* Pound confines most of his allusions to and uses of Dante to only two or three cantos per sequence, in *Rock-Drill* he scatters the references throughout the various cantos, sometimes merely one or two brief glimpses of Dante in heaven, sometimes long clusters of sustained use of Dante, with no apparent principle of organization. This is quite in keeping with the technique of the late sequences, in their radically fragmented and disjointed nature. I propose to gather most of the scattered allusions to the epic tradition (which for these sequences means Dante's work and the "Leucothea" episode from *Odyssey* V) and construct something of a narrative pattern from the accumulation. What justifies this procedure is the almost desperate need to find some principle on which to shape these very nearly shapeless cantos; what justifies my choice of Dante as the figure who provides a glimpse of organization is Pound's earlier, clearer but I think not more deliberate and precise use of Dante to announce his purposes and destination. What emerges from the accumulation of so many references to Dante's work, mainly drawn from *Paradiso*, is an understanding of Dante's paradise that forms the basis for Pound's effort to make his own.

The first explicit use of Dante comes in the midst of Pound's presentation of details from *Chou King*, the "Book of Documents" containing annals of the first three Chinese dynasties. As he over-whelms the reader with ideograms and with translated fragments from these documents, he includes a quotation from *Purgatorio* XXIV, "'ch' e' ditta dentro'"—"which he dictates within." This line is part of Dante's response to Bonagiunta's question, a response relevant to Pound's new intentions:

> 'But tell me if I see here him that brought forth the new rhymes, beginning with *Ladies that have intelligence of Love.*' And I said to him: 'I am one who, when love breathes in me, take note, and in that manner which he dictates within go on to set it forth.' (*Purgatorio* XXIV, 49–54)

As Dante includes his assessment of his own work as "new," so Pound, through this moment from *Purgatorio,* comments on his own new method of composition. There is some playful irony here in Pound's choice of this moment as a gloss on his own "new writ-ing"; the bewildering innovation of technique marking *Rock-Drill* is the result of the poet's scrupulous attention to the manner in which Love has dictated the matter at hand. But this is serious too, for in these cantos Pound wants to write history in the way Love inspires. It might seem strange and bewildering, but history as seen from the perspective of divine love differs significantly in form from that of the conventional historian. This moment from *Purgatorio* announces Pound's intention to write a new kind of his-tory and to place his ambition alongside Dante's.

One theme Pound isolates from the *Commedia* is Dante's self-consciously new understanding of history. The next allusion to Dante directs us to consider how earthly activity appears differ-ently to one who has experienced the inspiration of divine love than to a conventional historian:

To know the histories

to know good from evil

And know whom to trust.

Ching Hao.

Chi crescerà

(Paradiso)

"of societies" said Emanuel Swedenborg.

Mr Jefferson lining up for Louis Philippe,

a fact which shd have been known to

M. de Tocqueville.

(LXXXIX/590)

The Italian is from *Paradiso* V, where the souls of the second sphere say of Dante as he approaches them, "Lo one who will increase (*chi crescerà*) our loves!" (line 105). Pound notes what he considers an essential law governing paradise; namely, that the arrival of another soul to share God's love increases the amount of love in heaven. Swedenborg also reports that each society of angels in heaven increases in number daily and, as it increases, grows ever more perfect. These two allusions point to a fundamental difference between earthly goods and heavenly love, a difference Virgil explains to Dante on the terrace of envy:

> It is because your desires are fixed where the part is lessened by sharing that invidia blows the bellows to your sighs. But if the love of the highest sphere bent upward your longing, that fear would not be in your breast. For there, the more they are who say *ours*, the more of good does each possess and the more charity burns in that cloister. (*Purgatorio* XV, 49–57)

In contrast to earthly goods, the experience of divine love encourages sharing and fellowship; whereas on earth the grouping of a large number of individuals into a society can only decrease the amount of material wealth each person possesses and so increase envy and competition, in heaven the formation of societies causes an increase of wealth for each individual. Pound notes this principle of heavenly exchange immediately after he implies that he is the one to be trusted regarding history and the good and evil contained therein, and immediately before beginning the series of historical "facts" presented in the usual fragmentary and disjointed manner that will comprise the canto. We are meant to understand that the history being written is evaluated and organized according to a very different principle, by a man who has witnessed and achieved a very different mode of experience.

Through allusion to *Paradiso*, Pound begins to establish the new ground from which he is now examining human activity. Later in the same canto, he includes another allusion to *Paradiso*, this time in the context of Van Buren's effort against the Bank, to serve as an indication of the subtle but crucial shift in the poet's attitude toward "history":

> "Of great suavity and gentleness of deportment,
> Mr Van Buren"
> An experiment on his nerves was resolved on,
> Had Crab such crystal, winter were as a day.

You cannot make mariners out of slaves
and the mud, mud, said Guinicelli
(LXXXIX/599–600)

The first three lines are from Thomas Hart Benton's description of a conspiracy devised by pro-Bank forces against Van Buren; they hoped to bring such public pressure to bear on the President that his will to oppose the Bank would collapse. He did not yield and was able to resolve the financial crisis caused by the pro-Bank forces without rechartering the Bank. But his acts were unpopular and he was defeated for reelection. The following line is Pound's version of Dante's description of the brilliant light generated by the soul of St. John: "then one light among them shone out so that if Crab held such a gem winter would have a month of unbroken day" (*Paradiso* XXV, 100–102). This light shone just after St. James's examination of Dante on hope was completed. According to the catechism of this canto, Hope "is a sure expectation of future glory, and it springs from divine grace and precedent merit" (67–69). The puzzle, then, is to determine how the flash of light from paradise functions as a gloss on Van Buren's actions and fate (and we must note how Van Buren's fragment is joined to the line from *Paradiso* by a comma, as if the two go together). One might suggest that Van Buren was motivated by a glimpse of such light, that he was able to persevere in his difficult course because of the hope enkindled by such light. Such a reading would accord with Pound's earlier understanding of human history, as the place of final and ultimate value; if one had access to divine light, it would enable one to see how to act in the world; understood thusly, the light's value would be in its effect, in sustaining heroic action on earth. But it can be argued that Pound has shifted his sense of the relation between supernatural light and earthly activity: though Van Buren's efforts are destined ultimately to fail, he might maintain hope for personal fulfillment; that is, he might maintain his "sure expectation of a future glory" accorded by the conjunction of God's grace and the man's own merit. Earthly activity is still important, and it still might be guided by a vision of the supernatural; but the ultimate value now is in the "future glory," the transcendence won by proper action. If Van Buren is now shining in the heaven where hope is understood, it is not because he was able to make "mariners out of slaves"; it is not because he created an earthly paradise, for his side lost. He shines forth because he acted properly, heroically, for the good of the people. Action in history is the way to blessedness.

Pound might be suggesting that his own epic ambitions have
shifted: no longer does he hope to affect the world, to make the
slaves dominated by usury free men who can sail to blessedness;
but perhaps he can achieve his own transcendence and lead, more
modestly, a select few along the way. Guinicelli's poem sings of the
sun that beat against the mud but failed to make anything other
than mud from it; yet the sun's brilliance is not lessened. The
emphasis of this passage is on the light that cannot effect great
and permanent change on earth but still shines eternally. Pound's
own effort "to make a paradiso terrestre" (Notes for CXVII/802) is
reluctantly being revised as he now sets out to achieve paradise in
his own poem. Revised but not necessarily abandoned: for the
effort to make the earthly paradise, while no longer the ultimate
value for the poem, is still the means to the new end—personal
transcendence. Pound is not abandoning his commitment to
human action in the public realm of politics but subordinating that
action to a more personal goal.

    In his effort to complete his poem by "writing Paradise,"
Pound turns to an emphasis on one's private transcendence of the
human condition. But it is achieved, not by escaping from history
(as in the early cantos where he sought a return to origins, before
the corruption of history), but by committing oneself passionately
to history, to the details and causes informing the public order. In
the next canto he continues this revision by transforming a brief
phrase from *Paradiso* I into a ritualistic response in a prayer of
thanksgiving:

                         Sibylla,
         from under the rubble heap
                         m'elevasti
         from the dulled edge beyond pain,
                         m'elevasti
         out of Erebus, the deep-lying
             from the wind under the earth,
                         m'elevasti
         from the dulled air and the dust,
                         m'elevasti
         by the great flight,
                 m'elevasti,
                         Isis Kuanon
             from the cusp of the moon,
                         m'elevasti.
                              (XC/606)

The tag—m'elevasti, "you raised me"—comes from Dante's description of his own transcendence of the human condition:

> The passing beyond humanity cannot be set forth in words; let the example suffice, therefore, for him to whom grace reserves the experience. If I was only that part of me which Thou createdst last [i.e., the soul], Thou knowest, Love that rulest the heavens, who with Thy light didst raise me [*mi levasti*]. (*Paradiso* I, 70–75)

Dante praises the "Love that rulest the heavens" for granting him the experience of "passing beyond humanity"; that is, he thanks God for the grace permitting his transcendence of the human condition. Pound borrows the phrase to fashion a prayer of thanksgiving upon being taken out of history (the bounds of space and time that defines human being) and into the experience of paradise. This prayer is preceded by a defiant and troubling reference to Hitler—"not arrogant from habit, / but furious from perception." It is remarkable that Pound can make this apology for the Nazi leader, that he became furious (certainly an acknowledgement of excess and loss of control) only because he *saw* so clearly. Hitler fell into the error of genocide, it is implied, because he was a visionary whose efforts toward creating a different nature and destiny for humanity than those of the present were blocked by the forces of usury. Pound places this terribly contentious moment immediately before his prayer because it is from precisely this kind of difficult assessment of human behavior that he is grateful to be released by the grace of divine love. Hardly abandoning the realm of politics, Pound reasserts his defiant position but subordinates evaluation to the expression of relieved joy for having transcended, even if only for isolated moments, all human concerns. Once again, he uses Dante to indicate the divine, transcendent perspective from which he is now regarding history.

Towards the very end of the canto Pound makes a brief but pointed reference to *Purgatorio* XIV in the midst of a procession of souls freed from Erebus and ascending towards paradise:

> For the procession of Corpus
>> come now banners
> comes flute tone [. . .]
> to new forest,
>> thick smoke, purple, rising
> bright flame now on the altar

the crystal funnel of air
out of Erebus, the delivered,
          Tyro, Alcmene, free now, ascending
e i cavalieri,
          ascending,
no shades more.   (XC/608, my italics)

The Italian is spoken by Guido del Duca on the terrace of
Purgatory where the penitent souls are cleansed of envy; he is
recalling former days for Florence, "the ladies *and the knights,* the
toils and the sports to which we were moved by love and courtesy
where hearts have grown so wicked" (*Purgatorio* IV, 109–111).
Part of his purgation is to remember the better motives that
spurred him to noble deeds, but he also recalls the envy "that so
inflamed [...] my blood that if I had seen a man make merry thou
hadst seen me suffused with livid colour." This memory causes him
to castigate mortals: "O race of men, why do you set your hearts
where must needs be exclusion of partnership?" (lines 82–87). The
knights who were "moved by love and courtesy" in bygone days
were also stricken with the envy for material wealth and earthly
joys that keeps their eyes bent downward; but now, in Pound's
hands, they are "ascending, no shades more"; they have been freed
from invidia and now rise, along with the poet, "out of Erebus, the
delivered." The procession of freed souls is making its way "to new
forest," which both Flory and Bacigalupo see as a reference to
Dante's earthly paradise atop Mount Purgatory.[3] The souls move
toward the purity and goodness that was theirs before their corruption in and by history. Pound understands that Dante's *Purgatorio* is where human beings work and suffer to return to their
original health:

Wang: that man's phallic heart is from heaven
          a clear spring of rightness,
Greed turns it awry.   (XCIX/697)

The mind at the start had
                    cheng[4]
Greed defrauds it
Some want more than they can get in a lifetime.
                              (XCIX/701–02)

But to live as flowers reflected,
                    as moonlight,

free from all possessiveness in affections,
                    but, as Chu says, egoistical.
                                        (XCIX/703)

    Greed is the human affection that turns the phallic heart from its proper trajectory, from rising toward the heavens down toward earthly possessions. At its origin the human mind had cheng[4], the ability to hit the target squarely, but greed has cheated us of this natural ability. The souls at the end of Canto XC rise from such possessiveness toward their natural health in the new forest, and from there they will rise to the heavens. Pound manages to infuse this celebratory climax with a larger significance by means of the Dantesque allusions; for the triumph of these souls is their successful purgation of the envy that keeps them bound to the human condition and now they are rising to a new and utterly different mode of experience where sharing and partnership increase the amount of wealth. Once again, Dante is used to indicate the new perspective from which Pound is writing these cantos.
    In the first half of *Rock-Drill*, then, Pound has included several allusions to Dante's *Commedia*, especially *Paradiso*, to indicate that the history examined in this sequence is being written from the perspective of one who has achieved the transcendent experience of divine love. The brief fragments chosen with extreme deliberation continue the journey on which he sent his wanderer in Canto I. In each of the next three cantos he fashions a larger cluster of such allusions as Dante's presence is made more palpable and dominant. As *Rock-Drill* approaches its climax, which occurs in Canto XCV, the wandering hero is once again used to define the journey's direction and purpose.

Canto XCI

Canto XCI renews the wanderer's journey as it presents a sustained image of paradise given shape by Dante's heaven:

The GREAT CRYSTAL
                    doubling the pine, and to cloud.
          pensar di lieis m'es ripaus
Miss Tudor moved them with galleons
from deep eye, versus armada
from the green deep
                    he saw it,

in the green deep of an eye:
>   Crystal waves weaving together toward the gt/
>>   healing

Light *compenetrans* of the spirits
The Princess Ra-Set has climbed
>   to the great knees of stone,
She enters protection,
>   the great cloud is about her,
She has entered the protection of crystal
>>   convien che si mova
>>   la mente, amando.
>>>   XXVI, 34

Light & the flowing crystal
>   never gin in cut glass had such clarity
That Drake saw the splendour and wreckage
>   in that clarity
[. . .]
The golden sun boat
>   by oar, not by sail
Love moving the stars [beside the altar]
by the altar slope
>   "Tamuz!   Tamuz!"
They set lights now in the sea
>   and the sea's claw gathers them outward.
The peasant wives hide cocoons now
>>   under their aprons
>>   for Tamuz.
>>>   (XCI/611–12)

In this passage Pound indicates that his wanderer is now on a journey through "the flowing crystal" toward the "love that moves the sun and the other stars"; but even in his "golden sun boat" which moves "by oar, not sail" (that is, by effort, not grace), he insists on the relevance of history through the figure of Sir Francis Drake. "The GREAT CRYSTAL," according to Terrell, is a Neoplatonic metaphor for the source of the primal creative force; it is an image suggesting the exquisite bodies of light into which Dante enters in each sphere on his voyage through the various heavens. In fact, the movement of the Princess Ra-Set is strikingly like that of Dante's as he enters a new sphere. For instance, as he enters the sphere of the Moon:

It seemed to me that a cloud covered us, shining, dense, solid and smooth, like a diamond that is smitten by the sun; the eternal pearl received us into itself, as water receives a ray of light and remains unbroken. (*Paradiso* II, 31–36)

Dante enters the sphere of the Moon by entering "the eternal pearl" that "receives" him yet "remains unbroken"; that is, remains unified and whole though it takes in a foreign body. He enters and becomes part of the cloud of dense light, very much as Ra-Set "enters the protection of crystal" while "the great cloud is about her." Pound does create his own figure in Ra-Set, who, according to Boris de Rachewiltz, is a conflation of the male Egyptian gods of the Sun and of the Moon, respectively, into a single female entity (*Approaches* 181); but he sends her into a heavenly sphere very much like Dante's. For the light in Canto XCI is also a solid light best represented by exquisite jewels; for Pound, crystal and for Dante, diamond and pearl.

The passage contains several images of this flowing, almost solid light that recur quite frequently in the late cantos: "Light & the flowing crystal"; "Gods moving in crystal"; later in Canto XCI, "overflooding, light over light" and "the light flowing, whelming the stars" (613); and "'Ghosts dip in the crystal, adorned'" (617). These are important additions to *The Cantos* because they establish a new element on (or, perhaps more appropriately, in) which Pound's wanderer travels: no longer over the sea, making a periplum around coasts; nor like Hanno and Dante's Ulysses, beyond the Pillars of Herakles and out toward new experience; nor even, as with Drake, circumnavigating the globe; but now through the liquid, almost solid, light that comprises paradise for Dante and for Pound. "The golden sun boat" might well be a reference to the boat used by Ra as he traversed the underworld during the night so that he could rise the next dawn; but in Pound's hands this boat becomes the craft on which the epic wanderer now makes his journey, using his own labor to proceed through the liquid light toward "the love moving the stars," Dante's final vision. He creates an elaborate context, drawing mainly on Dante's *Paradiso* and some Egyptian mythology his son-in-law has been showing him, for his own journey through paradise.

But Dante does more than provide the nature of the liquid light through and into which the wanderer travels; he also provides the physical principle governing the movement of bodies in Pound's paradise. The Italian in the passage (which is so important that its source is noted as part of the poem) is from Dante's explanation about the relation of the mind to Love:

> To that Essence, then, in which is such pre-eminence that every good found outside of it is nothing but a light from its radiance, must be moved with love, more than to aught else, the mind of everyone who discerns the truth on which this reasoning rests. (*Paradiso* XXVI, 31–36)

"To that Essence . . . must be moved with love . . . the mind of everyone who discerns the truth." The nature of the mind is that it must move toward the highest heaven where God dwells once it discerns the truth, once it sees beyond the illusions of human vision and glimpses portions of the divine light. Pound's wanderer, then, is moving by the necessity of his nature toward the Love that draws the purified and strengthened mind. Dante is called upon here to provide the wanderer's journey with its medium, motive, and goal.

No longer is worldly good the ultimate source of value for the poem, for human activity on earth has become the means to the journey through the liquid light of paradise undertaken previously only by Dante. But the persistent presence of Sir Francis Drake suggests that the wanderer must still work in the realm of political, even military, action if he is to be propelled toward the experience of beatitude. As Princess Ra-Set moves into the protection of crystal drawn by the power of Love, Drake is moved by "the green deep of an eye" toward the political actions of fighting the Spanish armada and circumnavigating the globe. In the "deep eye" of Miss Tudor, Drake sees "Crystal waves weaving together toward the great healing" as well as "the splendour and wreckage in that clarity"; that is, he sees the effects of the warfare and the promise of great healing in the splendour of the divine light. The wreckage resulting from warfare is quite in keeping with the further journey through the light; though one's efforts in the realm of human activity fail and lead to wreckage (as Pound's commitment to Mussolini led to his own personal disaster), the effort, if inspired by and aiming at divine love, may still bring one through the liquid light to God. Drake, as a figure of the wanderer, journeys both in the world of historical action and through the liquid heavens.[4] Inspired by Love, his heroic action is the oar by which he moves through the flowing crystal toward union with that Love. History, even in its most violent form, is the medium through which the wanderer travels on his way to blessedness.

Canto XCII

Pound's decision to use Drake as the appropriate version of the wanderer for this sequence makes commitment to action central to attaining the experience of beatitude. Canto XCII continues and advances this understanding of paradise by using several moments from the *Commedia:*

>   ex aquis nata
>   [the birth out of the waters]
>   "in questa lumera appresso"
>   Folquet, nel terzo cielo.
>   "And if I see her not,
>   no sight is worth the beauty of my thought."
>   Then knelt with the sphere of crystal
>   That she should touch with her hands,
>   Coeli Regina,
>   The four altars at the four coigns of that place,
>   But in the great love, bewildered
>   farfalla in tempesta
>   under rain in the dark:
>   many wings fragile
>   [...]
>   And from far
>   qil tremolar della marina
>   chh   chh
>   the pebbles turn with the wave
>   chh   ch'u
>   "fui chiamat'
>   e qui refulgo."
>   (XCII/619–20)

This cluster opens with a reference to Aphrodite's birth out of the waters, which takes us back to the very opening canto where the wanderer, having sailed "outward and away," encounters a Botticellian vision of Aphrodite on the deep water. Her appearance on the waters slides smoothly into the fragment in Italian—which means "in this radiance that so sparkles"—spoken by the troubadour Folco (Folquet), who dwells in Dante's third heaven ruled over by Aphrodite/Venus. The third heaven is reserved for those whose love was inspired by sexual passion, for those whose divine love was achieved by what can be called the sublimation of eros but is still marred by wantonness. Folco is answering Dante's

unspoken question concerning the identity of the soul within the
sparkling light:

> Know then that within it Rahab is at peace, and, since she is
> joined by our order, it is sealed with her in its highest rank;
> by this heaven, where the shadow ends that is cast by your
> world, she was taken up before any other soul of Christ's tri-
> umph. It was indeed fitting to leave her in some heaven as a
> trophy of the lofty victory that was gained with the one and
> the other palm, because she favoured Joshua's first glory in
> Holy Land—a place that little touches the Pope's memory.
> (*Paradiso* IX, 115–126)

Dante gives to the harlot Rahab a special place: it is her position in its highest rank that seals this heaven, and she was the
very first soul to be taken up by one of the heavens—even before
the greatest of Old Testament figures. Rahab earned this lofty
place because of what she did in the realm of politics: she hid from
the king of Jericho the spies Joshua sent to learn how best to
attack the city, and so was instrumental in Joshua's victory there.
Dante implies that her behavior, which is in accord with the divine
will, was inspired by the sexual passion that so dominated her.
Sexual passion can destroy one's will to right action, as in *Inferno*
V, where Paolo and Francesca flit aimlessly about driven by the
passion they are helpless to direct; or it can inspire the righteous
action that leads to blessedness. Though sexual passion is still
bound to earthly joy, it has the potential to inspire the kind of
behavior that leads to transcendence. The emphasis of this reference falls not on Rahab's sexuality but on the heroic action she
undertook under its influence.

Pound notes that "Folquet" is the speaker of these lines
because he is a troubadour poet and thus a possible representative
of Pound the poet and translator. By identifying himself here with
Folco, Pound suggests a reassessment of his own earlier commitment to political action, most dominant in the 1930s and 1940s,
when he became a spokesman for Italian Fascism. His behavior in
those days, inspired as Rahab's by eros, was heroic and led him to
a place in Dante's heaven, albeit a place marred by wantonness.
The next two lines in the passage—"'And if I see her not, / no sight
is worth the beauty of my thought"—are a translation of another
troubadour's song, that of Bernart de Ventadorn, quoted in its
original in Canto XX. Beyond any significance that the emotion
expressed in these lines and the poem may have for Canto XCII,

the mere fact that they refer back to an earlier canto and earlier interests indicates that Pound is placing his former self—the poet who worked so hard to fit his work into a troubadour tradition—in the third circle of Dante's heaven.[5] But we also have, through this Provençal song, a reference to the ideal lady that does not have to be seen with the bodily eye to be enjoyed; Pound indicates that his erotic passion was always capable of transcendence, that his love of women was always able to be raised to an ideal level represented for Dante by the Queen of Heaven, "Coeli Regina." This tag refers us at once back to Pound's own Canto XXXIX, where it is referred to in the midst of a sexual encounter with Circe that leads to a manifestation of holy light; and also to Dante's *Paradiso* XXIII, where the Church Triumphant sing a hymn of praise to Mary that so delights Dante that "the delight has never left [him]" (line 129). Devotion to the earthly values of eros that may have dominated his earlier understanding of the powers of sexual passion has been sublimated so he can hear the song in praise of the Queen of Heaven (who, even if he cannot see her, is sufficient to delight him).

Pound then offers a slightly revised version of a line from *The Pisan Cantos*—"the four altars at the four coigns of that place," which was rendered in Canto LXXIV as "With the four giants at the four corners" (430). This is a reference to Wagadu, the Soninke legend of the ideal city that can be made manifest in earthly form through the actions of a purified humanity. The four giants at the four corners have been replaced by four altars; the heroic men who in Pisa gave shape to the earthly manifestation of the ideal city have been replaced by symbols of devotion that define the nature of the ideal city as a heavenly city, as a version of the City of God Dante witnesses and joins in the upper reaches of paradise. Not only does this signal once again the shift of ultimate value from earthly incarnation to visionary experience of the ideal city; but it marks Pound's new understanding of his own earlier action on behalf of Wagadu, that it was the means to a devotion that can make him a citizen of a heavenly city. He formulates this vision of the High City, only to admit then that he was "in the great love, bewildered"; that is, he was participating, as was Rahab, in "the love that moves the sun and the other stars" but was overwhelmed by it and perhaps led to some excess. This is as close as we get to a confession of fundamental error in his political thinking, for he will never revoke his advocacy of Mussolini and, as we have seen already, he is willing to make part of his poem an admiration for Hitler. The love inspired by the third sphere, which is the last sphere of heaven to bear the shadow of earthly fault, has brought him to a transcendent vision of the ideal city that he thought Mussolini and the Axis powers were working toward.

This passage comes to an end with a joining of two moments from the *Commedia,* one from the shores of Mount Purgatory, where Dante has a glimpse of "the trembling of the sea" (*Purgatorio* I, 117); and another from *Paradiso* IX, in which Cunizza identifies herself to Dante:

> Cunizza I was called, and I shine forth here because the light of this star overcame me; but I gladly pardon in myself the reason of my lot, and it does not grieve me,—which may seem strange, perhaps, to your crowd. (*Paradiso* IX, 32–36)

He claims to have experienced the arrival onto the island of Purgatory, on whose shores he sees "trembling of the sea"; and to have made it to the third heaven where Cunizza dwells. He once was in danger of being lost on hellish seas "in tempesta" but made it to the shores of Purgatory, as Cunizza was in danger of being lost in the excess of her passion. That he drops her name from the allusion ("fui chiamat") indicates that he is assuming her place and her words in this heaven. He has been through the process of purgation, has raised his erotic passion to sublime heights; and if the sphere of Venus seems marred by excess, those who dwell in it feel no shame or remorse for the errors made under its influence. Pound at once acknowledges and distances himself from the errors he might have made as a passionate man working for the incarnation of the ideal city. Though he ran to excess, he has reached beatitude.

Canto XCII insists on commitment to earthly action in the journey to beatitude and places Pound's own commitment to earthly affairs in the third heaven, action inspired by eros and thus subject to excess. He maintains previous positions and extends their significance: he still believes in the position taken before and during the war, but now recognizes that its ultimate value is in the blessedness it makes possible.

Canto XCIII

Canto XCIII is dominated by allusions to Dante's work which fall into two equal parts: the first half of the canto refers frequently to *Convivio* and the second half to *Paradiso.* It begins with a phrase from the opening of Dante's philosophic treatise, "panis angelicus"—"angel's bread"; Dante promises to distribute the never-dimishing bread of the angels to his readers. *Convivio* is a labored piece of reasoning in which Dante tries to make sure pronouncements, in prose and by means of scholastic logic, concerning divine knowledge. What Pound critics have not yet emphasized is that Dante abandons this work and takes up the great poetry of the *Commedia* in its place; that is, discursive language and logical thinking about the divine is made subordinate to the poet's intuition and imaginative presentation. Pound notes this shortcoming of *Convivio:* "tho' he puts knowledge higher than I should" (XCIII/626). Pound never rejects knowledge as a central value for his poem; to do so would be to reject his life's work, for what else has *The Cantos* been about but knowledge of the past and its relation to our present condition and future destiny? He can maintain the cohesion of his poem by revising his understanding of history; like Dante, he now makes it serve a higher end. In fact, one way to approach this canto is to watch how Pound follows Dante's movement from *Convivio* to *Paradiso.*

Pound uses *Convivio* to make the highest claims possible for the kinds of knowledge he has been presenting in *The Cantos* for over thirty years:

> Nine knowledges about
>
> chih[3]
> chih
>
> Avicenna and Algazel
> The 8th being natural science, 9th moral
> 8th the concrete, 9th the agenda,
> Agassiz with the fixed stars, Kung to the crystaline.
> (XCIII/625)

Pound is responding to an essential principle organizing the universe as described by Dante in *Convivio.* Dante's nine heavens, he understands, are arranged according to nine knowledges, each of which are "about chih[3]." When translating Confucius Pound came to believe that "there is no more important technical term than this chih(3), the hitching post, position, place one is in and works from " (*Con* 232). Wisdom "is rooted in coming to rest, being at ease in perfect equity. Know the point of rest and then have an orderly progression" (*Con* 29). According to Thomas Grieve, chih[3] is "the ground from which virtuous actions spring" (*Pai,* 4–2&3). Pound sees that this term can be used to identify the nature of the "rest" attained in

Canto XLVII, a rest associated by Pound with Dante's in the earthly paradise. For this poet, chih³ suggests the point of perfect rest from which one can "behave in the eternally sensible manner. That is to say, naturally, reasonably, intuitively" (*LE* 92). Pound fashioned that phrase in 1912 to describe the motivation behind the search for "a return to origins", and fifty years later he repeats the idea by means of this Chinese ideograph found in Confucius and used to understand Dante. From the point of rest indicated by chih³ one acts with such virtue in one's earthbound life that one glimpses, perhaps even achieves, the experience of beatitude.

Chih³, then, is the source of the various kinds of virtuous activity human beings may undertake. Pound follows Dante in admiring and calling for virtue in its various aspects. On the previous page he included a fragment from *Paradiso* VIII, "non fosse cive" ("if he were not a citizen"). This phrase is from an exchange between Dante and Charles Martel concerning the nature of citizenship:

> He continued therefore: 'Now tell me, would it be worse for man on earth if he were not a citizen?'
> 'Yes,' I replied, 'and here I ask no proof.'
> 'And can he be unless men below live in diverse ways for diverse tasks? Not if your master writes well of this.' (*Paradiso* VIII, 115–20)

A citizen is a member of a structured society that strives to meet the various human needs by a variety of organized activities all tending toward the well-being of the whole. This quotation from *Paradiso* marks Pound's awareness that a respect for the variety of virtuous activity carries over to form the organization of *Paradiso*.

Each sphere of human activity has its own wisdom, its own way of knowing; according to Pound, the nine knowledges that correspond to the nine heavens are "about chih³." In the second treatise of *Convivio*, Dante himself worked out a classification of the various heavens according to nine "sciences." Each of the first seven heavens, he tells us, corresponds to one of the sciences in the *trivium* and the *quadrivium*. He does not spell out the rest, but Étienne Gilson argues for the substance of the eighth and ninth spheres in a way Pound seems to follow (and Pound did exchange letters with Gilson and knew his work). The tenth heaven, the empyrean, the final goal where God and the heavenly host actually dwell, is beyond all our earthly human attempts at knowing, and so no science, no "knowledge," can belong to it. For the eighth and ninth spheres, the ones to which Pound sends Agassiz and Kung, Gilson argues that metaphysics and physics belong to the eighth, and ethics to the ninth (or, in Pound's terminology, natural science—which for Pound is a type of metaphysics grounded in careful observation of natural phenomena—and morals). Each heaven possesses a knowledge about how to regard and act in the world of human affairs and human concerns, and each of these knowledges is "about chih^3"; that is to say, each of these knowledges revolves "about chih^3." There are nine kinds of human knowing that are rooted in the perfect rest of chih^3 and bring us to beatitude. By placing Agassiz and Kung in their appropriate heavens, Pound plays at being the Dante who puts his intellectual and artistic heroes in relation to one another. With this perhaps humorous gesture of judgment, Pound indicates that knowing is somehow crucial to attaining beatitude.

Dante abandons the writing of *Convivio* most likely because he recognized, as Pound did, that he was attributing to human knowing transcendent powers. Later in the canto Pound translates a crucial line from *Paradiso* II—"'Oh you,' as Dante says/ 'in the dinghy astern there'"—that he quoted in an earlier canto and which marks the difference between Dante's conception of knowledge in *Convivio* and *Paradiso:*

> O ye who in a little bark, eager to listen, have followed behind my ship that singing makes her way, turn back to see your shores again; do not put forth on the deep, for, perhaps, losing me, you would be left bewildered. The waters I take were never sailed before. Minerva breathes, Apollo pilots me, and the nine Muses show me the bears. Ye other few that reached out early for angels' bread by which men here live but never come from it satisfied, you may indeed put forth your vessel on the salt depths, holding my furrow before the water turns smooth again. Those glorious ones who crossed the sea to Colchis were not amazed as you shall be, when they saw Jason turned ploughman. (*Paradiso* II, 1–18)

In this passage Dante mentions the "angels' bread" ("pan delli angeli") that opened *Convivio*. But this time he is not promising to give the reader this food that satisifies; rather, "those few that reached out early for" it are encouraged to continue and follow Dante on his journey, now on a journey through waters "never sailed before." Dante promises experience not known to mortality, experience of the divine that will amaze the daring voyagers. As he opens *Paradiso* Dante refers back to *Convivio* through this metaphor of the angels' bread in order to indicate that the way to transcendence is no longer through the discursive language and scrupulous logic of scholastic philosophy; but now the way is risky, a dangerous navigation through unknown waters that daunts the ordinary reader and that requires the utmost daring. As I argued in my first chapter, the navigational metaphor here is meant to connect Dante's successful voyage through the heavens to Ulysses' failed effort to discover new experience described in *Inferno* XXVI. Ulysses' thirst for knowledge and experience is very much like the abstract philosopher's, and Dante distinguishes his own poetic (that is, imaginative) journey to transcendent experience from the philosopher's journey of knowledge. Those who sought the angels' bread of human knowing are now called to follow Dante's "ship that singing makes its way." Discursive logic is abandoned when the voyager reaches the limit at which knowledge stops; beyond that point into the divine presence, only the song of the poet can bring us. This is hardly a denial of the value and worth of knowl-edge, for the heavens are still organized by various ways of know-ing and *Paradiso* contains long dense passages of speculative the-ology; and those who might be able to follow Dante are those who did reach out for angels' bread, who have already tried to gather divine food from their powers of reasoning. But such efforts at knowing do not in themselves suffice for the attainment of the transcendent experience described and claimed in *Paradiso*.

In the canto that might have seemed unreservedly to praise human wisdom, Pound alludes to Dante's own revision of *Convivio* and concludes it with the longest extended use of Dante's *Comme-dia*. With this paradisal passage he remarks that Dante's journey through paradise is not accomplished ultimately by the powers of human knowing but by the impulses set in motion by his love of Beatrice. But Pound does not merely follow Dante; he works to transform Dante's relation to Beatrice into an instance of his own version of the Eleusinian mysteries. For the Dantesque allusions in the passage (of which there are at least eleven) are ruled over by the hidden presence of Persephone, the daughter-goddess who brings the voyager into the presence of the light. The emphasis on human knowledge in the first half of Canto XCIII gives way to the daring sexual journey that catapults the wanderer to beatitude, a journey Pound compares to and measures by Dante's love of Beatrice.

The passage begins on the bottom of page 630 and continues to the end of the canto. Pound begins this lengthy cluster of Dan-tesque allusions with "nuova vita," a reference to Dante's story of his "new life" after meeting, loving, and losing Beatrice, the experience, in fact, that causes him to begin his epic. In this story Dante describes how the love of a mortal woman becomes the bearer of a vision which in turn leads the lover from erotic love to the love of God. *Vita Nuova* ends with "a miraculous vision in which I saw things that made me resolve to say no more about this blessèd one until I would be capable of writing about her in a nobler way. [...] I hope to write of her that which has never been written of any other woman" (*Vita Nuova* XLII). This is the appropriate opening for Pound's passage, for in it the poet works to make his Eleusinian ritual the way to the mysterium beyond knowing. Pound next quotes the opening phrase of *Paradiso* V, *"e ti fiammeggio,"* "if I glow"; Beatrice explains to Dante the source of her splendour: "If I glow on thee with the flame of love beyond all that is seen on earth so that I overcome the power of thine eyes, do not marvel, for it comes from perfect vision, which, as it apprehends, moves towards the apprehended good" (lines 1–6). Already we may observe that Pound is using Dante's relation to Beatrice to distance himself from the overreliance on humanity's rational powers. It is by looking on Beatrice that Dante has a glimpse of the source of all light; the splendour of Beatrice comes from her visionary power, her perfect vision, that allows her to see God and which brings her toward Him. Dante can move toward God only through his love for Beatrice (and not, it can be added considering the canto's earlier concern with "knowing," through rationality and logic). Pound ends this canto with an appreciation of the mystical and intuitive way one reaches the transcendent experience of union with God.

Pound then refers to the opening of his own Canto XCI, "Such light is in sea-caves"; there, the light generated by sexual passion calls forth "your eyes [...] to the surface/ from the deep wherein they were sunken" (610). Sexual passion generates the light that restores the eyes to their former and proper visionary capacity. This image moves immediately into a phrase from the opening of *Paradiso* VIII, *"e la bella Ciprigna,"*—"and the fair Cyprian"; as he enters the sphere of Venus, Dante recalls the "ancient error" believed by "ancient peoples" that Venus "rayed forth mad love." But for Pound it is no error, for the kind of love in Dante's third circle entails great risk in that, while it might bring our eyes back to the surface, it might also lead us to the excess that is madness. Having already associated himself with the third heaven of Paradise, he insists now upon the danger of the journey to blessedness. He then includes a light-filled line of his own, "where copper throws back the flame." That a common object or substance can be made to radiate divine light is a tribute to the visionary capacity of the resurrected eyes. The copper here is most likely meant to suggest pennies and other coins made from this metal; as such, it brings to the passage the poet's earlier (more obsessive) curiosity about the nature of money. A concern for money may seem out of place in such a passage; perhaps we are meant to marvel all the more at the renewed power of the eyes to see holy light, even in an image that once aroused his anger. Perhaps he has overcome the rancor and fury that kept him from a paradisal state of mind; so much is suggested by the next phrase, "from pinned eyes," which is a reference to the punishment/ discipline undertaken by the penitents on the terrace of Purgatory where envy is purged: "to the shades in that place I speak of heaven's light denies its bounty, for an iron wire pierces all their eyelids and stitches them up, as is done to an untamed falcon when it will not be still" (*Purgatorio* XIII, 68–72). Pound includes in his journey the discipline required to restore the eyes to their visionary power. It is worth noting that the "copper throws back the flame from pinned eyes." The poet seems to be suggesting the ritual for the dead in which the eyes of the deceased are "pinned down" by copper coins; the image suggests the power of money to blind us and the effort required to purge the effects of the envy generated by usury. This cluster forms the idea that, in addition to and more than the mind that knows, the eye is crucial to the journey toward beatitude.

Continuing the emphasis on vision, he then quotes from *Paradiso* V, *"alcun vestigo,"* "some trace"; Beatrice explains that "if aught else beguile your love it is nothing but some trace of this [eternal light], ill-understood, that shines through there" (lines 10–12). The "traces,"[6] the clues one finds of God's presence might be "ill-understood" and yet no less compelling as impulses to advance in the journey toward God. One moves toward beatitude perhaps aided by the understanding (after all, knowing that all objects of attraction participate in divine light might help the voyager search for the source of the splendour he sees); but the journey is one of the eye following the traces of God's presence until the voyager arrives in the Court of Heaven where the source of all Light is found. We are surely in a place modelled on Dante's *Paradiso* where knowledge has been subordinated to vision, where knowing might be an aid to vision but the power to see is essential to the attainment of transcendence.[7]

As he continues to define the nature of his paradisal journey, Pound conjures the landscape of the *Commedia:*

and as for the trigger-happy mind
>amid stars
>amid dangers; abysses
going six ways a Sunday,
>>how shall philologers?
A butcher's block for biographers,
>quidity!
>>Have they heard of it?
>>>(XCIII/631)

These lines emphasize the danger inherent in the journey through paradise: losing the trace of God's light in the radiance of any given object, one may lose direction, "going six ways a Sunday." As one proceeds through the spheres, "amid stars," one is also in danger of encountering "abysses," a word perfectly suited to Pound's "modern" sense of things. For the traces of presence that we can find only bring us to impenetrable darknesses, gaps, that daunt most of us; the careful following of traces is a difficult task that requires great courage, especially when one loses the light and finds oneself in an utter gloom. We can use our rational powers to follow the traces of our visionary experiences only so far, only to where an impenetrable darkness separates human knowledge from its divine goal. It is at this point that Pound quotes an odd word from Paradiso XX and XXIV, *"quiditate,"* quiddity, essence. In both cases Dante uses the word in connection with belief through faith: "I see that thou believedst these things because I tell them, but seest not how they can be, so that, though they are believed, they are hidden; thou are like one that knows a thing well by name but cannot perceive the quiddity of it unless some one set it forth" (XX, 88–93); "faith is the substance of things hoped for and the evidence of things not seen; and this I take to be its quiddity" (XXIV, 64–66). Through this strange word Pound manages to allude to the doctrine of faith that can supplement reason so that one can believe what one does not understand, faith that can supplement vision so that one can believe in what one cannot see. Encountering the abysses, one relies on faith; one continues the journey believing in the happy things to come. The next line is the translation of the opening line of *Paradiso* II, "Oh you in the dinghy astern there," in which Dante tells the "few who have reached out early for angels' bread" that they can proceed through paradise only if they hold the furrow of Dante's ship before the water turns smooth again; that is, they can make their way through paradise if they follow Dante's traces and have faith in his guidance. The dangerous journey to blessedness requires a skillful reader who can follow the traces toward presence and a degree of faith in the master of the "ship that singing makes its way"; the knowledge that we can share is limited to bringing us to the abyss separating us from the divine splendour and is supplemented by the poet's love songs that carry us over these awesome gaps.

Pound's version of the opening line from *Paradiso* II makes Dante's navigational metaphor into something entirely "Amurkin"; he captures the urgent note of a sailor's warning in words hardly "as Dante says"; he makes of Dante something wholly his own. He brings the medieval Italian text into the modern American world by means of such transformations, and he continues to indicate that he is using, and not following, Dante by including a line from Guido, "un lume pien' di spirit"—"a light full of spirits." This may sound as if it comes from one of Dante's descriptions of the spirits he meets throughout *Paradiso* but actually comes from "Ballata V" in which Guido praises the light in his lady's eyes that is full of the spirits "d'Amore." As we saw in Canto XXXVI, Guido functions in Pound's text as a "modern" version of the truths that Dante describes in more "orthodox" fashion. The light of the holy that Dante witnesses more clearly and understands more fully than his friend is given its accurate source in eros through this allusion to the more defiant Guido. A few lines further down Pound includes a line—"Blind eyes and shadows"—that seems to come from *Purgatorio* but actually is from an early poem of his own, "Ballatetta":

> The light became her grace and dwelt among
> Blind eyes and shadows that are formed as men;
> Lo, how the light doth melt us into song.
>
> (*Personae* 38)

He recalls his early work to provide Dante's paradise with its honest origins, in the light generated by sexual love. It is a mark of Pound's subtle poetic genius that he can take these lines, from Guido and his younger self, render them Dantesque by placing them in a Dantesque context, and still make them function as revisions of Dante, as crucial moments that highlight what Dante was eager to hide. If this argument of mine is similar to the argument I advanced in my first chapter about Canto XXXVI, it is because Pound's effort once again is to appropriate Dante's world for his own poem. The light of the divine that Dante sees and that Pound wants to claim for his own comes from the light in the eyes of one's beloved.

Sandwiched between these two lines is a passage that clearly brings the Eleusinian mysteries of Canto XLVII to this Dantesque world:

Shall two know the same in their knowing?
    You who dare Persephone's threshold,
    Beloved, do not fall apart in my hands.
E "chi crescerà" they would be individuals,
    Swedenborg said "of societies"

                                        by attraction.
                                        (XCIII/631)

The act of knowing is given its limits and thus once more made to seem an inadequate means for attaining the visionary experience of the heavenly community, in that each individual's knowledge differs from his fellows. Pound again combines the line from *Paradiso* V, where the blessed spirits welcome an additional individual into their community, with the fragment from Swedenborg's theory on the angelic communities, that additional members can only increase their various perfections. In this way the poet wonders about the relation of the individual to the High City, which was a central problem for him when he was approaching Italian Fascism in the 1930s; the claims made on behalf of the state seem to go against his intuitive respect for the rights and powers of the individual. His tender words to his "beloved" serve as a solution of sorts to this problem. "Persephone's threshold" refers to the mysteries depicted obliquely in the pivotal Canto XLVII, where the "beloved" is transformed from daughter (in the sense of substitute) to the mother. The "threshold" is that massively protected border that separates the woman from being the mother, and Pound here expresses the hope that, as he and his beloved cross this boundary, they can continue the journey and reach the ecstatic experience described at the climax of Canto XLVII. Implied in the arrangement of these fragments is that the ecstasy achieved in and through the Eleusinian mysteries, and not ultimately any degree or kind of knowing, brings individuals into the heavenly community described by Dante and Swedenborg; the potentially conflicting demands of the individual and the community are resolved by the common ground achieved by means of the "mysterium." Pound's "anti-intellectualism" (a charge with which I shall soon take issue) does exist to this extent, that he insists that ultimate experience—what I have been calling transcendence—is not achieved by the human capacity to know but by means of certain rituals that bring each initiate to the experience of divine light.

The canto ends as Pound fits Dante's example into relation with the Eleusinian rituals, which are yet again presented in an oblique fashion:

> Without guides, having nothing but courage
> Shall audacity last into fortitude?
>> You are tender as a marshmallow, my Love,
>> I cannot use you as a fulcrum.
>> You have stirred my mind out of dust.
> Flora Castalia, your petals drift thru the air,
> the wind is 1/2 lighted with pollen
>>> diafana,
> e Monna Vanna . . . tu mi fai rimembrar.   (XCIII/632)

The question about fortitude may suggest the arrogant claim that this poet, unlike Dante, has no guide and so reaches beatitude completely on his own, a self-reliance which, in an American tradition shaped largely by Emerson, makes the modern poet greater than his medieval precursor. But the question can also be read to express the need for guidance; only with a guide can the audacity to seek the blessed "last into fortitude." Pound implies as much when he ends the passage with a cryptic set of references to the medieval tradition culminated by Dante. "Monna Vanna" is an endearing diminutive for the beloved of Guido Cavalcanti. In *Vita Nuova* Dante has a dream in which it is explained that Giovanna has been given the name Primavera because she is the precursor ("she will come first") of the lady Beatrice. The last words—"tu mi fai remembrar," "you make me recall"—are from *Purgatorio* XXVIII where, standing in the earthly paradise, Dante addresses Matelda: "You make me recall well where and what Persephone was at the time her mother lost her, and she the spring" (lines 49–51). Both allusions are to women whose importance lies in what they signify, in what they lead one to think of. As Giovanna reminds one of the richer presence of Beatrice who will bring Dante to the empyrean, so Matelda reminds Dante of the daughter goddess of Eleusis who, now in Pound's poem, brings the wanderer to blessedness. The poet deftly fashions a Dante who was secretly a part of an Eleusinian tradition. He places his own journey to the mysterium in a tradition that even the orthodox Dante knew and obliquely included as part of his progress to blessedness.

Pound brings Dante's story about Beatrice's meaning and power into such relation to his own Eleusinian ritual because, in his utter isolation from the world, he needs the support and comfort of Dante's example (even if the example is Pound's own fiction). Pound doubts if he can rely on the girl he embraces in the ritual (who, critics tell us, is usually identified as Sherrie Martinelli) to function "as a fulcrum"; that is, the "tender marshmallow" might not be able to provide the support that prevents the traveller from falling into one of the abysses encountered along the way. By being placed in the Dantesque context of the passage, the young woman is able to bear the larger significance required by Pound's ritual; she acquires greater power by being associated with Dante's story of Beatrice's growing power. She can become the mother goddess and propel the voyager over the abyss separating him from the divine goal. The image of the girl as fulcrum insists on the presence of dangerous gaps along the path to blessedness that the wanderer passes over by means of Eleusis.

In the context of the entire canto, these gaps represent the limits of human knowledge, the darkness into which our rational attempts at knowing can never penetrate. Knowledge is not any less important for the poet now than earlier in *The Cantos,* but he has pressed its power to the limit and leaves the wanderer seeking blessedness at the abyss. At the limits of knowing he turns to the Eleusinian ritual from Canto XLVII to propel him over the yawning darkness and onto the solid ground of supernatural light. The work of Canto XCIII is to place knowledge in its proper subordinate position to the Eleusis in the journey to blessedness, a journey given shape by Dante's progress through paradise.

Canto XCV

Perhaps one of the more recalcitrant problems facing Pound as he tries to "write Paradise" is how to continue writing "a long poem including history" now that he seeks to transcend the very conditions of history. When he turned to write the purely personal dimension of the beatific experience, he must have wondered if he had to abandon his commitment to "history" and so create a radical fissure in the integrity of the poem. A mere glance at *Rock-Drill* and *Thrones* reveals that Pound does not by any means reject history as subject matter for his poem; but it is more difficult to decide whether the historical material is integrated into the fabric of the paradise being attempted, or if earthly history and heavenly beatitude run parallel to one another with no point of meaningful intersection ever occurring.

Pound manages to resolve this difficulty by making the written presentation of human history the means by which one can transcend the human condition. A particular kind of historical knowing brings the wanderer-historian near the apprehension of ideal justice, to which he unites himself through a commitment to action. While in earlier sections of *The Cantos* the claims of the personal life were subordinated to those of the public realm, in *Rock-Drill* and *Thrones* a commitment to public affairs becomes the means to a private end as the facts and details from history become the material by which one seeks beatitude. In this way he is able to maintain the cohesion of his poem continuing the investigation of history with which he came to early in the poem (at the latest in Cantos VIII through IX, when Malatesta's life is made part of the poem).[8] While the role and value of history is revised significantly in these late cantos, he does not suddenly have to exclude it from his poem. What he has done is fashion a radically new mode of presentation, the swift succession of cryptic fragments Bacigalupo calls "atomic facts," a metaphor designed to suggest the highly charged nature of these disjointed details. This extraordinarily swift movement of swirling facts, which is the overriding characteristic of these sequences, is the material used by the historian-wanderer to form a pattern of ideal justice that reaches the stillness of beatitude.

Canto XCV is the clearest example of Pound's attempt to "write paradise." Its goal is to present a carefully chosen and arranged array of historical facts in such a way that the reader is led to a blessed state of mind. The apparent chaos of Canto XCV is in reality a deliberate effort to bridge the distance between the poet and the reader in the figure of the wanderer travelling through a sea of facts drawn from a variety of texts, a wanderer who labors to organize the fragments into the perfect pattern of divine justice. Pound writes a poetry with the loftiest of all ambitions, to bring the reader to the same transcendence that he has been claiming for himself. What we witness in the strenuous poetry of the late cantos are the effects of the mode of historical action taken by this poet as he attempts to bring his long poem to conclusion. Pound's commitment to knowledge and history is hardly abandoned but brought to a climax as he finds the way for words to bring a reader into the presence of the divine.

The opening lines present the appropriate context for the reading of the canto, in images of swiftness, permanence, and order:

LOVE, gone as lightning,
    enduring 5000 years.

Shall the comet cease moving
　　or the great stars be tied in one place!
"Consonantium demonstratrix"
[demonstration of harmonies]　　　　　(XCV/643)

We are still in a universe propelled by and towards Love. The
phrase "gone as lightning, enduring 5000 years" suggests the sudden and brief brilliance of a lightning bolt that, though it departs
from the field of perception in an instant, nevertheless endures as
a shadow in memory. Love flashes for an instant with incredible
swiftness but leaves a permanent trace in the mind of the perceiv-
er. This description of Love's motion is followed by an exclamation
suggesting awe and wonder about the perpetual motions of
heavenly bodies, the even and orderly movements of comets and
constellations that science has discovered. The Latin, taken from
the Venerable Bede, provides a medieval tag for what one ought to
seek in studying science, concrete and verifiable instances of order
at work in the universe, an order governed by Love. We are in a
universe similar to Dante's paradise, where the perfect motion of
the heavenly spheres is both the cause and the result of the perfect stillness of the highest sphere, the empyrean, where God
dwells. The light generated from that sphere flashes through the
various spheres of the physical heavens and eventually reaches
the mind that might perceive traces of it in the physical world.
　　The mind can reach the stillness of the empyrean by contemplating the order that underlies all objects of perception, by discerning and following the perfect motion of details that creates
stillness. Pound suddenly plunges the reader into a sea of historical facts, which constitute the set of details appropriate to the epic
poem's attempt to present divine order:

Mist weighs down the wild thyme plants.
　　"In favour of the whole people". "They repeat"
　　　　said Delcroix
Van Buren unsmearing Talleyrand,
　　　　Adams to Rush before that, in 1811
And there were guilds in Byzantium.
　　"Not political", Dante says, a
　　　　　　"compagnevole animale"
Even if some do coagulate into cities [. . .]
There were many sounds in that oak-wood.
Benton: when there was plenty of metal,
Van Buren already desmearing Talleyrand

J. A. "the whole people (devaluation)."
Alexander paid the debts of his soldiery
    And over an arch in Vicenza, the stemma,
the coat of arms, stone: "Lapo, ghibbeline exile".
    "Who knows but I also from some vento di siepe?"
six centuries later "de gli Uberti".
          Queen of Heaven bring her repose
          [Daughter of Cadmus]
          bringing light *per diafana*
[white Leucothea]
          white foam, a sea-gull
And damn it there were men even in my time
    Nicoletti, Ramperti, Desmond Fitzgerald
      (the one alive in 1919)
That the crystal wave mount to flood surge
                      $chin^4$
                      hu^1
                      $jên^2$
The light there almost solid.   (XCV/643–44)

One hardly needs to point out the dizzying speed with which a fragment of historical detail is presented and then abandoned by the poet, who moves abruptly to another "atomic fact" presented and left just as rapidly; I want to emphasize this speed because it marks the essential difference of these sequences from the rest of the poem and signals the meaning and purpose of the late cantos. We are meant to undertake the strenuous labor of putting all these details together, discovering what they share and making of the fragments a unity. The reader is intended to create the order here and, in so doing, approach the apprehension of ideal justice (in which each fact participates and serves as a dim copy).[9]

Both *Rock-Drill* and *Thrones* in their entirety are composed according to this radically new technique, and in the early cantos of *Rock-Drill* Pound alludes to the medieval tradition of contemplation that explains this innovation. Early in Canto LXXXV Pound includes this line: "Dante, out of St Victor (Richardus)" (546); and two cantos later:

    "Cogitatio, meditatio, contemplatio."
      Wrote Richardus, and Dante read him.
  Centrum circuli.   (LXXXVII/570)

In both cases the reader is led to consider the relation

between Richard of St. Victor and Dante. In fact, Richard is one of the spirits Dante meets in *Paradiso*. In the sphere of the Sun where the wise dwell, Thomas Aquinas (usually considered the philosopher whose thinking informs Dante's poem) notes Richard: "See, flaming beyond, the glowing breath of Isidore, of Bede, and of Richard who in contemplation was more than man" (*Paradiso* X, 130–32). As Pound insists, "Dante read him" and noted the power of his contemplative method to make one "more than man"; that is, to transcend the human condition. There is, then, the possibility for a human, in his knowing, to reach beyond humanity. The knowledge of history that has been Pound's subject for so long is now the kind to be used to "write paradise."

Richard makes the distinction between three kinds of thinking, cogitation, meditation, and contemplation. According to Pound, "In the first the mind flits aimlessly about the object, in the second it circles about it in a methodical manner, in the third it is unified with the object" (*GK* 77). As Pound returns to a serious study of Richard in the 1950s,[10] he decides to write his paradise under Richard's (and thus under Dante's) influence. He presents a variety of significant "facts" with no sense of context or order, and, for these sequences to reach their goal, the reader must agree to work with these fragments as the material for an act of contemplation. Even the most sympathetic reader of *The Cantos*, I imagine, must be bewildered by the lengthy passage quoted above. Not only does the first-time reader have a difficulty in making these notes cohere, he is troubled with understanding the facts presented in Pound's dislocating and cryptic fashion. The mind of the reader, at first, practices "cogitation" as it flits about these facts without discerning any principle of order or sign of pattern. After one understands the references somewhat and can call to the passage the various contexts, perhaps some sense of cohesion may be felt and gradually deepened until the mind now "circles about [them] in a methodical manner." Only after a further dedication to these facts might the mind become unified with the ideal pattern they form. This "unity" is Pound's entry to a Platonic realm of ideas, where justice can be seen and joined. Pound's paradise is the pattern of ideal justice the mind enters through a contemplation of concrete historical facts. By patiently accumulating a sufficient number of particular instances of human attempts to realize justice, one may glimpse the idea of justice they imitate.[11]

Whether or not the reader can actually follow Pound's arrangement of facts and reach something transcendent is not something I wish to decide; my own skepticism about such lofty intentions might only indicate my own failings; it certainly does not invalidate my argument, that *Pound* thought he was actually bringing a handful of his most ambitious and daring readers, those "who reached out early for angels' bread," to the particular brand of beatitude achieved by those who apprehend justice. I wish to offer a brief sketch of what kind of activity and what kind of results are expected by the poet of his reader in this most ambitious enterprise.

If we return to the lengthy passage quoted above, we first note that it begins with a line recording a "lyric sensibility," the state of mind that attends closely to the natural world and notes clearly its beauty: "Mist weighs down the wild thyme plants." Only the most loving attention would notice the subtle effect of the mist on the plants. This line is, I suggest, the governing sensibility: one must feel the "union with nature" achieved by the sexual ritual of Canto XLVII in order to begin this paradisal investigation of history. We must still be grounded in the "home" achieved by the wanderer in the first phase of his journey to participate now in this movement toward paradise. Pound then presents a series of historical "facts," some of which are new to the poem and some called forth from previous cantos. We must first learn that Delcroix was an Italian Fascist (and a poet) who argued that Mussolini was a leader working "in favour of the whole people"; we thus note that Pound has not recapituated his advocacy of Mussolini's efforts, that the political stance adopted with such vigor in the 1930s and 1940s is still part of the poem's particular ideology. We then must learn the significance of Van Buren's reassessment of Talleyrand, whom he "unsmears"; and then wonder if the "facts" about Delcroix and Van Buren are meant to go together to indicate that Pound is willing to revise his previous opinions (as Van Buren did) if the opinions require; but his advocacy of fascism, apparently, does not need revision. The poet then makes an extraordinarily vague reference to a letter of John Adams to Benjamin Rush in 1811 concerning Adams's growing hostility toward banks and their conspiracy against "the whole people" in favor of the few; this is juxtaposed to a detail far removed in time and place from Adams, the mere fact that "there were guilds in Byzantium." Mussolini's work to take charge of the economic machinery of Italy, Van Buren's efforts against the Second Bank of the United States, Adams's hostility toward financial institutions, and the guild system of Byzantium imitated by the Fascists in their "corporations"; these facts drawn from three entirely different historical periods are brought together and begin to form a pattern of the kind of political commitment and action that leads to justice.

The student of this canto will continue to assemble the atomic facts, give them meaning, postulate connections and patterns (that are constantly challenged by the new fact and so always open to revision and expansion), and seek the elusive pattern that is ideal justice. To the cluster already formed Pound adds Benton's understanding of the money problem, Alexander's act of generosity in paying the debts of his soldiers, and an anecdote about another official from the Fascist regime, to the already established pattern; additions that cause the student to revise and extend the patterns he must constantly be finding. It is evident that Pound abandons neither politics in general nor Italian Fascism in particular as appropriate material for the epic. But cultural regeneration through political reform is no longer the goal of Pound's commitment to history; rather, politics is the realm of experience the poet has chosen to contemplate. History is the epic poet's material to be used to write paradise.

I want to skip to the end of the long passage in question, where Pound deploys his wanderer whose journey is now through this sea of texts toward the paradise the poet has described by his previous use of Dante. Pound prays to the "Queen of Heaven" (a name for the Virgin Mother already made part of his thinking about eros and beatitude) for the repose of "the daughter of Cadmus," "white Leucothea." At one stroke he brings to his unique brand of historiography both Dante's journey through heaven and Odysseus's voyage back home. "Daughter of Cadmus" has become Pound's shorthand for "Ino, Kadmos' daughter, slim-legged, lovely, once an earthling girl, now in the seas a nereid, Leukothea" (*Odyssey* V, Fitzgerald's translation). In Homer's story, Odysseus, having finally been freed from Calypso's island, is tossing about in a storm generated by Poseidon's wrath when Leucothea sees him and takes pity on him. She offers him her veil that, she promises, will keep him from harm and bring him to the safety of the nearest shore. He accepts the gift but does not leave the raft until it is broken by the fury of the storm. Odysseus strips himself of the cloak given him by Calypso and wraps Leucothea's veil around his chest, plunging into the water and eventually emerging onto the safety of Phaeacian shore.

We must recall at this point that this episode from the *Odyssey* has already been made a part of Pound's epic, that he used it as the climax of his purgative journey undertaken in *The Pisan Cantos*. He returns to another aspect of the wanderer already established to provide a degree of continuity to the poem, for the wanderer who reached the purity and strength of a

prophetic identity now is plunged into a stormy sea of texts that
has become the poem's subject matter. He turns from Dante's
example (which has been dominant in determining the shape and
purpose of the epic journey thus far in *Rock-Drill*) to this story
from Homer in order to make sure that he does not lose his own
voice and purpose in Dante's example. He calls upon this episode
from *Odyssey* V so forcefully in the last canto of *Rock-Drill* to
stamp the journey as quite his own, as a continuation and revision
of the journey developed up to and through *The Pisan Cantos*.

Canto XCV contains two more references to *Odyssey* V:

> Among all these twerps and Pulitzer sponges
>   no voice for the Constitution,
> No objection to the historic blackout.
>   "My bikini is worth yr / raft". Said Leucothae
> And if I see her not
> No sight is worth the beauty of my thought.
> The immense cowardice of advertised litterati.
>
> (XCV/645–46)

As he gives voice to his paranoid theory that the production of
discourse is tightly controlled by those with power who want to forget the Constitution, as he accuses fellow writers of cowardice and
capitulation, he includes a reference to *Odyssey* V in which Leucothea offers her veil to Odysseus to save him from drowning. It
seems that the voyage to the realm of the ideal is dangerous, in that
the historian might be so roused to anger by what he discovers in
his study that he might lose himself in bitterness and hatred. But
the historian is right to feel strongly and commit himself to a particular set of belief and actions. Pound's study of history is not a neu-
tral description of human action, but a search for particular human
acts tending toward justice; as he discerns the existence of an ideal
justice, the wanderer-historian thirsts for the actualization of the
ideal on earth, a thirst which grows more and more intense with the
deepening awareness that the ideal will never be realized. Leucothea is called on to provide the wanderer with the supernatural
grace needed to overcome the bitterness and hatred afflicting those
who thirst for justice. In Pound's version of the story, the veil she
takes off that saves Odysseus is her bikini; her naked beauty brings
the wanderer through the storm of excessive emotion and brings
him to the safety of sacred ground. The knowledge of history being
presented requires the beauty of the naked sea-nymph to bring the
wanderer to the full apprehension of the ideal.

Canto XCV also contains the longest allusion to the Homeric episode, with which *Rock-Drill* ends:

> That the wave crashed, whirling the raft, then
> Tearing the oar from his hand,
> > > broke mast and yard-arm
> And he was drawn down under wave,
> > The wind tossing,
> Notus, Boreas,
> > > as it were thistle-down.
> Then Leucothea had pity,
> > > "mortal once
> Who now is a sea-god:
> > > [to reach
> the land of the Phaeacians, . . ."]   (XCV/647)

As the very last lines of Rock-Drill, this passage is made to loom large in the overall meaning of the sequence. Having maintained the treacherous voyage through the sea of texts that are subject to tempests of excessive emotion, the wanderer-historian loses his raft to the storm's fury and falls into the water. But the nature of the water has been shifted by means of all the Dantesque images of flowing light; in the long passage quoted earlier we read "That the crystal wave mount to flood surge/ [. . .] The light there almost solid." The wanderer has lost his balanced moderation as he studies history, but such righteous anger is the very quality that brings knowledge of history to the abyss beyond which lies beatitude. It is Pound's commitment to the realm of public affairs which incites his wrath, and this emotion plunges him beyond knowing and into the liquid sea. Leucothea has pity on him, and her beauty brings him to the safety of shore; that is, supernatural powers grant grace to the historian and bring him into the solid light of the great crystal.

It is not anything in knowing that brings us the transcendent experience; rather the thirst for justice that causes intense commitment to politics brings one to the place where one can jump into the sea and find it solid light. Pound's extraordinary desire to see economic justice practiced in earthly human affairs leads him to contemplate history until he can enter the realm of the ideal and become immersed in the divine light of ideal justice.

Thrones de los Cantares

Pound was still in Saint Elizabeth's with no end in sight to his incarceration when *Rock-Drill* was published and work was begun on the next sequence of cantos. There is no demonstrable technical difference between *Thrones* and Rock-Drill; and, since shifts in technique have thus far been signs of important shifts in direction and purpose, it seems safe to conclude that *Thrones* represents no swerve from but rather a continuation of the journey defined and executed in *Rock-Drill*. Pound indicates as much by beginning the new sequence with the episode from *Odyssey* V:

> [Veil]...
> [veil]...
> and the wave concealed her,
> > dark mass of great water.
> > > (XCVI/651)

The veil that rescues the wanderer from destruction and brings him to the safety of the shore opens *Thrones* to suggest that, once the transcendent experience achieved by contemplating history is over, the wanderer-historian decides to continue the program of contemplation and hopes to be able to repeat the experience, again and again. It is important to consider that in *Thrones* the poem approaches the one hundredth canto, which was long anticipated as the finale that, by concluding the epic, would explain all the difficulties encountered along the way; according to Bacigalupo, even as he was working on the late cantos Pound was suggesting that Canto C would be his last (243). The utter lack of ceremony with which this long awaited canto comes and goes can be read as the poet's way to demonstrate that no ending is possible for this kind of historiography; that one can only repeat and repeat the process as long as one lives. To emphasize further that *Thrones* makes no significant advance from *Rock-Drill* but rather represents another attempt to write paradise, Pound also ends the sequence with *Odyssey* V, this time juxtaposed to *Paradiso* II:

> Over wicket gate
> > INO [daughter of] Kadmeia
> Erigena, Anselm,
> > > the fight thru Herbert and Rémusat
> Helios,
> > [of the beautiful ankles] Ino Kadmeia,
> San Domenico, Santa Sabina,
> > > > Sta Maria Trastevere
> > > > > in Cosmedin
> Le chapeau melon de St Pierre
> You in the dinghy (piccioletta) astern there!　　(CIX/774)

As *Thrones* ends, Pound is still drilling away, now presenting mere names as "facts" to be pondered. Certain admired religious thinkers are placed next to several well-crafted churches (in contrast to the "internal horrors" of St. Peters observed in Canto XCIII/623) to form yet a final pattern of right behavior; by communicating "clear thought about holiness," people like Erigena and Anselm begin the process that leads to the construction of beauty. As he presents this final cluster, he calls on the daughter of Cadmus yet again and repeats his translation of the opening of *Paradiso* II. We are voyagers still on a sea of historical detail who, by the grace of the supernatural, might be able to transform the waters into the flowing light in which Dante immerses himself at the upper reaches of paradise.

The allusions to *Paradiso* are far fewer in *Thrones* than in *Rock-Drill*, primarily because Pound does not need to revise significantly the nature and direction of the journey undertaken by his wanderering hero. Nonetheless the poet does include several moments drawn from his private version of the epic tradition that provide a final understanding of his paradise.

First, the choice of title for the sequence indicates that these cantos take shape and meaning from the thrones in Dante's heaven. In the third heaven Cunizza explains to Dante, "Above are mirrors—you call them Thrones—and from them God in judgement shines upon us, so that we think it right to say such things" (*Paradiso* IX, 61–62). According to Pound,

> The thrones in Dante's *Paradiso* are for the spirits of the people who have been responsible for good government. The thrones in *The Cantos* are an attempt to move out from egoism and to establish some definition of order possible or at any rate conceivable on earth. One is held up by the low percentage of reason which seems to operate in human affairs. *Thrones* concerns the states of mind of people responsible for something more than their personal conduct. (Hall 58)

We must be careful to limit the amount of authority we grant to explanations by poets of their own work, but we are safe in saying that Pound was conscious of using Dante's *Paradiso* as a model for his *Thrones* and that the primary concern of the fragmentary and disjointed late cantos is to define an "order possible or at any rate conceivable on earth." This subtle distinction, between the possible and the conceivable, demonstrates Pound's awareness of the crucial shift in his thinking about the nature of history.

Thrones does not celebrate those who made actual a possible earthly order but those whose actions were based on a vision of a conceivable order. The emphasis is on the vision of divine justice that their behavior indicates; they function as mirrors in that the representations made in history of their public actions reflect God's shining judgments; it is through these people that we attain glimpses of the transcendent vision inspiring them. Therefore we investigate history because we can see in these mirrors the original source of their brilliance, a reflection of divine light manifested in human history.

    Thrones includes a cluster of allusions drawn from *Paradiso* XVIII through XX that brings Dante's thrones clearly into the sequence; he carefully chooses fragments from the fifth sphere of Dante's heaven where the spirits of just rulers appear:

> "That Virginia be sovreign," said Andy Jackson
>   "never parted with . . ."
>   Oh GAWD!!! that tenth section . . .
> "any portion of . . . "
>   DAMN IT.
> George Second encouraged,
>   the tariff of 1816 murdered indigo.
>   Freemen do not look upward for bounty.
> Barley, rice, cotton, tax-free
>   with hilaritas.
> Letizia, Dante, Canto 18   a religion
> *Virtù* enters.
>   Buona da sè volontà.
> Lume non è, se non dal sereno
>   stone to stone, as a river descending
> the sound a gemmed light,
>   form is from the lute's neck.
>   (C/715–16)

Pound manages to allude to each of the three cantos of *Paradiso* where divine justice is explained and celebrated. First, several lights containing certain spirits of just rulers appear to Dante:

> I saw a light drawn through the cross at the name of Joshua
> as soon as it was spoken, nor did I note the speech before the
> fact; and at the name of the great Maccabaeus I saw another
> move wheeling, and joy ["*letizia*"] was the whip to the top [. . . .
>] (*Paradiso* XVIII, 37–42)

It is joy, or hilaritas, that drives these men to their acts of justice; it is their joyous participation in the divine vision that makes them able to continue their dedication to earthly affairs where they make manifest the light of God's judgments. The next allusion explains the nature of justice:

> The Primal Will, which is itself good [*Buona da sè volontà*], from itself, the Supreme Good, never was moved; whatever accords with it is in that measure just [....] (*Paradiso* XIX, 86–88)

The measure of justice in any particular act is the degree to which it accords to the Primal Will which always is united to Supreme Good; it is the act of vision revealing the Supreme Good ever willed by God that inspires the ruler to will that good. The ruler acts justly when he succeeds in making his will one with God's. The evidence of this union is the ruler's actions taken to procure a portion of that good. The next allusion, also from *Paradiso* XIX, explains why divine justice is so hard for mortals to see:

> [...] the sight that is granted to your world penetrates within the Eternal Justice as the eye into the sea; for though from the shore it sees the bottom, in the open see it does not, and yet the bottom is there but the depth conceals it. There is no light but that which comes from the clear sky [*"Lume non è, se non dal sereno"*] that is never clouded; else it is darkness, either the shadow of the flesh or its poison. Now is laid well open to thee the hidingplace that concealed from thee the living Justice of which thou hast so often made question. (*Paradiso* XIX, 58–69)

The light of Eternal Justice shines always brightly in God's judgments but either ignorance ("the shadow of the flesh") or sin ("its poison") blocks the sight from our eyes. Because most of us are thus incapable of achieving a vision of living justice, we ought to turn to the thrones, the mirrors that reflect it for our lesser faculties. Those individuals who see Eternal Justice, direct their will toward it, and act upon its dictates in the earthly world of human affairs are the thrones that reflect God's light; this reflected vision is one kind of beatitude. Pound is writing a series of cantos on such individuals to maintain and further his program of writing paradise. The last cryptic allusion in this cluster brings the wanderer to an ecstatic moment of transcendent bliss:

For all those living lights, shining still more brightly, began
songs that slip and fall from my memory. O sweet Love that
mantlest thyself in a smile, how glowing didst thou show in
those flutes that were filled with the breath of holy thoughts!

After the bright and precious jewels with which I saw the
sixth light gemmed had made silence in their angelic chimes
[*the sound a gemmed light*], I seemed to hear the murmur of
a stream that fell limpid from rock to rock, showing the abundance of its mountain sources [*stone to stone, as a river
descending*]; and as the sound takes its form at the neck of
the lute [*form is from the lute's neck*] and the wind at the vent
of the pipe it fills, so, keeping me waiting no longer, that murmur of the Eagle rose up through the neck as if it were hollow. (*Paradiso* XX, 10–27)

The living lights of those who in this life were just rulers sing
sweetly and shine brightly for the pilgrim who experiences divine justice only through them (at least in this part of paradise). Pound uses
this moment from Dante's journey to indicate that his own experience
of transcendence is reached through the mirrors of those whom his
textual investigation has found acting justly. If *Thrones* differs significantly from *Rock-Drill*, it is not in technique but in material, in the
increased attention to actual laws devised to procure a share of justice—Byzantine law, the natural law of Chinese metaphysics in Canto
XCIX, the legal work of Coke—all the laws and lawgivers of *Thrones*
are instances of shining lights and sweet songs that give to the wanderer-historian the transcendent experience of a reflected vision of
divine justice. This cluster of allusions, all drawn from the sphere of of
divine justice, governs the meaning of the entire sequence.

Another allusion to Dante, this one from *Inferno* and included
in *The Cantos* only after the fall of the Fascist State and Pound's
political hopes, is presented and repeated in *Thrones*. While ideal
or divine justice, which is permanent and unchangeable, might
govern the heavenly sphere, earthly human existence is governed
by "Fortuna." *Thrones* contains four distinct allusions to Dante's
conception of Fortuna:

> With eyes pervanche
> > all under the Moon is Fortuna
>
> > > CHEN,
>
> e che permutasse.   (XCVI/656)

All neath the moon, under Fortuna,
        splendor' mondan',
beata gode, hidden as eel in sedge,
        all neath the moon, under Fortuna.
                            (XCVII/676)

Earth under Fortuna,
                each sphere hath its Lord,
with ever-shifting change, sempre biasmata,
        gode.   (XCVII/677)

"Mortal blame has no sound in her ears"   (C/720)

Pound includes various aspects of Dante's Fortuna in *Thrones* to provide an understanding of the nature of earthly affairs of which we are reading the history. Virgil explains to Dante Fortune's role in history:

> [. . .] He ordained for worldly splendours [*"splendor' mondan'"*] a general minister and guide who should in due time change [*"che permutasse"*] vain wealth from race to race and from one to another blood, beyond the prevention of human wits, so that one race rules and another languishes according to her sentence which is hidden like the snake in the grass [*"hideen as eel in sedge"*]. Your wisdom cannot strive with her. She foresees, judges and maintains her kingdom, as the other heavenly powers do theirs. Her changes have no respite. Necessity makes her swift, so fast men come to take their turn. This is she who is so reviled by the very men that should give her praise, laying on her wrongful blame and ill repute. But she is blest and does not hear it. Happy with the other primal ceatures she turns her sphere and rejoices in her bliss [*"beata gode"*]. (*Inferno* VII, 77–96)

For Dante, Fortune is one of the "primal creatures" ordained by God to rule the various spheres; as each sphere of heaven is ruled by its particular power or agent, so earth is "under Fortuna." God establishes for "worldly splendours" a minister who causes swift and unpredictable changes in the distribution of wealth and power among states; earth differs from paradise in this one crucial respect: that it is the sphere in which mutability exists and acts as an essential principle regarding human action. Any attempt to control the economy of wealth is doomed to failure; economic justice on earth is simply not possible because no kind of human intelligence is capable of directing and controlling the machinery toward the just distribution of wealth. By including these references to *Inferno* VII, Pound records his radical revision of his earlier political hopes and views, as he denies the possibility of the establishment of an earthly paradise based on such a just exchange.

Since earthly affairs are "under Fortuna," history consists only of ultimately unsuccessful attempts to make the earthly paradise. But, as we have seen again and again in the late cantos, Pound does not reject human history as a value. For the unsuccessful efforts of select men in history to defy Fortune and establish justice are still the stuff that gives us the reflected vision of God's light. By including the references to Fortune, Pound underscores the fortitude required constantly to overcome the historian's bitter frustration and despair and bravely continue the journey. There is no "end," that is, no final resolution to *The Cantos* because its use of history as raw material out of which one achieves the state of mind that contemplates ideal justice can yield only brief moments of transcendence and never a permanent state of affairs on earth. As *Rock-Drill* ends and *Thrones* begins with the shipwreck of Odysseus, so, Pound implies, all one can do is begin again and repeat the process of contemplation. The wanderer-historian plunges into the sea of historical detail which he then makes into the flowing light of paradise. When the ordered vision of justice is over and the sea becomes mere chaos again, he does not drown but finds himself on the solid ground of Phaeacia, from the safety of which he can begin the process again.

The episode from *Odyssey* V plays a central role in *Thrones* in the only two instances in *The Cantos* where Pound claims to have achieved such ground:

> They still offer sacrifice to that sea-gull
> est deus in nobis
>   [veil]
> She being of Cadmus line,
>   the snow's lace is spread there like sea foam
> But the lot of 'em, Yeats, Possum and Wyndham
>   had no ground beneath 'em.
>
>   Orgae had.
>   Per ragione vale
> Black shawls for Demeter.
> "Eleven literates" wrote Senator Cutting,

"and, I suppose, Dwight L. Morrow."
Black shawls for Demeter.   (XCVIII/685–86)

And after 500 years
                    still offered that shrub to the sea-gull,
Phaecians,
              she being of Cadmus line
The snow's lace washed here as sea-foam

          But the lot of 'em, Yeats, Possum, Old Wyndham
          had no ground to stand on
Black shawls still worn for Demeter
          in Venice,
                    in my time,
                              my young time.
                                        (CII/728)

Pound suggests boldly that only he among his contemporaries has indeed found what the modernists were seeking, a ground on which one can erect a totalizing vision of humanity's relation to history. Both instances of this claim are presented in the context of references to *Odyssey* V and to his own Canto XLVII. Pound refers to the two places in his own poem where he feels he achieved a purity and strength which ground his strenuous effort required for his paradise. The Eleusinian mysteries of Canto XLVII and the purgative experience of the Pisan sequence were presented as successful efforts to achieve a new identity purged of former stains and weaknesses, and it is this purified self that can overcome the frustration and despair attendant to an investigation of history and continue the journey to blessedness. If the wanderer falls into bitterness, he calls upon these "grounding" moments that soothe him and renew the effort. We are now in a position to understand why Pound includes in *Thrones* an allusion to the very end of *Purgatorio*, "New fronds, / novelle piante" (XCVII/675). For after his immersion in Eunöe, the stream that restores memory of all good, Dante feels ready to ascend to heaven: "From the most holy waters I came forth again remade, even as new plants ("piante novelle") renewed with new leaves ("novella fronde"), pure and ready to mount to the stars" (*Purgatorio* XXXIII, 142–45). Pound has grounded his late efforts to write paradise in these two earlier moments that provide him with the purity and strength to continue the treacherous journey. For the late cantos are either chaos or paradise, and the wanderer-historian constantly is falling from a contemplation of ideal forms into the madness of utter chaos. These moments give him "a ground to stand on" so he can continue and repeat his efforts, over and over, until death puts an end to the project.

In short, *Rock-Drill* and *Thrones* bring Pound's "long poem including history" to its climax, to its most ambitious phase. For in these sequences he seems to believe that he has found a way for poetry to include history that brings the poet and his most attentive reader to beatitude. He thinks he may have found a way "to write Paradise."

Conclusion
Palinode and Silence

Released from Saint Elizabeths and living with his daughter back in Italy, Pound writes and adds to *The Cantos* a set of poems whose failure to bring the long epic to a satisfying conclusion is underscored by its title, *Drafts and Fragments of Cantos CX–CXVII*. In these last cantos the poet sings palinode to his earlier political ambitions, reflects upon the success of his effort to "write Paradise," yet asks the reader still to consider the veracity of the visionary experience to which his work with "history" led him, a visionary experience he sets out once again to describe. What I said about the way *Thrones* follows *Rock-Drill* still holds true, there can be no true end to the effort to write paradise except the profound silence of death. I shall argue that the *Drafts and Fragments* do make, if not a conclusion, a fitting end to Pound's life work by bringing the wanderer to such silence.

Before turning to an examination of *Drafts and Fragments*, I want to review the effects created by the persistent presence of Pound's multifaceted and ever-changing wanderer throughout *The Cantos*. What Pound succeeded in doing by means of his wanderer is to provide an elastic framework for the heteroclite material that enters the epic through its four-plus decades of composition. He manages to give to his long and complex poem a certain sense of continuity and integrity by means of the deployment of a multilayered wanderer, by means of the not-so-simple fact that Pound's Odysseus is the consciousness recording the various material. I hope I have shown that this device is not some facile mechanical ploy fashioned in anticipation of criticism that he failed to organize his poem; rather, as I shall now argue in review of my analysis, Pound's wanderer allowed the poet to announce his changing needs and aims while still providing the reader with a sense of continuity. By adding layer upon layer of meaning to this organizing figure, he was able to relate, in precise and meaningful ways, each part of his poem to what had preceded and so continue the same journey, begun in 1917, through all its unexpected detours, to the very end of the poet's life. The figure of Pound's composite wanderer provides the poem with a sense of continuity sufficient to make *The Cantos* a recognizable entity overcoming its centrifugal tendency toward chaos. In fact, the poet makes the achievement of order through this figure the primary goal of his modern epic, as the chaos of the world is given shape and integrity by the poet's heroic "will to order."

The most important goal I have set for my examination of *The Cantos* is to demonstrate that it is a cohesive poem with a subtle but discernible organization, a "plot," if that word does not sound too reductive. Pound made the writing of his epic part of the story itself, in that he set for himself in his opening canto the task of returning humanity to some original experience, the way to which is not yet known but to be discovered in and by the writing of the poem. The dominant theme of wandering, then, began at the very start of the poem, for he committed himself to something that he did not yet know how to achieve; moreover, he did not know what he would find along the way, what the implications of his search would be, and what material might become important to his quest. When he wrote that opening canto, he had no idea that he would become fiercely political in his advocacy of an Italian autocrat; that commitment was unexpected, in retrospect almost seeming inevitable and necessary given the nature of the journey he set upon but really a conjunction of various "accidental" circumstances (those that place him in Italy in the 1920s) and his growing understanding of history with its subsequent strenuous demands on the poem. Like any other human being, he had no idea what lay ahead but wanted to be able to include any possible set of events in his poem and labored to find a device that would allow him to change, revise, expand, and continue the journey of his life as a work of art. Whatever seemed interesting or important along his journey would have to be included *and* made part of the poem, not merely included but integrated into the artifice he was creating: such was his unique ambition as he began his "modern" epic. In fact, one of the chief characteristics making *The Cantos* "modern"—that is, unique and different from the previous attempts in the epic mode—is this radical commitment to the unknown and open-ended; and it is the device of the multilayered wandering hero that permits Pound to embark on his own poetic journey to the unknown while still having clear ties to a great tradition of epic poems. It is this tradition made part of the poem through the composite wanderer that provides the poet with guidance as he makes his own wholly original journey. Part of the final assessment of *The Cantos* must derive from an application of Harold Bloom's thesis, that a great poet works with precursor texts struggling to make his own "modern" version of traditional material unique and supreme. Or, employing T. S. Eliot's terms which assumes a more genial relation of great poet to precursor than Bloom posits, Pound manages to fit his "individual talent" into a "tradition" of his own construction.

But despite the supreme importance he places on order and tradition, no other poet of any age has ever committed himself to as rigorous a representation of the fragmented and chaotic as Pound does in *The Cantos;* no other poet—not even Eliot or Joyce —was as faithful as Pound to the conviction that modern culture is radically unloosed from any tradition that might provide stability and coherence. Pound's devotion to mimesis results in the poem's overwhelmingly anarchic appearance as fragment after fragment is assembled in what seems a frenzy of random selection. Nevertheless, the cardinal virtue of *The Cantos* is order: as we saw, for this poet beauty itself is understood as the the perfect achievement of order in a given material. *The Cantos* is the supreme example of the attempt to mime chaos with the hope that a natural order will arise from the faithfully represented material; of the attempt to imitate with intense and unrelenting devotion the fragmented anarchy of modern reality and, through the sheer force of the poet's directed will, make an order perceptible to a scrupulous reader. Pound's goal in his epic poem exhibits a central modernist hope, that the poet can become the hero who provides the basis of a new order from the material of a world in tatters. We can begin an assessment of modernism with *The Cantos,* as the poem most poignantly revealing the tension between an artist's fidelity to realism and his desperate hope that the poetic imagination can drive its ideals through its material and achieve a satisfying form.

The elastic form of the wandering hero allows Pound to develop his ideas and ideals as the poem unfolds. Most importantly, his understanding of history and its relation to his poetic talent undergo subtle but significant changes. In the four chapters of this study may be isolated four distinct but related attitudes toward history. In fact, we can organize *The Cantos* into its major components by examining the changing ways in which history is understood by the poet as he continues his epic quest for home. It is not too bold to claim that there is a "progressive organization" to *The Cantos* discernible in the major shifts of attitude toward history announced with deliberation and precision through the figure of Pound's wanderer.

In the first chapter, history is regarded chiefly as a zone of activity in which humanity has suffered a decline from an original wholeness and health to its present enervated state, in which humanity finds itself corrupted by a mysterious force called *"usura"* so that the civilization it has built is mean and hostile. This much is implied by the wanderer's decision to sail "outward and away," to move away from the present and before all history in search of some lost home figured as an original consciousness that feels delight and sees the holy operating within the natural order. In the first fifty-one cantos Pound's Odysseus makes a mighty effort to leave the conditions of the present and return to a lost consciousness that constitutes this aspect of "home." It is a private journey of an alienated man seeking vital connection with the universe, something lost in history and regained, it is claimed, in Canto LXVII.

But even in the first fifty-one cantos Pound knew that history cannot be escaped, that the most he can hope for in the centrifugal movement is a return to the point of human origin where history began and can be made to begin again, this time "in the eternally sensible manner" toward a healthy civilization that is home for everyone. In the second chapter we were able to follow, in the same fifty-one cantos, a significantly different attitude toward history than the one implied by the centrifugal movement of the wanderer; as the wanderer was moving "outward and away" on his imaginative journey to human origins, the poet was looking at the records of human activity for examples of people who, rooted in the health of such origins, worked, in history, toward the creation of a new home for all the people, an ideal state that transformed the world into a satisfying home for everyone. Whereas in chapter one we followed the private journey of an alienated wanderer back to a consciousness that feels vital union with the world, in chapter two we watched the poet begin to assemble a series of "heroes" who acted for the public good based on such "unity with nature." The private vision of the wanderer-poet becomes the public goal of political action, as the centrifugal movement away from the present culture, climaxed in Canto XLVII, becomes the centripetal reordering around the poet's vision of an ideal state recorded in Canto XLIX.

It is important to realize that Pound's activities at this time are represented in the poem, as he comes to consider himself the poet of the ideal Fascist state he describes in his prose and poetry written in the thirties. His allegiance to the Italian Fascist State and his devotion to Mussolini are products of his poetic mission, to return the world to a lost but recoverable home. As war approaches he begins to convince himself that he has attained genuine political wisdom through his work in the epic mode and that he has the responsibilty to return to his homeland and advise Roosevelt about the best course of action through the oncoming violence. In the spirit of Confucian sage he returns to America in 1939 to meet the President and the other powerful men running the United States, but he is not recognized by others as he sees himself. He returns to his poem, not forsaking politics but understanding that he is not to have an immediate impact on the course of events called "history." He writes the Chinese History Cantos and the Adams Cantos as an effort to provide for future American leadership a tradition of political wisdom that can be used to return America to its original greatness under the guidance of Jefferson and Adams, an American tradition with roots in Confucian principles. These twenty cantos represent a radical break in technique, as the poet becomes teacher who copies out pages from Chinese history and from John Adams's personal papers; no longer on a dangerous quest for home, he loses his poetic intensity as he sees his task as the recording of documents not yet central in the understanding of American history. The sudden noticeable shift in style signals Pound's assumption of a new role for himself and a new purpose for his poem: no longer the imaginative wanderer searching for a private home and its subsequent traces in human history, he becomes a strident and partisan teacher, and the didactic voice makes for what is usually regarded as the weakest poetry in all of *The Cantos.*

The Fall of the Fascist State, the ignominious death of Mussolini, and his own arrest and internment as an accused traitor bring Pound to the painful acknowledgement that his dream of justice, to be realized by Mussolini, had been utterly destroyed. His hope for the realization in history of the ideal city gone, he makes another adjustment in the course his poem now takes. It is essential to my purposes to note the way in which "external" events have affected the purpose of the "internal" workings of the poem: as the failure of the 1939 trip to America resulted in the didactic style of the Chinese History Cantos and the Adams Cantos, so the failure of Mussolini to create an ideal state caused Pound to work strenuously on the recuperation of his epic ambition. A third phase of *The Cantos* occurs in *The Pisan Cantos* when Pound works to convince the reader, and himself, of his own enormous significance in the course of events known as history. He has not so much changed his evaluation of the value of history, for his goal is still to cause the construction of the ideal state through historical action, even if its realization is now conceived as a far-off distant event; what has changed is the focus of the poem from the world of public events to the private history of the man named Ezra Pound. His purely personal past, his present and unique predicament, even his body are the central focus of this sequence as he struggles to become the prophet of the ideal order, the recorder of a dream still and always possible to be made real in history. The tremendous strain on the man results in the most moving verse of his entire poetic career, as he purges himself of a personal identity and works to become the bearer of a vision vital to the maintenance of hope for the future. The personal mood of this sequence is unique in *The Cantos,* and again such a change in material and technique signals the abrupt shift in the poem's goal. It is still "a long poem including history," but the way history is incorporated into the poem has undergone significant adjustments announced and undertaken by shifts in the composition of Pound's wanderer.

Confined indefinitely to a psychiatric institution as mentally incompetent, the man who sought to attain epic status for his poem and for his understanding of history is forced to reevaluate his role as epic poet. *Rock-Drill* and *Thrones* represent Pound's most radical reassessment of his understanding of history and the goal of his poem, and, following the central thesis of this study, we should regard the accompanying innovation in technique as a certain sign that the poem is undergoing an important change. As he implies in *Drafts and Fragments,* his earlier mistake was in working for earthly political goals—"that I tried to make a paradiso/ terrestre" (Notes for CXVII/802)—and not for the higher goal of beatitude. In these late sections Pound turns to the purely personal goal of reaching a blessed state akin to those described by Dante in *Paradiso;* but unlike the early cantos where the wanderer sought a private return to a happy consciousness by leaving history, the wanderer is, more fully than ever, committed to history in the form of textual fragments now understood as the means to the personal end. Whereas in the first fifty-one cantos the personal is subordinated to the public as the private vision becomes the center for political action, in *Rock-Drill* and *Thrones* the public is subordinated to the private goal as fragments from textual history become the material out of which one reaches the realm of Ideal justice. No longer working primarily for the good of the whole, the poet nonetheless is able to maintain his commitment to historical material as he writes his version of paradise. The goal of the poem has changed drastically in these late sections, but they are successfully integrated into *The Cantos* in that the wanderer is still on a journey through history, travelling through a sea of texts on his way to the realm of ideal justice. Though now the goal is no longer to make an earthly paradise but to "write Paradise," the briefest glance at *Rock-Drill* and *Thrones* demonstrates that they are part of "a long poem including history."

The technique of *Rock-Drill* and *Thrones* fashions the most innovative "package" for "containing history" ever devised by any poet working in the epic mode. The extraordinarily fragmented nature of these late cantos testifies to Pound's absolute devotion to miming the preceived chaos of his world but should not blind us to the poet's continued effort to achieve some sort of order from the chaos. Pound hoped that these cantos would form a design that would provide the reader with a hard-won glimpse of the pattern of ideal justice, a pattern to be fashioned by the reader's disciplined contemplation of the carefully assembled fragments. In no other poetry can we find so clealry embodied the twin impulses of modernism, the movement toward chaos and the vigorous effort demanded of the reader to pull the particulars together into a perfect synthesis. I suggest that these late cantos, if not his greatest achievement, constitute Pound's most important contribution to modern literary art, representing the urgent need for a shared "will to order" of poet and reader in a broken world of fragmented chaos.

In *Drafts and Fragments* Pound evaluates his past ambitions and brings his epic to its conclusion by announcing that his effort to write a modern version of Dante's *Paradiso* has not been wholly successful. He opens the final section with an image that connects *Drafts and Fragments* with *Rock-Drill* and *Thrones:*

> Hast'ou seen boat's wake on sea-wall,
> how crests it? [. . .]
> here the crest runs on wall
> che paion' si al vent' (CX/777)

As we saw in the previous chapter, Pound borrowed Dante's image from *Paradiso* II of a boat's wake to indicate that his reader must be careful to follow the traces the poet leaves behind on the risky way to beatitude. But now the poet asks his reader if he has seen "boat's wake on sea-wall,/ how crests it?"; that is, no longer in the position of poet whose ship "singing makes its way" through heaven, he turns to his reader as an equal asking for any help he may be able to offer the poet. Occupying more than ever a position of importance in the dynamics of the poem, the reader is called upon to find the traces of the wanderer's presence that can make the poem intelligible. The reader, by finding these traces, makes the poem readable. It seems as if the boat's crest is seen, but Pound alludes to a moment from *Inferno* V to describe the sighting that renders his position even more tentative; he compares the sighting of the guiding traces to the movement made by Paolo and Francesca through the murky air of hell: "Poet, I would fain speak with these two that go together and seem so light upon the wind" (lines 73–75). No longer firmly in control and navigating smoothly through treacherous waters, the reader and the poet are lucky if they can find traces of the Dantesque wanderer and, when they do, these traces appear swirling as aimlessly and helplessly as these two lovers through the darkened air. This revision of the image from *Rock-Drill* and *Thrones* suggests that Pound is no longer certain he can hold a steady course through the chaos of history and that he is perhaps flitting about as skittishly as the lovers whose sin was to subject reason to desire.

Here is a curious paradox that lies, I believe, at the heart of *The Cantos* and what is called "high modernism" in general: that the modern poet calls on a tradition even when expressing a profound sense of being lost and overwhelmed by difficulty. When he wants to announce that his wanderer is now aimless and helpless, he refers to Dante's lovers to make the point. No matter how lost, how rootless, how isolated the modern artist feels, in his desperation he still has access to a tradition of great poems for support and solace. For a modern poet like Pound, a tie to tradition is always necessary, even if it is available only to speak of one's despair or failure. After my analysis of *The Cantos* which has revealed the continuous and persistent presence of an epic traditon over which the poem is written, we can conclude that Pound never wavers—even in this late moment of palinode—in his estimation of the central importance of a reliable "tradition" to the life of a culture.

Later in the canto Pound continues to sing palinode to his earlier convictions: "and there is no *chih* and no root" (781). Much was made in the previous chapter about the poet's understanding of this crucial term learned from reading Confucius, the chih[3] which represents a point of rest from which progresses to excellence. Now, the poet clearly asserts, there is no place of rest, no sure ground from which one can act, no steady point from which one can progress toward blessedness. Without this chih³, there can only be movement without order, there can only be chaos. By renouncing this conviction, Pound suggests that the mighty ambitions of the entire poem were resting on an illusory point of rest that never was able to provide the ground from which history could be judged and ordered into a pattern that reaches the stillness. The pattern of ideal justice he hoped would be formed by the accumulation of fragments is not possible if there is no chih³ from which one can begin the work. Without this secure ground to stand on, the hope for a permanent order fashioned from the fragments was ill-judged. Yet the effort is not renounced.

Nor are its results, though they are now severely qualified. In the next canto, whose title—Notes for CXI—underscores the provisional and tentative nature of the last cantos, Pound uses another moment from *Inferno* to describe the degree of validity he can accord the visionary experience set forth throughout the epic, especially in *Rock-Drill* and *Thrones:*

> Cold mermaid up from black water—
> Night against sea-cliffs
> the low reef of coral—
> And the sand grey against undertow
> as Geryon—lured there—but in splendour,
> Veritas, by anthesis, from the sea depth
> *come burchiello in su la riva*
> (Notes for CXI/783)

The image describing the visionary experience—the "cold mermaid" rising "up from black water"—presents a mythical creature of beauty surfacing from darkness, suggesting that the fragmentary moment of vision is won in the midst of, and despite, a dense night of emptiness. This experience is rather unexpectedly placed in the context of *Inferno* XVII, where Virgil summons Geryon to assist his and Dante's descent to the lowest depths of hell where the various kinds of fraudulent sinners are punished. The line in Italian, italicized by Pound to emphasize the allusion, is a conflation of two lines from this canto of *Inferno* which describes how Geryon lies on the shore defining the edge of the pit from which Dante and Virgil wish to move. Only the head and chest of Geryon can be seen, for he "did not draw his tail *on to the bank"*—*"in su la riva"* (line 9); Geryon's position is *"as boats* which sometime lie at the shore, part in water and part on land"—*"Come* tal volta stanna a riva i *burchi,* che parte sono acqua e parte in terra" (lines 19–20). Pound conflates these two lines so he can describe Geryon fully yet still include the reference to boats, keeping the navigational metaphor of the wanderer prominent in his own poem. He manages to suggest that his vision of the "cold mermaid" resembles Geryon, whose gracious and just face attached to a vile serpent body is Dante's image of fraud. Pound's visionary experience, then, may be as fraudulent and misleading as Geryon, who seems just and lovely at top but is corrupt and horrible beneath. The mermaid is the proper mythical creature at this point in the poem for she is beautiful and seductive from the waist up but cold and scaly below, unable to fulfill the desire she arouses in a human observer. One is tempted to conclude here that Pound renounces the truth of his moments of vision, except that he does use a strong Latin term—"Veritas"—to describe the mermaid's significance, and he notes that Geryon, lured by Virgil's call (and so under a poet's mastery) appears "in splendour." Truth comes "by anthesis"; that is, it blossoms into its splendour from the unlikeliest origins and has a beauty that belies those origins. Pound seems to suggest here that, though the moments of vision that he has been able to sketch might spring from some fairly vile sources (his persistent endorsement of the Axis powers, for instance), they still possess the quality of eternal truth. His errors and wrecks, we may say, have, by the poet's power, blossomed into fragmentary moments of absolute truth out of the most unpromising soil. The order achieved is now carefully qualified and itself only a fragmentary and momentary appearance; but it nonetheless possesses the crucial quality, "veritas."

Pound seems to be admitting that his earlier arrogant claim to a masterful understanding of human behavior has been fraudulent but that the visionary experience of ideal justice to which it led still has the quality of eternal truth. He ends Canto CXIII with a series of fragments suggesting that the effort to reach the stillness of sphere of ideal justice may have failed but should not be surrendered:

> And for a little magnanimity somewhere,
> And to know the share from the charge
>   (scala altrui)
> God's eye art 'ou, do not surrender perception.
>
> And in thy mind beauty, O Artemis
>   Daphne afoot in vain speed.
> When the Syrian onyx is broken.
>   Out of dark, thou, Father Helios, leadest,
> but the mind as Ixion, unstill, ever turning.
>   (CXIII/790)

Pound still sees fit to hammer away his economic principles—in this case, that a significant distinction must be maintained between a share and a charge; such persistence is an example of "a little magnanimity" in that he has the strength and
largeness of character to stand by and repeat unpopular and discredited opinions and still offer such as wisdom to an unreceptive
audience. Such persistence has brought him to utter isolation, in
fact a state of exile so profound that only Cacciaguida's words to
Dante in the course of *Paradiso* XVII can describe:

> Thou shalt leave everything loved most dearly, and this is the
> shaft which the bow of exile shoots first. Thou shalt prove
> how salt is the taste of another man's bread and how hard is
> the way up and down *another man's stairs* ("altrui scale").
> And that which shall weigh heaviest on thy shoulders is the
> wicked and senseless company with which thou shalt fall into
> that valley, which shall become wholly ungrateful, quite mad
> and furious against thee [. . .]. Of their brutish folly their
> doings shall give proof, so that it shall be to thine honour to
> have made a party by thyself. (lines 55–69)

His insistence on certain matters of historical judgment have
indeed brought Pound to the position described so movingly by
Dante's ancestor: separated from all things beloved, the poet has
lived, and is still living (though now in his daughter's castle), the
painful life of an exile who has "made a party of himself." The
intelligence of his own perceptions, which is one of God's ways of
making the divine manifest in the human order, shall not be surrendered even if they have not led to any happy result in the poet's
life. He makes a break in the lines at this point, as if a new
thought has occurred to him at this juncture. For he turns to
female beauty, in the persons of the chaste Artemis and the
beloved Daphne, as a source of consolation for the loneliness he
has suffered in exile, working on his own and in his own unique
way, for the realization of ideal justice. He repeats a line he wrote
over forty years earlier in *Homage to Sextus Propertius*—"When
the Syrian onyx is broken"—which referred to the wish of that
poem's narrator that his beloved kiss his lips mournfully when he
is dead. As an old man (he is seventy-eight when the last cantos
are published), Pound returns to one of his most successful early
poems, one written before *The Cantos* is undertaken, as a gesture
of hope that he can be consoled by those who love him despite the
maddening chaos to which his epic has brought him. For the last

two lines speak of the failure of *The Cantos* to bring him to the
stillness that the late sections of the poem aimed at. While the god
of the sun can lead him to glimpses of the light, the old sun-god,
Ixion—the one deposed by Helios—is the one with whom Pound
feels his own quest has made him associate; for his mind, like
Ixion's, is "unstill, ever turning." The work of *Rock-Drill* and
Thrones did not bring the poet to any still point achieved by the
perfect ordering of a multitude of historical facts; indeed, the poet
admits that his mind never could reach that moment of stillness to
which the the accumulation of historical texts was meant to bring
him, even if momentarily. The late sections are now seen as "Error
of chaos" (788), "flowing, ever unstill" (787); that is, no pattern of
ideal justice was ever reached and maintained in any way that
would allow the poet to claim at his conclusion the achievement of
a blessed state. Like Ixion's, his mind is "unstill, ever turning" as
it seeks the peace that passes understanding. The centrifugal
energy of the fragments reaching outward toward chaos is too
much even for this poet's strong "will to order" to tame and fashion
into a final harmony reaching absolute stillness.

    Canto CXVI contains some of Pound's most important reflec-
tions on the nature of the poem he has been writing for almost
fifty years. He acknowledges that he was not able to make *The
Cantos* "cohere":

> "Have made a mass of laws"
>   (mucchio di leggi)
> Litterae nihil sanantes
>   Justinian's,
> a tangle of works unfinished.
>
> I have brought the great ball of crystal;
>   who can lift it?
> Can you enter the great acorn of light?
>   But the beauty is not the madness
> Tho' my errors and wrecks lie about me.
> And I am not a demigod,
> I cannot make it cohere.   (CXVI/795–96)

    Pound compares his effort in the late sections to Justinian's,
in that both attempt to reduce a tremendous amount of textual
material to its essential minimum, making the past useable for the
present. But the result has been "a tangle of works unfinished"; the
literature resulting from the attempt has not achieved a unity that

reveals a principle of coherence for the material accumulated and so has not been able to cure anything ("Littcrac nihil sanantes"). But the two questions that follow seem to imply a certain degree of success on the poet's part; after all, he has "brought the great ball of crystal" to us, even if we cannot enter it. It seems consistent with Pound in these last cantos to admit failure yet still claim a measure of success in his effort, a success usually associated with the presentation of a visionary substance even if it is not final and clear. After all, whose fault is it if we cannot "enter the great acorn of light," ours or the poet's? We cannot lift the ball of crystal he has shown us, nor enter the light he has presented, most probably because the poem has not achieved a lucidity and order that would allow the reader to follow the poet's trail to a full and lasting conclusion. But he has seen what he has seen (to recall Acoetes' words from Canto II), and these moments of qualified failure seem only to reinforce the poet's claim to vision; though he may not have been successful in presenting a permanent order arranging the vast array of material that could with certainty bring the reader to a lasting beatitude, he insists on the validity of his own visionary experience of which he has offered glimpses to the faithful reader. He implies that though the poem has taken on the appearance of "madness" (that is, absolute chaos), he has also achieved a "beauty" (i. c., an order) not to be denied; though his errors and wrecks lie about him, a vision of beauty has nonetheless been sketched for others to share. He realizes his limitations; he has not been able to make all the material cohere; he has not been able to bring the reader to a final, secure, and permanent vision of ideal justice that should have concluded the poem. But we should take some measure of satisfaction in the implied success of the poet regarding the veracity of such visionary experience and the momentary glimpses we have gleaned through his mighty efforts.

Later in the same canto, Pound insists again that he has indeed seen and been to the realm of ideal justice, and he insists on the validity of his vision even if he has not been able to make the reader a full participant in it:

> again is all "paradiso"
>   a nice quiet paradise
>   over the shambles,
>   and some climbing
>   before take-off,
>   to "see again,
>   "the verb is "see," not "walk on"

                    i. e. it coheres all right
                                even if my notes do not cohere. [. . .]
                    And as to who will copy this palimpsest?
                                                (CXVI/796–797)

Pound insists that he has achieved a state of blessedness similar to Dante's, but his "nice quiet paradiso" has been constructed
gingerly "over the shambles" of the poem; again, the poem is
assessed as a chaotic failure that nonetheless has created something lasting and valid in its fragments of vision. The poet then
offers a clear distinction between the twin aims of the poem, the
early mistake that poetry could lead to the construction of an
earthly paradise "to walk on" and the later understanding that
poetry can provide glimpses of a paradisal state only to be "seen."
Poetry does not make anything happen in the "real" world of political action but can testify and sketch a world of eternal beauty,
even if the poem does not achieve the coherence needed for true
success. He refers to his poem as "notes," a "palimpsest," and earlier in the canto as a "record"; each image emphasizes the written
and provisional nature of the poem, a series of fragments without
coherence that nonetheless have somehow offered glimpses of the
eternal realm of absolute justice. "Palimpsest" is the most provoca-
tive metaphor offered as assessment of *The Cantos,* for it suggests
that Pound's poem is written over the partially erased words of
previous texts that still may be read through the words Pound has
written; the "notes" Pound writes give rise to sudden fragments of
visionary splendour (and the canto ends with "a rushlight/ to lead
back to splendour") because these partial notes provide the outline
of a modern journey that reaches out toward the realm of the absolute over the still perceptible marks of an epic tradition.

One of the fragments included in "Notes for CXVII et seq."
offers another statement renouncing earlier ambitions. Pound recognizes that, despite all his efforts, he was unable to reconcile the
demands of the personal and the public as their various claims
clashed and led to disaster for the poem and the poet:

                    M'amour, m'amour
                                what do I love and
                                        where are you?
                    That I lost my center
                                fighting the world.
                    The dreams clash
                                and are shattered—

and that I tried to make a paradiso
terrestre.
(Notes for CXVII/802)

This fragment emphasizes the poet's sense of himself as lost, as finally separate from the objects of love he sought for so long to become united with. He blames his final alienation on his vigorous effort to "make a paradiso terrestre," on the extraordinary ambition to fight the present order in the hope of establishing an earthly paradise. The work for the construction of an ideal state in the public realm clashes with the personal effort to become united with the sphere of ideal justice. The work on earth for a just state leads one to excesses figured here as "losing one's center"; the private journey toward beatitude might require an equanimity not compatible with the violent passion incited by the work in the political sphere for earthly justice.

Pound renounces the effort dominant through the first eighty-four cantos, even through *The Pisan Cantos* which are designed to recuperate the project of prophesying and working for an ideal state, the effort of making the poet's vision the center of political action aiming at the construction of a "paradiso terrestre." A clearer statement of palinode than this could not be made, that the effort to make the earthly paradise led to the shattering of the poet's dreams. If the poem has become questionable in its conclusion, it is because of the poet's mistaken belief that poetry could change the world and facilitate the coming of the millenium. As far as his poetry was concerned, it would have been better if he had not worked so vigorously for the Axis powers and made that commitment so important to his epic. The effort of the later cantos, to become one with the sphere of ideal justice through the close examination of textual history, is the one ambition to which *The Cantos* may claim some measure of success, even if the visionary experience sketched in Rock-Drill and *Thrones* can only take shape from an impassioned accumulation of partisan facts. The poet "lost his center" when he thought fit to oppose the present order in the political arena, and should never have tried to "make a paradiso terrestre." The proper verb, we now know, is "see."

The canto that used to end the poem, formerly numbered Canto CXX and now part of Notes for CXVII et seq., provides the fitting end to this study, as it brings the movement of the poem to the profound silence where all activity has been forsaken and one can only passively listen for paradise:

I have tried to write Paradise

Do not move
   Let the wind speak
      that is paradise.

Let the Gods forgive what I
     have made
Let those I love try to forgive
     what I have made.   (Notes for CXVII/803)

Since he cannot achieve a lasting stillness by the perfect
ordering of the whirling material, he calls for a different kind of
stillness, that of an absolute lack of motion, a surrendering of
effort. The wanderer's movement that became so dizzying in the
later cantos comes to a full stop, as the poet calls for the reader to
join in his utter stillness: "Do not move." No more hurried activity
of presenting fragment upon fragment of historical data to be
pieced together, like some monstrous jigsaw puzzle, into an order
that brings the reader to stillness of beatitude. No more frenzy but
instead an absolute surrender of motion and activity and, in their
place, an acceptance of a passive role where one listens to the
wind's voice speaking of paradise. The effort "to write Paradise" is
acknowledged by the poet to have failed, and he calls for stillness
and silence, and asks for forgiveness for writing his chaotic poem,
as the wanderer's movement finally comes to an end. Not a conclusion that brings the poem's pieces into a coherent pattern, but an
abrupt and final halt.

When we ask whether *The Cantos* achieves success or not, it
is to *Drafts and Fragments* that we should first look for an answer.
For Pound sees fit to make such an evaluation of his life's work the
subject of the last section of his epic, primarily because the writing of the poem has become the dominant subject of this epic.
Pound's response to the question of the success of *The Cantos* is
that he has failed to make all the material cohere in a pattern that
explains the Western world in a satisfying way. It seems rather
obvious, but worth saying anyway, that no one else has been able
to do so much in a poem, and Pound's failure stems from the
extraordinary nature of his ambition to include all relevant material from the past and present of Western culture and discover the
principle that unifies all the accumulated data into perfect order.

We do not need to rehearse the testimony of late interviews
in which Pound calls his life's work "a botch," "a hodge podge," and

"a mess." He said as much, and more precisely, in *Drafts and Fragments* anyway. We are not required to take Pound's verdict as the most authoritative concerning the success or failure of *The Cantos*, especially considering the state of depression into which he sunk in the last years, where the deep and total silence called for in the last lines of the poem is reflected in the man's life. The evaluation offered in *Drafts and Fragments* seems, however, quite perceptive and fair. He recognizes that he never could find a way for the personal experience of beatitude to be made available for the public through political activity. Perhaps what we learn from a reading of *The Cantos* is the danger of applying the testimony of poets regarding the personal states of ecstasy and blessedness to the world of politics, for such application seems to lend itself to totalitarian brutality. Perhaps the poet's personal vision of the good and beautiful can become the center of a political regime only through, or at least most easily through, violence and oppression.

A reader of *The Cantos* must recognize that Pound's experimental epic begins with expectations that he later renounces when his efforts to realize his ambitions meet the resistance of political realities. He began his epic with the impassioned hope of creating a "paradiso terrestre"; in his opinion, no other poet in the western literary tradition except Dante ever believed in and sought to realize the powers of poetry to affect the external world as Pound does through most of *The Cantos*. From a poet deeply committed to politics and history comes the lesson that poetry can ultimately only affect the private consciousness of the individual reader; that even when the poetry is about history (as *Rock-Drill* and *Thrones* still are), the the real effects of poetry are only to be imprinted on the sensibility of a sympathetic reader. While it always "contains history," *The Cantos* is finally a private poem about personal transcendence addressed to those few whose thrist for justice will impel them to follow the poet's eccentric journey.

Pound suggests that his poem achieves its most lasting value in its late effort to erect a paradise by reading history. In subordinating the claims of the public to purely personal ends, Pound is able to use history in a radically innovative way for the same goal as Dante, the presentation of the state of beatitude. Pound regards the poetry of *Rock-Drill* and *Thrones* as only a qualified success that is nonetheless his most important achievement; even if his poem only wrote the "notes" for paradise, glimpses of the vision are sketched "above the shambles." Only Dante before him ever realized the ambition to present through poetry (that is, through words carefully chosen and arranged on paper) what it is to transcend the human condition.

We are, of course, free to evaluate the poem on different terms than the ones Pound provides, but only after following the poem to its end and realizing that evaluation of the poem is the poem's ending. I want to suggest that my reading of the wanderer motif throughout *The Cantos* has placed us in a better position to assess whether the poem does achieve a kind of unity, at least a clear sense of continuity and integration of material. For my reading of this motif allows us to follow the poem's changing intentions and new demands sequence by sequence, and allows us to account for the major changes in technique Pound sees fit to make. My assessment of the poem emphasizes Pound's achievement in attempting an epic poem in the modern age, in trying to find a way to "include history" when all the things that go into the meaning of that term have become so diverse and numerous. The effort to find a way to make any relevant fact a part of this work of art is an enormous challenge, and one he was able to undertake only after the development and deployment of the wanderer. Pound exhausts various stances one can take toward history in a poem—as a nightmare to escape, as a set of events needing the poet's vision as guiding principle, as raw material for the construction of an ideal realm of absolute justice. Other stances might well exist, but Pound succeeds in trying out for the epic poem what has traditionally been its attitudes toward history and finds them all inadequate to the age's demands. Perhaps we can begin to assess Pound's epic achievement by testing the thesis that he has brought the epic mode to the modern world and found it unable to provide a satisfying principle of organization for the heteroclite materials of the modern mind.

For the advances in the modern age, with its extraordinarily powerful technologies of production and communication, have made the containment of all relevant history a task beyond any poet's powers. There is simply too much material available for a modern epic to contain: not only too many records of the past now readily accessible, but too many images from the present disseminated through the agency of modern mass media. According to Pound in the 1962 interview with Donald Hall, the epic poet must now fight against what he calls "the propaganda of terror and the propaganda of luxury" (Hall 52) whose images now control the modern mind. Pound had tried to bring the poet's voice to the radio during the Second World War only to lose his lyric sensibility as he devolved into a bitter, mean-spirited, and embarassingly reductive crank. The poet, it seems, must confine himself to his proper space, pieces of blank paper to be filled in with precious language in elegant arrangement; such limitation puts the poet at serious disadvantage in combatting the "propaganda of terror and luxury" dominating the west in the post-War years. When he returns to the task of including history in *Rock-Drill* and *Thrones,* he manages to include more historical references than in any other part of the poem; the sheer prolifertaion of detail in the late cantos testifies to his acute awareness of the epic poet's need to fight against the images of the mass media. But these cantos, for all their accumulated facts, only leave the reader with the impression of partiality. The more he includes, it seems, the more we become aware of the amount of material left out. And how can words in obscure books ever compete with images disseminated through the mass media? The epic poet's ambition to provide order to his culture is dashed by these media whose domination in the public mind can hardly be challenged by highbrow and allusive poetry. We begin to see the impossibility of realizing the epic ambition in the modern world and begin to conclude that the epic, at least as Pound envisioned it, may no longer be a genre available to our poets.

In fact, Pound's highly ambitious but ultimately failed epic may indicate that the two contemporary literary artists most like him in ambition and in devotion to Dante, namely T. S. Eliot and James Joyce, undertook more successful adaptations of this genre to the conditions of the modern world. For neither of them took as their obligation the mastery of the historical and political worlds by their poetic packages. Instead, both understood the private nature of their communication and made the epic a genre describing personal modes of heroic fulfillment. In *Four Quartets,* Eliot sees history as a "pattern of timeless moments" (*Little Gidding* V), which is a radical denial of the usual definitions of history as events in the public sphere of communal interests; for this poet, history is design made by a series of special moments of heightened sensibility ultimately understood as moments of "Incarnation" (*The Dry Salvages* V) where the divine enters the human world. The images Eliot uses to suggest these moments are drawn from the inner world of the private imagination, never from the world of public events. (Images such as "winter lightning" and "wild strawberries" are purely lyric and personal in implication and make no reference whatsoever to politics or public events.) Even when he walks along the streets of London after an air-raid, the historical scene dissolves into a visionary encounter with a dead master in which the speaker hears lessons about the liberating fires of purgation. While Pound in the late cantos also seeks a perfect pattern of discrete moments that can give rise to the experience of beatitude, his particulars are overwhelmingly historical in nature. Eliot never undertook the effort to master the historical and so *Four Quartets* is more readily perceived as an integrated and successful depiction of personal transcendence made available to an elite readership.

In *Ulysses* Joyce also refrains from confronting the world of history as something for his epic to master, though in *Finnegans Wake* he does turn to the public world of myths and legends and history for his material. Leopold Bloom is elevated to epic status as an heroic example for the modern world not for any action taken in the world of public events. He is, as the commonplaces of Joyce criticism have it, an obscure man in a large city exerting no effect on the general paralysis of Dublin, with the significant exception of his genial influence upon Molly, Milly, and Stephen. It is the story of a man who brings to those in his family (and Stephen, as we all now know, is a possible substitute for the deceased Rudy) a sense of freedom and kindness. His heroic achievement is almost hidden in the catechism of "Ithaca": he is so far above the petty emotions of possessiveness and jealousy that he is able to brush the crumbs of Plumtrees' potted meat left in bed by Blazes and Molly earlier in the day, lie down next to his adulterous wife, engage in friendly conversation, kiss her good night in his usual manner, and fall asleep. He rises above the expected responses and allows his wife the freedom to live her life as she sees fit, a magnanimty for which Joyce rewards him by ending Molly's monologue not with images of Boylan drawn from that very day but of Poldy on Howth sixteen years earlier. Having done nothing at all to dominate his wife, he nonetheless has emerged as the most tender and important figure in her life. Bloom's "apathy of the stars"—a sublime indifference to the usual assortment of petty emotions—is the highest ideal for human behavior. This is transcendence in Joyce's secular world, and it has nothing whatever directly to do with politics or history.

This brief glance at his closest contemporaries highlights the central decisions made by Pound not to deny the effect of history on the individual and to find a way for poetry to change those effects. Even in the late cantos when his goal becomes more like Eliot's and Joyce's in their epic efforts, Pound's way to personal transcendence is still the world of history. That is Pound's contribution to the epic poem, to bring the "heteroclite materials of the modern mind" into poetry and allow these diverse and multifarious elements free play and equal privileges. Only Pound of these three high modernists considers the epic essentially a poem containing history, and the attempt for a work of art to contain history in a totalizing manner is the unifying principle of the poem. And the various attitudes toward history exhibited by Pound throughout the long life of the poem, the different ways of confronting and including the world of public events, are always announced and enacted by the poet in the figure of the wanderer he has created.

The main objective of this study, then, has been to initiate a reassessment of *The Cantos,* not as a ragbag randomly stuffed with any material the poet found handy, but as an organized poem with a significant degree of continuity and integrity provided by the figure of Pound's multifaceted wanderer. I do not pretend that *The Cantos* can be reduced only to those moments in which the wandering hero does appear, nor that this figure magically explains all the diversity of material that does get into the poem in its long life. What I hope is that this analysis can provide the student of this poem with a sense of its loose and complex structure so that *The Cantos* can be treated as a single entity straining to achieve order and unity. Despite the appearance of a chaotic swirl of charged and interesting fragments from a great poet's mind, *The Cantos* may be seen as an epic project approaching integrity only if Pound's innovative structural device, his ever-changing composite wanderer, is recognized and applied to future studies. In other words, we must be able to recognize in the poem both its centrifugal tendency toward anarchy resulting from the poet's scrupulous representation of history and his centripetal efforts to bring order to his epic and his culture through the presence of his multifaceted wanderer. If my study can refute the most hostile charges levelled against *The Cantos,* namely that it is ultimately an unintelligible jig-saw puzzle or a haphazard assortment of occasionally beautiful fragments, Pound's epic may brought to the center of modernist studies as the most ambitious effort by a poet to discover poetry's power and role in the world we call modern.

Notes

Introduction

1. "High modernism" is a term that has come to be applied to the thinking and work of certain artists of the early twentieth century, any listing of which always features in prominence the names Pound, Joyce, and Eliot. It is no mere coincidence that these three writers, who do so much to determine the artistic sensibility of the modern period, each claim Dante as their most important and lasting literary influence. For in Dante they find expression of their own most basic and urgent need, the need to give unity to a world in fragments. For Dante inherits several traditions that he hopes to synthesize: a Christian tradition of dogma and philosophy; a classical (or pagan) tradition of artistic masterworks (most prominent of which is the *Aeneid*); and the troubadour tradition of erotic love songs (to name three of the most important such traditions). So the "high" in "high modernism" may indicate the great reach, the ambition, manifested in the modernists who follow Dante.

The adjective "high" also serves to suggest the search for the holy or the sacred in these modernists, and this also leads us back to their devotion to Dante. The fragmented world they mime in their art is to be placed in relation to an elusive supernatural order. Like Dante, the "high modernists" are interested in the sacramental function of their art, its power to render certain aspects of our experience holy. These moments out of time are used to measure the temporal order. As Dante grounds his comprehensive judgment of his world in a vision of the eternal God at the center of the holy City, so Pound, Joyce, and Eliot all seek to find such a point of stability from which the apparent anarchy of the "real" world is given satisfying shape and order.

2. While many critics consider Pound's relation to Dante in the course of their own project, only James J. Wilhelm in *Pound and Dante: The Epic of Judgment* has made Pound's study of Dante the explicit and primary focus. Wilhelm's book begins promisingly: "What kind of man purports to have the design by which he can put all things into order or at least into some coherent perspective?" (1). But this question already indicates the shortcoming of the study: he wishes to consider the "kind of man" who undertakes the "epic of judgement" instead of the workings of

those epics; Wilhelm indulges in speculation about the characters of the poets instead of investigating the search for "the design" that can order a complex world. The first half of the book is mainly biographical, noting similar details in the two poets' lives and personalities that are often conjectural and seldom helpful in explaining the nature of their poetry.

When in the second half of the book Wilhelm does begin to consider the poetry, he does not advance a rigorous or consistent thesis that aspires to explain how *The Cantos* responds to the *Commedia*. In fact, he comes to a conclusion that baldly rejects such a response: "Pound uses the Italian master almost the way a painter uses his colors: for emphasis and dramatic effect" (113). But, it is implied, Pound does not turn to Dante for structure, organization, or material. Wilhelm's study is the basis of Reed Way Dasenbrock's neat statement: "Dante and his works are continously relevant in The Cantos but not in any continuous way" (*Paideuma*, Winter 1980, 504). I shall argue that the use Pound makes of his chosen precursor is a coherent and continuous reading that aims at "modernizing" the medieval "epic of judgment."

3. Giuseppe Mazzotta argues that Dante's Ulysses is a traveller after origins: "His model is the sun: to go left is to return to the point of origin. . . . As he goes leftward, Ulysses follows the motion by which the universe returns to its point of origin" (101–02). Dante measures his journey to origins (Eden) by showing his taking a radically different path: instead of journeying beyond the Pillars, he approaches and reaches the island of Purgatory by descending to hell and then going through the bowels of the earth to the other side of the globe.

I should like here to acknowledge my debt to Mazzotta's reading of Dante: while he is certainly not the first to study Dante's use and theory of history, he demonstrates that Dante comes to his position by reading other texts and including them in the poem. My own reading of *The Cantos* is inspired and shaped by Mazzotta's study insofar as I follow Pound's reading and inclusion of other epic texts in his own epic.

4. In his chapter on Pound in his study *Dante and English Poetry*, Steve Ellis claims, "Pound secularizes the *Commedia* and . . . models his own epic journey upon it toward a non-transcendent light" (190). But Pound's early reading of *Paradiso* focuses mainly on images that describe a supernatural and transcendent light; for example, "the vigor of sunlight in the *Paradiso* is unmatched in art, even by Blake's design" (*SR* 150). One of the complexities of Pound's poem is its religious sensibility, its witnessing of a light whose meaning and nature is constantly explored and developed.

5. Dante's journey through paradise opens with the central belief of Neoplatonic light metaphysics: "The Glory of Him who moves all penetrates through the universe, and shines in one part more and in another part less" (*Paradiso* I, 1–3). As Joseph Mazzeo asserts, "From the beginning of the *Divine Comedy*—'where the sun is silent'—to the final vision of light the

poem is a carefully ordered hierarchy of light and shadows" (56). Mazzeo demonstrates Dante's commitment to the tradition of light metaphysics being advanced in his time. In this tradition, "Light is an ontological principle . . . which runs through the whole of vitality, ordering it in a hierarchy of graded intensity and purity of light leading to a light that is both supersensuous and supernatural" (85). We can follow Pound's attempt to organize his material (which aims at exhaustive comprehension of all reality) in a visionary capacity to see various kinds of light shining through the universe. Pound's own dedication to medieval philosophers who study the nature of light (Eriugina and Grosseteste especially) is well known.

6. Harold Bloom's thesis from *The Anxiety of Influence* might provide a useful theoretical tool in discussing Pound's relation to Dante: in learning from Dante, Pound comes to fear becoming overly imitative of the master, of producing a "servile" body of work merely repeating Dante's accomplishment. As a result, the later poet looks for (and discovers) places where the precursor fails to communicate to a modern reader, places where the medieval sensibility of Dante limits his vision and requires "updating" by the modern poet.

I find T. S. Eliot's terminology more apt for Pound's relation to Dante: in writing *The Cantos* Pound seeks to find a way for his unique skill to add to the already established epic tradition; that is, he seeks to fit his "individual talent" into a long-standing "tradition" which Dante has culminated for his age. Pound's rivalry with Dante is better understood through Eliot's more genial understanding of the way a poet works with tradition, than through Bloom's often hostile and unconscious "oedipal" struggle.

7. In this interview conducted when only "Drafts and Fragments" remain to be made part of *The Cantos*, Pound provides an assessment of the aims and successes of his epic. His emphasis is on the enormous difficulties facing the poet whose ambition leads him to undertake an epic project in "an experimental age" (57). This interview is a crucial document in understanding how Pound chooses to view the overall intention of and obstacles to the "modern epic."

8. Pound does not follow his friend and sometime mentor T. E. Hulme in a complete rejection of "romanticism." Hulme's work is helpful in this regard, for he defines the romantic sensibility for his generation and provides the challenge to a poet such as Pound who was, by nature, drawn to that sensibility. According to Hulme, the romantic follows Rousseau in the belief

> that man was by nature good, that it was only bad laws and customs that had suppressed him. Remove all these and the infinite possibilities of man would have a chance. This is what made [people of the romantic temperament] think that something positive could come out of disorder, this is what created the religious enthusiasm. Here is the root of all romanticism: that man, the individual, is an infinite

resevoir of possibilities; and if you can so rearrange society by the destruction of oppressive order then these possibilities will have a chance and you will get Progress.

One can define the classical quite clearly as the exact opposite to this. Man is an extraordinarily fixed and limited animal whose nature is absolutely constant. It is only by tradition and organisation that anything decent can be got out of him. (*Speculations* 116)

Pound learns early from Hulme to be suspicious of the romantic aspects of his own personality and the project to which that personality leads him; he will not reject "romanticism" so much as temper it by a careful reading of Dante and the epic tradition.

9. It seems worth noting that in the works left unfinished by their premature deaths, Shelley and Keats both turn to Dante for a model. In *The Triumph of Life* and *The Fall of Hyperion*, these two Romantic poets undertook to write long poems of comprehensive and visionary scope based on Dante's heroic journey and his ambition to understand the effects of history on human nature. We have in these poems precedent for considering Dante's influence on those poets with Romantic aims: Dante seems to discipline their verse and provides a model of rigor to follow as they try to express their frustration with their present culture and their hopes for the poetic imagination to construct something better.

10. With this much said about Pound's use of the wandering figure most frequently called either Odysseus or "no man" in *The Cantos*, it is striking to note that W. B. Stanford completely overlooks Pound's epic in his classic study of *The Ulysses Theme*. Its subtitle—"A Study in the Adaptability of a Traditional Hero"—indicates the usefulness of this book to the present study, for one of Stanford's aims is to explain why Ulysses has been adapted successfully to a variety of situations and for so many different purposes. Stanford offers an explanation that might help us imagine how Pound came to rely on this hero: "Ulysses was by far the most complex in character and exploits. . . . His character was both more varied and more ambiguous than the character of any figure in Greek mythology or history until Archilochus. And, most significant of all for the possibility of later adaptations of his myth, one of his chief qualities, as Homer portrayed him, was adaptability" (7). One might wish to argue that Pound's use of this figure is the culmination of the tradition defined by Stanford; for this poet not only adapts Ulysses to his own needs but makes this adaptability itself, this flexibility, this elasticity the organizing principle of his epic project.

Chapter 1

1. Pound believes that "The Nekuia shouts aloud that it is *older* than the rest" (*SL* 274); Kenner states that the poet "ascrib[es] the under-

world journey to 'fore-time'" (Bornstein 10), to the earliest moment of human time. This is highly suggestive of Pound's theory of poetry: if the earliest artifact of Western culture describes a descent for knowledge about the way back home, might not the very impulse to make and record verse be the attempt to return to the state originally enjoyed? If the first hero in Western literature is a wanderer searching for a lost home, Pound joins an epic tradition at its source, in its original impulse.

2. In 1912, the same year he wrote about the importance of a "return to origins," Pound translated "The Seafarer," in which he explores the pain and hardship of the exile's life:

> May I for my own self song's truth reckon,
> Journey's jargon, how I in harsh days
> Hardship endured oft.
> Bitter breast-cares have I abided,
> Known on my keel many a care's hold,
> And dire sea-surge, and there I oft spent
> Narrow nightwatch
> nigh the ship's head
> While she tossed close to cliffs.   (*T* 207)

The speaker compares the hardship of the wanderer to the ease and joys of those lucky enough to remain "home":

> Lest man know not
> That he on dry land loveliest liveth,
> List how I, care-wretched, on ice-cold sea,
> Weathered the winter, wretched outcast
> Deprived of my kinsmen [....]   (*T* 207)

This early work informs the manner and meaning of Canto I: Pound's wanderer is no sentimental hero whose wandering is easily accepted as an alternative to the comforts of the bourgeois world he abandons; his adoption of the status of wanderer accepts all the pains and hardships the Anglo-Saxon poem depicts in its sound and sense.

3. This attitude toward visionary experience is fundamentally the same as T. S. Eliot's:

Dante's is a visual imagination . . . in the sense that he lived in an age in which men still saw visions. It was a psychological habit, the trick of which we have forgotten, but as good as any of our own. We have nothing but dreams, and we have forgotten that seeing visions—a practice now relegated to the aberrant and uneducated—was once a more significant, interesting, and disciplined kind of dreaming. (*Selected Essays* 204).

Eliot's choice of words implies that the substance of the vision does not have to be "true" to be significant or interesting; the visionary capacity is a "trick" or a "dream" that yields results. It is worth noting how the two poets, close friends who nonetheless have sharp differences in religious outlook, share this attitude toward the experience that draws them to the medieval mind and to Dante in particular. Perhaps poets, in their conscious appreciation of the power of words to construct reality, understand that any version of "origins" is not literally true nor logically developed, but rather the result of powerful images fostered by creative writers.

4. It is illuminating to read his account of how he first came to the economic theme that will become an obsession: "Autobiography if you like. Slovinsky looked at me in 1912: 'Boundt, haff you gno bolidigal basshuntz?' Whatever economic passions I now have, began *ab initio* from having crimes against living art thrust under my perception" (*I* 88). He did not, I presume, sense the "historical" or, more properly, "political" implications of his youthful capacity for visionary experience "that year," but by the time he writes these he has sensed the opposition serious art meets in the bourgeois world of marketplace competition: "twenty years ago, before 'one,' 'we,' 'the present writer' or his acquaintances had begun to think about 'cold subjects like economics' one began to notice that the social order hated *any* art of maximum intensity and preferred dilutations. The best artists were unemployed" (*I* 83). His belief in a conspiracy against health and the natural order began with the conviction that his own talent made him an outcast from his culture: "I have blood lust because of what I have seen done to, and attempted against, the arts in my time" (*I* 86). The forces behind the present culture sense in the artist's power a threat against their privileged position.

5. Pound complains that "After the Trecento we get Humanism. . . . Man is concerned with man and forgets the whole and the flowing. And we have in sequence, first the age of drama, and then the age of prose" (*SR* 93). In the main, literary history describes a decline from poetic art that registered a perception of the divine and supernatural to a prosaic art that documents a fallen human nature. In an essay about Henry James, written in 1918 in memory of James and using the same Dantesque description of his slow and dignified movement as in Canto VII, Pound cites Flaubert's observation of the artist's role in "the age of prose": "If it is the business of the artist to make humanity aware of itself; [in *Education Sentimentale*] the thing was done, the pages of diagnosis" (*LE* 297). Pound reads in Joyce's art a "disgust with the sordid [that] is but another expression of a sensitiveness to the finer thing. There is no perception of beauty without a corresponding disgust" (*LE* 415). Prose brings the depiction of beauty to the modern world only in its negative manifestation, disgust with the present version of reality lacking beauty. Pound sees the great prose tradition of Flaubert-James-Joyce as preparing the scene for the emergence of the great poet whose epic recovers the realm of beauty in the positive.

6. Joyce provides a reading of the dangers of love songs in "Sirens," where Leopold Bloom listens to sentimental songs of love that threaten to

diminish his pain and lull him to a dangerous ease. Bloom chooses to feel the pain of his loss and continue his wandering rather than yield to the soothing comfort that, like the Sirens, would drown him.

Both Pound's version of Odysseus and Joyce's accept the pain attendant to exile, and we can use Eliot's insight about Dante's penitents in *Purgatorio* to see how their wanderer can be placed in a Dantesque framework: "In purgatory the torment of flame is deliberately and consciously accepted by the penitent. . . . The souls in purgatory suffer because they *wish to suffer*, for purgation" (*Selected Essays* 217). In accepting the suffering attendant to exile and regarding it as essential to the reaching of their home, Pound's and Joyce's versions of Odysseus both have the purgatorial motive and mentality.

7. Here is a place of fundamental difference between Pound and Eliot, for Eliot denies that nature can yield knowledge or experience of the supernatural. Pound believes that by bridging the gap between nature and humanity, by bringing the natural and the human worlds into intimate contact, one becomes open to the perception of the divine; the holy inheres in nature, and we must return to our place in a natural order if we are to see the manifiestation of the holy. He reads Dante in just this way, as one who returns to Eden (our natural origin) so he can ascend to heaven; Pound sees in Dante a relation between the return to nature and the vision of the holy.

Eliot posits that a sharp and irreconcilable gap exists between the natural and the supernatural:

> . . . I am convinced that if this "supernatural" is suppressed . . . , the *dualism* of man and nature collapses at once. Man is man because he can recognize supernatural realities, not because he can invent them. Either everything in man can be traced as a development from below, or something must come from above. There is no avoiding the dilemma: you must be either a naturalist or a supernaturalist. (*Selected Essays* 433)

Eliot advises to choose against a relation to nature if one is to have a relation to the supernatural. Eliot sees for humanity the need to raise our affections toward the supernatural instead of lowering them to the level of animal affections (see Gordon 123). These radically different evaluations of the results of a return to nature, I suggest, can explain many other poetic decisions the two authors make.

8. Pound has some striking affinities with the Romantic tradition as it is embodied in the "nature-feeling" of Wordsworth. We can see in his belief that the human needs intimate union with the natural order something similar to Wordsworth's marriage between the mind of Man and Nature:

> Paradise, and groves
> Elysian, Fortunate Fields—like those of old
> Sought in the Atlantic Main—why should they be

> A history only of departed things,
> Or a mere fiction of what never was?
> For the discerning intellect of Man,
> When wedded to this goodly universe
> In love and holy passion, shall find these
> A simple produce of the common day. [...]
>   my voice proclaims
> How exquisitely the individual Mind [...]
>   to the external World
> Is fitted:—and how exquisitely, too—
> Theme this but little heard of among men—
> The external World is fitted to the Mind [....]
>   (*"The Recluse,"* 800–21)

Both Pound and Wordsworth believe that a correspondence exists between the structures of the mind and the external universe, that the same laws govern both orders. And both poets believe that if the current gap between these two realms is closed, an earthly paradise is made real again. The ways to this "return of the human to nature" and the ensuing results differ in important ways, but Pound's modernism shares this attitude toward nature with Wordsworth's Romanticism.

9. In his final chapter entitled "The Heretics of 'Provence,'" Peter Makin documents the history of the Church's persecution of the heresy centered on Languedoc and Aquitaine. He works hard to show that Pound's reading of this episode from Provençal history was essentially correct, that the heresy was not ascetic but celebratory; not Manichean but pagan and even Eleusinian. Whether Pound was right or not is not the question for my argument; rather, Makin "proves" that the poet did associate the troubadours with an outlawed and persecuted cult descended from the rites at Eleusis. This reading appeals to Pound because he wants his hero to be outside, even against, the current law of his culture, as my argument about Canto XLVII emphasizes.

10. It is interesting that Pound first presents a ritual from the worship of Tammuz/Adonis rather than from Eleusinian legends. The rites associated with Tammuz/Adonis also celebrate fertility and the miracle of renewed growth. The inclusion of these rites highlights Pound's decision to use the Eleusinian mysteries as one of the pivots of his epic; the Eleusis story appeals to this poet because of the presence of the mother-daughter unity that he will use to challenge the law providing the foundation of the present culture, the law prohibiting a return to the mother.

11. In discussing the taboo against incest, Freud quotes Frazer, "The law only forbids men to do what their instincts incline them to do.... Instead of assuming, therefore, from the legal prohibition of incest that there is a natural aversion to incest, we ought rather to assume that there is a natural instinct in favour of it ..." (*Totem and Taboo* 123). The law of

the father that prohibits the return to the mother is poised against a natural desire for the mother. Since we all desire this return, we are all punished by the imposition of guilt for this "horrible" wish. The present culture is founded on guilt instead of joy, fear of punishment instead of courage and confidence; Pound's efforts as a poet may be regarded as "against guilt and fear."

Chapter 2

1. We do not watch the active man enact the imaginative return to origins; at first, these two movements are kept separate. Instead of waiting for a return to healthy conditions, he finds a way to act, in the midst of economic corruption and artistic decadence, that might make the world conform to the vision of home that the imaginative wanderer glimpses and finally records in Canto XLIX. Pound quotes Lord Palmerston's instructions to fellow political leaders in Canto LII: "Begin where you are" (261). One cannot wait for a return to purity but must do what one can in the here and now. The two types of action, the imaginative return and the political construction, eventually come together in Canto XLIX as Pound makes his own poetic vocation central to the political reawakening he hopes for.

2. The Poundian hero is inspired by his vision that "humanity" did not have to become, nor must it remain, what it is. He knows that "humanity" is constructed in time, that it is a product of historical activity:

> If a man has not instincts, he ought to be in the way of making them. He has numerous instincts, and makes more everday: a part of his consciousness is constantly crystallizing itself into instincts. (*The Natural Philosophy of Love* 21)

Instincts are the product of human effort; tendencies that seem "natural" and "necessary" are really constructed over time; new instincts, and thus a new version of humanity, are possible. Pound recalls Gourmont's insight often in the 1930s, as he becomes increasingly an admirer of and advocate for Mussolini:

> Gourmont then got round to defining intellect as the fumbling about in the attempt to create instinct, or at any rate on the road towards instinct. And his word instinct came to mean merely PERFECT and complete intelligence *within a limited scope* applied to recurrent conditions.... (*J/M* 18)

> Gourmont's instinct as the result of countless acts of intellection, something after and not before reason.... (*GK* 195)

Pound believes that a "perfect and complete" human nature is possible if the scope and conditions of human being are so efficiently controlled that new forms of behavior become "instinctive." The political implications of these views become even sharper as he translates Confucius:

When right conduct between father and son, between brother and younger brother, has become sufficiently instinctive, the people will follow the course as ruled. (*Con* 65)

3. Miller demonstrates that the Bay Company was motivated by a sense of mission, "to realize in America the due form of government, both civil and ecclesiastical" (*Errand* 12). The Puritans who left England for America did so for the opportunity to work in a wilderness—"in a bare land, devoid of the already established (and corrupt) institutions, empty of bishops and courtiers, where they could start *de novo*" (12). While Jefferson is no Puritan, Pound's reading of his efforts places him in a distinctly American tradition.

4. It is interesting to note how Odysseus pops up in the most unlikely places and in a most casual tone, as if he were always on Pound's mind. Here, Jefferson is associated with the exiled wanderer. The argument can be made that, when Odysseus sails westward beyond the Pillars of Hercules, the land he sights is not Mount Purgatory but the new world, also a place never before seen. As we shall see for Hanno, the centrifugal movement becomes a political journey, a search for a place where one can begin again without the distractions and opposition of the corrupt institutions of Europe. Those who use the theme of the wanderer in the post-Columbian world are forced to think about the journey as circumnavigation; both Whitman and Crane make good use of that motif, in *Passage to India* and *The Bridge* respectively. The wanderer who breaks the confines of the old world and finds a wilderness in which to make a new Adam: this is an American trope Pound inherits and assumes in his epic.

5. Pound's call for a return to the original principles of the founding fathers from which subsequent generations have fallen is reminiscent of the Puritan rhetoric of the jeremiad, which has been closely studied by Perry Miller (*The New England Mind: From Colony to Province*) and Sacvan Bercovich (*The American Jeremiad*). One must merely replace the founders of the Bay Company with the founders of the American nation as the referents in the urgent call for a fallen America to return to the values and intentions of the "founding fathers." When Pound writes of America, he is drawn to the same structures and rhetoric as the Puritan writers who also saw America as an experiment in creating a perfect state in the new world, a garden out of the wilderness. Pound's reading of Dante—as a return to Edenic conditions from which one can work toward an ideal city—might ultimately be best considered an "American" reading.

6. Pound reads the *Commedia* primarily as a study of the political implications of human will. The pilgrim descends to hell observing the fate of those who failed to direct their will to the proper goals; climbs Mount Purgatory purifying his own will until Virgil can say, "Free, upright and whole is thy will and it were a fault not to act on its bidding" (*Purgatorio* XXVII, 141–42); ascends through heaven learning from those whose strong and pure wills directed their virtuous behavior; and

achieves union with God which is described as the perfect motion of the will: "my desire and will, like a wheel that spins with even motion, were revolved by the Love that moves the sun and the other stars" (*Paradiso* XXXIII, 143–45). Pound reads Dante's epic as a treatise on the political will to order, and he prepares for the introduction of Mussolini into his own epic by bringing *Paradiso* into play. In Canto XXXVI, he follows his translation of Guido's "Canzone d'Amore" with a reference to "thrones"; he begins Canto XXXVIII, which is almost entirely devoted to economic detail, with a quotation from *Paradiso* XIX in which Dante alludes to the misery created by the debasement of the currency; and in the same canto, he finishes a long verse explanation of Douglas' "A + B theorem" with

> and the light became so bright and so blindin'
> in this layer of paradise
> that the mind of man was bewildered.   (190)

Heavenly vision is associated with understanding economic justice. As we saw in chapter I, *Paradiso* is also made part of Cantos XXXIX and XL. In this way Pound implies that his study of Mussolini is a result of his reading of Dante.

7. Aristotle, *Physics*, Book II, section three. Pound is certainly thinking of Aristotle's "four causes"—the material, the formal, the efficient, and the final explanations of change. In a radio broadcast, he isolates the efficient cause as most pertinent to a study of history: "Nothing is without efficient cause. You can't beat Aristotle on that statement. Something causes the destruction of mosques, and museums" (Doob 292). He emphasizes in his study of Mussolini the role of the efficient cause, the agent that sets new events in motion. Pound makes an heroic act of the efficient cause, a triumph of the will to create a new form on given material toward visionary ends.

8. I assume that Pound did not take the compliment at face value; that is, he did not hear the normal usage of "divertente" as "entertaining" or "amusing." I feel sure that he would not have included in his poem such a light evaluation of his epic intentions.

9. Charles Norman (*The Case of Ezra Pound*) presents the texts of the court sessions leading to the ruling that Pound was not able to stand trial. Dr. Wendell Muncie, for instance, testified that Pound had "a number of rather fixed ideas which are either clearly delusional or verging on the delusional." Among these were the beliefs that he was "designated to save the Constitution of the United States for the people of the United States" and that he had "the key to the peace of the world through the writings of Confucius" (110–11). This physician also spoke of Pound's "remarkable grandiosity." Dr. Marion King diagnosed Pound's condition as "a paranoid state of psychotic proportions" (132). E. Fuller Torrey (*The Roots of Treason*) reviews the psychiatric reports, casting doubt on their sincerity and arguing that the psychiatrists conspired with the govern-

ment to keep Pound from standing trial. I call on Torrey's book to indicate the difficulty of asserting a definitive diagnosis of Pound's mental state from a psychiatric viewpoint and to pose as a question still to be settled whether the conventions of an epic poet's self-evaluation are invalidated by the conventions of a scientific community.

10. Pound's sexual theories are relevant to his politics, in the association of the phallic heart with the Fascist ruler. The phallus is both the giver of order and of pleasure, at one and the same time. Pound looks to an order that creates the conditions for the free flow of pleasure.

11. A. James Gregor reviews Fascist ideology, primarily through the speeches of Mussolini and the philosophical writings of Gentile. He notes the Fascist motto: "Everything within the state, nothing outside the state, and nothing against the state" (*The Ideology of Fascism* 189). The individual as distinct from and independent of the social fabric is a fiction of the liberal state, for the individual is born into an already existing structure of relations and duties that determine his sense of self. No one is ever free from, independent of, or anterior to the state, and one becomes a determinate and meaningful person only in relation to the state that precedes his existence (see pp 183–218). The call for a totalitarian state, then, is the result of a dissatisfaction with a liberal ideology that pretends to respect the individual while preventing the ordering of the state that would bring him into his true and full selfhood.

12. Both Hannah Arendt (*Totalitarianism*) and Gregor testify to the ultimate goal of a totalitarian state, the "transformation of humanity itself" (Arendt 432), to create "homines novi"—a new humanity (Gregor 195). While Pound's goal is the same as the Fascist and Nazi goal of the creation of a new version of humanity, it can be argued that a poet with this aim seeks not to dominate but to free, not to reduce passion but to increase the flow of pleasure. One might even wish to trace in the literary tradition of the West, especially from the Romantic poets onwards, the increasing frequency with which poetry is assigned the messianic role of redeeming a fallen people; and then contrast the poet's gentle seduction of the reader to a new consciousness with the politician's often violent imposition of new conditions on the citizenry, both aiming at the same goal of a "new humanity." The case of Pound is rendered even more important to literary history because he brings the Romantic sensibility and ambition to the era in which the state has the material and technological resources that might allow for total control of the people; we must watch him negotiate the dangerous line between poetic and political conventions. Pound's solution is to have poetry provide the context for the politician's action, to elevate poetry to the role of mastery over the political.

13. John Tytell notes and registers a negative assessment of Pound's "Confucian" ambition: "he became seduced by the Confucian notion of the writer as political advisor to a ruler. But it was an illusory notion. Confucius had been regarded as a quirky, rambling talker in his

time; he was not taken seriously by those in power, he was never given political office, and he never enjoyed any real power" (234). Oddly enough, Tytell does not notice that, in this description of Confucius, he describes Pound's relation to the political world of his time. Perhaps Pound was aware of this and used Confucius to indicate that his own hopes for "power" lie in the future. See my argument below.

14. Mary de Rachewiltz testifies to her father's tremendous ambition as he undertakes his trip to America in 1939: "he was going to America not for any private gain or motive but because he felt he knew more about Italy than American officials, thought he knew of a remedy against war if the President or a sufficient number of men in power were ready to hear him out" (118). But, she claims, the trip was not motivated by "megalomania, but a sense of responsibility carried to the extreme" (124). She quotes Pound in defense of his undertaking the series of radio broadcasts: "A responsible citizen must do everything in his power to prevent his country from entering an unjust war" (135). I assemble these sympathetic assessments of Pound's wartime activities to indicate that he was still trying to attain a position of power and to affect the course of events. But I want to draw a distinction between what he does and what he writes, for it seems to me that in *The Cantos* he understands his role more clearly and is more patient in his attempt to change the world. I simply do not see in the Dynasty Cantos the urgency and desperation to attain power and influence events that Makin and Nicholls suggest and that the radio broadcasts certainly reveal.

Chapter 3

1. It seems most probable that Pound is most inspired when under the strain of his enormous ambitions. Most readers agree that he achieves a sublime style in Cantos XLVII and XLIX where the challenge is to earn and demonstrate his role as visionary poet of "a people of leisure." The Dynasty Cantos exhibit an abrupt fall in beauty and splendor, I suggest, because they are written from the perspective of a man who has assumed an epic status; that is, when he no longer has to earn or convince his readers of his status, the poetry suffers. The arrest and internment cast grave doubts over the poet's credentials, and he rises to the occasion with what are usually acclaimed as his greatest poems.

2. It is a "startling identification" because until that point in Pound's own periplum, Aeneas was a most uncongenial figure. Pound was fond of "one of Yeats' favourite anecdotes":

> A plain sailor took a notion to study Latin, and his teacher tried him with Virgil; after many lessons he asked him something about the hero.
> Said the sailor: 'What hero?'

Said the teacher: 'What hero, why, Aeneas, the hero.'
Said the sailor: 'Ach, a hero, him a hero? Bigob, I t'ought he waz a priest.' (*ABCR* 44)

Aeneas's piety that permits him to renounce passion and desire is not a value for Pound until he is forced to abandon all hope for personal happiness. Even in Pisa, Pound is careful to qualify his admiration for Aeneas's capacity for self-sacrifice with an awareness of his lack of passionate ardor. As in Canto XXIII, Pound uses Anchises' affair with Aphrodite to prevent this aspect of Aeneas's character from entering the makeup of the wanderer.

3. As we saw in the previous chapter, Pound opposes any explanation of historical causality that relies on the concept of necessity, any explanation that mitigates the place of human will in the chain of events. His attitude is very much like that of Michel Foucault, who in *The Archaeology of Knowledge* launches a polemic against "historians" who seek continuities and development underlying any sequence of events:

in the disciplines that we call the history of ideas, the history of science, the history of philosophy, the history of thought, and the history of literature . . . , in those disciplines which, despite their names, evade very largely the work and methods of the historian, attention has been turned . . . away from vast unities like 'periods' or 'centuries' to the phenomena of rupture, of discontinuity. Beneath the great continuities of thought, beneath the solid, homogeneous manifestations of a single mind or a collective mentality, beneath the stubborn development of a science striving to exist and to reach completion at the very outset, beneath the persistence of a particular genre, form, discipline, or theoretical activity, one is now trying to detect the incidence of eruptions. (4)

One can use Foucault's method of historical investigation as a sophisticated model that Pound's method resembles in its emphasis on radical breaks and ruptures in what others have conceived as a relatively seamless process of gradual and inevitable growth or development. There are also some striking differences that will be discussed in the next chapter when Pound turns archaeologist in *Section: Rock-Drill* and *Thrones de los Cantares*.

4. Anthony Woodward claims that *The Pisan Cantos* are "the great modern elegy not only of one man over his individual fate but over a whole civilized order for which he had some claim to speak" (8). If elegy is a formal lament on the death of a particular person that, in expressing sorrow for the loss, eventually comes to find grounds for consolation (see M. H. Abrams, *Glossary of Literary Terms*), then *The Pisan Cantos* can be placed in this category, for Pound does find consolation. But I still want to claim that these cantos establish a tension between elegy and epic, for Pound's lament is overcome not by the traditional consolation that the one

who has died lives on in some form of eternal state but the consolation afforded by his own assumption of the position vacated by the deceased. He consoles himself by reaching an "epic" status.

5. It does not account for Pound's radical decision to include these prophetic voices from a book he "had virulently abused in previous years" to point out that the Bible was one of the precious few books allowed the poet while in Pisa (Bacigalupo 134). Pound's attitude toward the Old Testament does not undergo a change; instead, we must marvel at his resourcefulness that finds in a text he abhors the one aspect he can use in the construction of his epic.

6. Pound is paraphrasing a line from Micah, "For all the people will walk every one in the name of his god, and we will walk in the name of the LORD our God for ever and ever" [Micah 4. 5]. As Flory notes (229–230), this prophet seems to hold out the hope that in the Heavenly Kingdom the various peoples of the earth will be judged according to the god they have chosen to follow. Pound chooses this one moment in the Old Testament that includes and validates the pagan gods to begin the process of paganizing the Hebrew voices he has been accumulating.

7. The presence of Jeremiah and related Hebrew prophets in these cantos may alert students of early American literature to consider an application of Sacvan Bercovich's study of *The American Jeremiad* to this sequence and *The Cantos* in general. Bercovich argues that while the Puritan jeremiad is a response to an apparent fall in the present generation from an original promise and destiny, it "turn[s] threat into celebration" (8); the jeremiad "invariably joined lament and celebration in reaffirming America's mission" in a "litany of hope" (11). What Bercovich testifies to is the relationship between failure in history of a mission and the creation of a rhetorical form based on the prophetic voices of the Hebrew prophets. While still on board the *Arabella*, John Winthrop pointed at the certainty of failure: even before reaching America (and so before any actual failure), a prophetic voice is gained and a belief in a high and mighty mission begun by an appeal to eventual and inevitable backsliding of the people. As a result, the prophetic strain revels in accumulating evidence of the fall and rejoices in the hope so conceived. The sense of mission is created only by the prospect or fact of failure. Pound's dream of a just city is not crushed by the avalanche but rendered as exquisite and permanent as a diamond. Both *The Pisan Cantos* and the American jeremiad find consolation in actual or potential historical failure because only failure creates the hope of a prophetic voice.

8. *De Monarchia* III, 16:

Thus the reins of man are held by a double driver according to man's twofold end; one is the supreme pontiff, who guides mankind with revelations to life eternal, and the other is the emperor, who guides mankind with philosophical instructions to temporal happiness.

And since none or very few (and these with difficulty) can reach this goal, unless a free mankind enjoys the tranquility of peace and the waves of distracting greed are stilled, this must be the constant aim of him who guides the globe and whom we call the Roman Prince, in order that on this threshing floor of life mortals may exist free and in peace. (p. 79)

Paradiso XXII:

The little threshing-floor that makes us so fierce all appeared to me from hills to river-mouths, while I was wheeling with the eternal Twins. (lines 151–53)

Human activity takes place on a threshing-floor, a place where the chaff is sorted out from the wheat. The Roman Prince aims at tranquility to create a place where humans are free to work for their salvation. Seen from the upper reaches of heaven, the earth is now a "*little* threshing-floor"; the concerns that make us fierce in life seem unimportant in themselves seen from their true end, beatitude.

9. Two other passages describe the stillness of the water at Lake Garda, (LXXIV/427) and (LXXVI/458); the three passages recall his contemplative ease beside Lake Garda during the days of the Salò Republic. The first of these reminiscences notes the presence of the Villa Catullo on the lake, where Catullus lived for a time. It is as a love poet in a tradition that features Catullus that he lays beside Lake Garda "dreaming the Republic"; it is as lyric poet that he aspires to political significance.

10. In his chapter on "The Pisan Black-out," Furia argues that Pound comes to see himself as the lone survivor who can preserve the documents that testify to the dream-city; his own memory is politically significant because it alone can fight against the forces that want to efface all traces of the dream.

11. From the earliest cantos, Pound tried to focus the reader's eye on the solidity of light: "Thus the light rains, thus pours, *e lo soleills plovil* / The liquid and rushing crystal" (IV/15). In Pisa he registers such "seeing" when he says, "The poplar tips float in their brightness" (LXXXIII/531). The substance in which these trees grow is not transparent air but semi-opaque brightness; the brightness so thick that the polar tips "float" in it: the air has become flowing liquid. Pound claims to see "a sky wet as ocean/ flowing with liquid slate" (LXXX/494). The ocean the wanderer now journeys through is the "wet" sky; he is trying to reach the holy realm Dante recorded in *Paradiso*. He is on a Dantesque journey through the "sea of air strip" when he is overwhelmed. The moment from *Odyssey* V has been transformed into journey through a water associated with divine properties.

12. Woodward notes that Odysseus's immersion in water in Canto LXXX may be patterned on the ritual immersion of baptism: "waters can

be redemptive as well as destructive; they have baptismal overtones; immersion in water is an act of lustration in many ancient cultures" (78).

Chapter 4

1. Makin (*Pound's* Cantos) notes Pound's unusual environment: deprived of new sensory material for his poem, he was "instead flooded with all the printed matter he could wish for, from that Tower of Babel of universal information, the nearby Library of Congress" (254). With a small army of disciples doing research for him, he had access to an almost unlimited supply of textual detail. The texture and perhaps the purpose of Pound's poem is, to a significant degree, determined by the changing circumstances of the poet's life. His field of experience largely limited to texts and his public authority discredited, he makes of his textual experience the means to the private end of reaching beatitude.

2. Because he cannot find a "progression in poetics" between the two, Makin (*Pound's* Cantos) also considers *Rock-Drill* and *Thrones* as if they were a single unit (252). My study has been watching for changes in technique because they signal changes in purpose. The two sequences are almost identical in technique and so we can conclude that in both Pound's wanderer is moving through the same medium and toward the same end.

3. Flory argues that Pound is reminded by the pines of St. Elizabeths of the "pineta," the pine-wood near Ravenna "where the last stanzas of *Purgatorio* were written and from which Dante takes his description of the Earthly Paradise in which he finally sees Beatrice" (245). Bacigalupo also believes that the forest in Pound's Canto XC is meant to suggest Dante's earthly paradise (274). That these critics, who are not explicitly pursuing Dante's presence in the late cantos, feel Dante's presence in this scene testifies to the extraordinary care with which Pound makes Dante's poem part of his effort to write paradise.

4. Drake is an English incarnation of Pound's wanderer prepared for by the presence in this canto of Layamon's *Brut*, which tells the story of the founding of Albion by Brutus, the great-grandson of Aeneas. Brutus brings Aeneas's destiny to the English-speaking tradition in which Drake fits. As an actual historical figure given a mythical dimension, Drake functions as a manifestation of the prototypical wanderer who now commits himself to historical action as he journeys to beatitude. The infamous passage distinguished by italics from the rest of the canto registers as part of the journey through history the ugliest kind of rhetoric possible, a rhetoric that disturbs but does not negate the journey to blessedness. The shift from beautiful images of light to brutal scatology (*"a dung flow from 1913/ and, in this, their kikery functioned"*) suggests that the wanderer committed to historical action, exemplified in Canto XCI by Drake, must take the risk of falling into such hostility if he is to be propelled through history toward paradise.

5. Wilhelm claims that the *terzo cielo* is, "properly speaking, the locus for the entire last third of the poem" (151); that is, all of *Rock-Drill* and *Thrones* can be regarded as written by a man in the state of mind represented by Dante in the heaven ruled by Venus. While this claim is too extravagant (for other scenes from Dante's paradise are equally relevant to an understanding of Pound's paradise), Wilhelm does help us appreciate the role of erotic love in attaining beatitude.

6. Pound highlights Dante's understanding that words are only traces of a fuller presence seen by the poet, an understanding of the relation between language and reality put to different use by contemporary literary theories. We are following traces left by the poet's attempts to represent his journey through paradise; a careful and strong reader can make of the traces a trail along which he can travel and hope to reach the same *real* end as that described by Dante. Pound implies that, like Dante, he has found a language that can lead a select few on the way toward beatitude.

7. While each heaven has its own kind of knowledge and action, Dante makes clear that the visionary capacity, and not the act of knowing, is essential to beatitude:

> And thou must know that all [circles of paradise] have delight in the measure of the depth to which their sight penetrates the truth in which every intellect finds rest; from which it may be seen that the state of blessedness rests on the act of vision [. . .] (*Paradiso* XVIII, 106–110)

The intellect finds rest in the vision of the truth; our attempts to know are made complete by the visionary capacity that sees the divine light.

8. The briefest glance at the Malatesta Cantos (VIII through XI) after the dizzying whirl of the late cantos is enough to demonstrate the striking difference in presentation of historical detail. Pound's early effort to register the life of a neglected hero is leisurely and anecdotal, and from such technique we can conclude that this particular man's life is a value in and of itself. The dizzying speed of the presentation of facts in the late cantos suggests that value inheres not in the details themselves but in the relation of the facts; the value lies in the pattern that can be made. History is equally essential to the poem both early and late, but in radically different ways.

9. With my choice of language here and in the following paragraphs, I mean to suggest the relevance of Plato's theory of forms to Pound's thinking in *Rock-Drill* and *Thrones*. We are moving toward a Platonic realm of ideas as we work to find the ideal form of justice made by any particular set of instances. Whereas earlier in the poem an idea is something thrown out by the mind as a plan to be realized in activity (see Davie, *Pound* 64 ff.), now the idea is a form constructed by contemplating human action in history. The idea is no longer a plan but the pattern of ideal justice made from the material of experience.

10. That Pound translates and publishes "Quotations from Richard of St. Victor" as he writes the late cantos makes clear that he has rediscovered the value and use of this theologian's thinking.

11. Donald Davie anticipates my argument in his chapter on *Rock-Drill* in *Poet as Sculptor.* He defends the late cantos from the charge of being too demanding by arguing that they are written in a way designed to reach the infinite through a contemplation of form. Davie cites an early essay of Pound's (from 1921) to indicate how *Rock-Drill* has ties to Pound's earliest thinking:

> '[. . .] with the ideal form in marble it is an approach to the infinite *by form,* by precisely the highest possible degree of consciousness of formal perfection; as free of accident as any of the philosophical demands of a *"Paradiso"* can make it.' *(231)*

It takes until the 1950s for Pound to fashion a poetry that seeks to approach the infinite, a poetry modelled on *Paradiso.*

WORKS CITED

Abrams, M. H. *Natural Supernaturalism*. New York: W. W. Norton and Company, 1971.

Arendt, Hannah. *The Origins of Totalitarianism*. New York: Meridian Books, 1958.

Aristotle. *Physics*. Translated by Richard Hope. Lincoln: University of Nebraska Press, 1961.

Bacigalupo, Massimo. *The Formed Trace: The Later Poetry of Ezra Pound*. New York: Columbia University Press, 1980.

Bercovitch, Sacvan. *The American Jeremiad*. Madison: University of Wisconsin Press, 1978.

Bernstein, Michael André. *The Tale of the Tribe: Ezra Pound and the Modern Verse Epic*. Princeton, N.J.: Princeton University Press, 1980.

Brooks, Van Wyck. *Writers at Work: The Paris Review Interviews*, second series. New York: The Viking Press, 1963.

Bush, Ronald. *The Genesis of Ezra Pound's* Cantos. Princeton, N.J.: Princeton University Press, 1976.

Cassirer, Ernst. *Language and Myth*. New York: Harper and Brothers, 1946.

———. *The Philosophy of Symbolic Forms*, volume two. New Haven: Yale University Press, 1955.

Dante. *The Divine Comedy*. Translated by John D. Sinclair. New York: Oxford University Press, 1948.

———. *On World Government*. Translated by Herbert W. Schneider. Indianapolis: Bobbs-Merrill Educational Publishing, 1982.

———. *Vita Nuova*. Translated by Mark Musa. Bloomington: Indiana University Press, 1973.

Dasenbrock, Reed Way. "Dante's Hell and Pound's Paradiso." *Paideuma*, Winter 1980.

Davenport, Guy. "Persephone's Ezra." In *New Approaches to Ezra Pound*, edited by Eva Hesse. Berkeley: University of California Press, 1969.

Davie, Donald. *Ezra Pound*. Chicago: The University of Chicago Press, 1975.

———. *Ezra Pound: Poet as Sculptor*. New York: Oxford University Press, 1964.

Doob, Leonard W., editor. *"Ezra Pound Speaking": Radio Speeches of World War II*. Westport, Conn.: Greenwood Press, 1978.

Dronke, Peter. *The Medieval Lyric*. London: Cambridge University Press, 1977.

Durant, Alan. *Ezra Pound: Identity in Crisis*. Totowa, N.J.: Barnes and Noble Press, 1981.

Eliot, T. S. *Selected Essays*. New York: Harcourt, Brace, and World, Inc., 1964.

———. *Selected Prose*. New York: Farrar, Straus and Giroux, 1975.

———. *On Poetry and Poets*. London: Faber and Faber Limited, 1957.

Ellis, Steve. *Dante and English Poetry*. Cambridge: Cambridge University Press, 1983.

Espey, John. "The Inheritance of Tò Kalón." In *New Approaches to Ezra Pound*. Edited by Eva Hesse. Berkeley: University of California Press, 1969.

Fergusson, Francis. *Dante*. New York: Macmillan, 1966.

Flory, Wendy Stallard. *Ezra Pound and* The Cantos: *A Record of Struggle*. New Haven: Yale University Press, 1977.

Foucault, Michel. *The Archaeology of Knowledge*. Translated by A. M. Sheridan Smith. New York: Pantheon Books, 1972.

Frazer, Sir James George. *The Golden Bough: A Study in Magic and Religion*. Abridged Edition in one volume. New York: Macmillan Publishing Company, Inc., 1978.

Freccero, John. *Dante: The Poetics of Conversion*. Cambridge: Harvard UniversityPress, 1986.

Freud, Sigmund. *Civilization and its Discontents*. New York: W. W. Norton and Company, 1961.

Furia, Philip. *Pound's* Cantos *Declassified*. University Park: The Pennsylvania State University Press, 1984.

Gilson, Étienne. *Dante and Philosophy*. New York: Harper & Row, 1963.

Gordon, Lyndall. *T. S. Elliot's Early Years*. New York: Oxford University Press, 1977.

Gourmont, Remy de. *The Natural Philosophy of Love*. Translated by Ezra Pound. New York: Liveright, Inc., 1922.

Gregor, A. James. *The Ideology of Fascism*. New York: The Free Press, 1969.

Greive, Thomas. "Annotations to the Chinese in 'Section: Rock-Drill'." *Paideuma*, Fall and Winter 1975.

Hulme, T. E. *Speculations: Essays on Humanism and the Philosophy of Art*. London: Routledge and Kegan Paul Ltd, 1949.

Kenner, Hugh. *Gnomon: Essays on Contemporary Literature*. New York: McDowell, Obolensky Inc., 1958.

————. *The Poetry of Ezra Pound*. Norfolk, Conn.: New Directions, 1953.

————. *The Pound Era*. University of California Press, Berkeley, 1971.

Kerenyi, Karoly. *Eleusis*. New York: Pantheon Books, 1967.

McDougal, Stuart. *Ezra Pound and the Troubadour Tradition*. Princeton, N.J.: Princeton University Press, 1972.

Makin, Peter. *Pound's Cantos*. London: George Allen and Unwin, 1985.

. *Provence and Pound*. Berkeley: University of California Press, 1978.

Mazzeo, Joseph Anthony. *Medieval Cultural Tradition in Dante's Comedy*. Ithaca: Cornell University Press, 1960.

Mazzotta, Giuseppe. *Dante, Poet of the Desert*. Princeton, N.J.: Princeton University Press, 1979.

Miller, Perry. *Errand into the Wilderness*. Cambridge, MA: Harvard University Press, 1956.

————. *The New England Mind: From Colony to Province*. Boston: Beacon Press, 1961.

Mussolini, Benito. *Fascism*. Rome: Ardita Publishers, 1935.

Nicholls, Peter. *Ezra Pound: Politics, Economics, and Writing*. Atlantic Highlands, N.J.: Humanities Press, 1984.

Norman, Charles. *The Case of Ezra Pound*. New York: Funk and Wagnalls, 1968.

Otto, Rudolf. *The Idea of the Holy*. Translated by John W. Harvey. London: Oxford University Press, 1923.

Pearlman, Daniel D. *The Barb of Time: On the Unity of Ezra Pound's* Cantos. New York: Oxford University Press, 1969.

Pound, Ezra. *ABC of Reading.* New York: New Directions, 1960.

————. *The Cantos of Ezra Pound.* New York: New Directions, 1986.

————. *Confucius.* New York: New Directions, 1969.

————. *Gaudier-Brzeska: A Memoir.* New York: New Directions, 1970.

————. *Guide to Kulchur.* New York: New Directions, 1970.

————. *Impact.* Chicago: Henry Regnery Company, 1960.

————. *Jefferson and/or Mussolini.* New York: Liveright Publishing Corporation, 1935.

————. *Literary Essays.* New York: New Directions, 1968.

————. *Personae.* New York: New Directions, 1971.

————. *Selected Letters of Ezra Pound.* Edited by D. D. Paige. New York: New Directions, 1971.

————. *Selected Prose.* Edited by William Cookson. New York: New Directions, 1973.

————. *Spirit of Romance.* New York: New Directions, 1968.

————. *Translations.* New York: New Directions, 1963.

Rachewiltz, Mary de. *Discretions.* Boston: Little, Brown and Company, 1971.

Singleton, Charles. *Dante Studies I.* Cambridge: Harvard University Press, 1965.

Stanford, W. B. *The Ulysses Theme.* New York: Barnes and Noble, 1964.

Stewart, Douglas. *The Disguised Guest: Rank, Role, and Identity in the* Odyssey. Lewisburg: Bucknell University Press, 1976.

Surette, Leon. *A Light from Eleusis: A Study of Ezra Pound's* Cantos. Oxford: Clarendon Press, 1979.

Terrell, Carroll F. *A Companion to* The Cantos of Ezra Pound. Volumes I and II. Berkeley: University of California Press, 1980 and 1984.

Torrey, E. Fuller. *The Roots of Treason: Ezra Pound and the Secret of St Elizabeth's.* New York: Harcourt Brace Jovanovich, 1984.

Tytell, John. *Ezra Pound: The Solitary Volcano.* New York: Anchor Press, 1987.

Wilhelm, James J. *Dante and Pound: The Epic of Judgment.* Orono: University of Maine Press, 1974.

Woodward, Anthony. *Ezra Pound and* The Pisan Cantos. London: Routledge and Kegan Paul, 1980.

Wordsworth, William. *Selected Poems and Prefaces.* Edited by Jack Stillinger. Boston: Houghton Mifflin, 1965.

INDEX